3rd Edition

# MONEY MATTERS

## Englisch für Bankkau[illegible]



*von*
*Susan Lau*

*in Zusammenarbeit*
*mit der Verlagsredaktion*

Cornelsen

Verfasserin: Susan Lau, Hamburg,
Irene Eckart, Flensburg *(KMK exam practice)*,
Manfred Thönicke, Hamburg *(KMK mock exam)*
Berater: Christian Schmidt, Nördlingen
Projektleitung: Jim Austin
Verlagsredaktion: Laura Spratling, Merlene Griffin (KMK-Materialien)
Redaktionelle Mitarbeit: Christine House, Lauren Chexal, Rosalind Higman
Christiane Großkopf, Fritz Preuss (Wörterverzeichnisse)
Bildredaktion: Gertha Maly
Gesamtgestaltung und
technische Umsetzung: Katrin Nehm, Sabine Theuring, Berlin (KMK-Materialien)
Illustrationen: Oxford Designers & Illustrators

Erhältlich sind auch:
Audio-CD (ISBN 978-3-06-024141-5)
Handreichungen für den Unterricht mit CD-ROM (ISBN 978-3-06-024142-2)

**www.cornelsen.de**



1. Auflage, 5. Druck 2013

Im 4. Druck wurden *KMK exam practice*-Seiten sowie ein *KMK mock exam* im Anhang eingefügt. Außerdem wurden die Incoterms© 2010 aktualisiert.

Alle Drucke dieser Auflage sind inhaltlich unverändert und können im Unterricht nebeneinander verwendet werden.



Druck: H. Heenemann, Berlin

ISBN 978-3-06-024140-8

Inhalt gedruckt auf säurefreiem Papier aus nachhaltiger Forstwirtschaft.

# Vorwort

**Money Matters 3rd Edition** ist die komplett aktualisierte Neubearbeitung des bewährten Lehrwerks für angehende und erfahrene Bank- und Sparkassenleute, die am Berufsschulunterricht oder betrieblichen Fortbildungsmaßnahmen teilnehmen. Das Werk basiert auf den Lehrplänen der Bundesländer für Berufsschulen und bereitet auf die KMK-Zertifikatsprüfungen vor (Stufe II bzw. III).

**Money Matters 3rd Edition** richtet sich an Lernende, deren Englischkenntnisse dem Niveau eines soliden mittleren Bildungsabschlusses bzw. dem eines durchschnittlichen gymnasialen Grundkursabschlusses entsprechen, bietet aber in allen Units fakultative *Extra Materials*, um Lernende mit fortgeschrittenen Englischkenntnissen gezielt zu fördern. Ein Grundwortschatz von ca. 800 Wörtern wird vorausgesetzt und in einem gesonderten Vokabelverzeichnis aufgeführt.

**Money Matters 3rd Edition** lehrt in erster Linie die sprachlich korrekte und angemessene Bedienung und Beratung von englischsprachigen Privat- und Firmenkunden in allen wichtigen Bereichen des deutschen Bankgeschäfts. Das Werk setzt Grundkenntnisse der deutschen Bankbetriebslehre voraus und erarbeitet die fremdsprachlichen Kompetenzen, die am Arbeitsplatz erforderlich sind. Jede der zehn Units behandelt ein in sich abgeschlossenes Thema, jedoch wird empfohlen, wann immer Zeit und Lehrpläne es ermöglichen, die gegebene Reihenfolge einzuhalten, um einen kontinuierlichen Aufbau des Vokabulars zu gewährleisten.

**Money Matters 3rd Edition** ist ein handlungsorientiertes Lehrwerk. Die Lernenden werden aufgefordert, an den dargestellten Handlungen, z.B. einer Kontoeröffnung oder einem Kredit- bzw. Anlagegesprächs, aktiv mitzuwirken *(case-study approach)*. Dabei übernehmen sie Aufgaben, die im täglichen Bankgeschäft anfallen: Telefonate entgegennehmen, Kunden am Schalter bedienen, Abläufe beschreiben, auf Sicherheitsvorschriften hinweisen, E-mails schreiben, Inhalte aus englisch- oder deutschsprachigen Quellen in der jeweils anderen Sprache weitergeben *(Mediation)* und vieles mehr – bis hin zur kompletten Durchführung eines Beratungsgesprächs.

Banktypische Dialoge mit Gesprächspartnern unterschiedlicher Nationalitäten schulen das Hörverständnis. Praxisrelevante Auszüge aus Bankbroschüren und Presseartikeln, authentische Dokumente, Zahlenmaterial und Bilder bieten eine Vielzahl fachbezogener Sprechanlässe. Grammatik wird in jeder Unit punktuell wiederholt, um die Grundstrukturen zu festigen.

**Money Matters 3rd Edition** trägt den jüngsten didaktischen und pädagogischen Entwicklungen Rechnung. In Eigen-, Partner- und Gruppenarbeitsphasen werden selbständiges Lernen und Sozialkompetenz gefördert. In jeder Unit werden in den Rubriken *Learning* und *Culture* Tipps vermittelt, die zu mehr Lernerfolg und besserer interkultureller Verständigung führen können.

Um in einer globalisierten Welt erfolgreich beruflich tätig zu sein, ist Englisch als Fachsprache unerlässlich. Wenn dieses Werk einen Beitrag leistet, die beruflichen Chancen der Lernenden wesentlich zu verbessern, hat es sein Ziel erreicht.

*Susan Lau*
*Hamburg 2009*

*Neu an dem vorliegenden Druck ist die zusätzliche Vorbereitung auf die KMK-Zertifikatsprüfung. Dies geschieht anhand von *KMK exam practice*-Seiten sowie einem *KMK mock exam* im Anhang des Buches. Sie können die Hörtexte zu den KMK-Hörverstehensaufgaben anhören, indem Sie den jeweiligen Webcode im Webcode-Suchfeld auf www.cornelsen.de/matters eingeben. Die Transkripte und Lösungen zu den KMK-Materialien sind auf der Cornelsen-Webseite unter *Money Matters 3rd Edition* zu finden.

# Table of contents



**Appendix**

(Transcripts are printed in the teacher's book.)

# Working in a Bank

## 1 Warm-up

The savings bank *Hamburger Sparkasse* and the *Commerzbank* used these advertisements to attract new trainees.

Look at them and then do the tasks below.

Source: *www.haspa.de*

Source: *www.commerzbank.de*

a good team worker | able to work under pressure | communicative
creative | friendly | good-looking | helpful | interested in people | polite
reliable | serious | trustworthy

**a** Describe the photos used in the two advertisements.

**b** What should a bank trainee be like? Choose the three most important qualities from the box.

**c** Decide which photo expresses the qualities you have chosen and say why.

**d** Tell your fellow students why you applied for a traineeship at your bank.

## Culture  Training in banks

In Britain and the USA people who work in banks train on the job, learning by doing. There is no standard 'dual system' of *Ausbildung* like there is in Germany and so there is no direct translation for the word *Bankauszubildende(r)*. The word 'apprentice' is only used for people learning a manual trade, like electricians and builders. Like many UK and US banks, this book uses the word 'trainee' to describe people training to work in a bank. 'Traineeship' means *Ausbildung*.
The word 'bank clerk' for *Bankkaufmann/-frau* is old-fashioned. Bank staff use their job title (e.g. cashier, financial adviser, personal banking manager, branch manager) to describe their position.

## 2 An e-mail

Robert Schmidt, a trainee with the *Haspa*, sent this e-mail to a friend in the USA. Read and do the activities on the next page.

**Neue E-Mail**

Senden Chat Anhang Adressen Schriften Farben Als Entwurf sichern

**An:** justine26@mailUSA.com
**Kopie:**
**Betreff:** Greetings from Germany!

Hi Justine,

Thanks for your news. I'm pretty busy too right now because I started my traineeship at the bank on August 1st. For the first week we had a course at the head office but now I'm working in a branch. I was a bit nervous at first but my colleagues are really nice and help me a lot.

My bank has got about 180 branches in and around Hamburg but I'm staying in the same one during my training. The branch is open from 9 a.m. till 4 p.m. on weekdays except on Thursdays when we are open till six. We have to be at work by 8 a.m. each day. It's a long day, but the time goes quickly because there is so much going on. My branch is near the university so most of the personal customers are students but quite a few wealthy people have accounts there too and there are business customers as well. Some of the foreign students can't speak much German so we serve them in English.

I'm working on the counter at the moment – we call it the service desk. My bank doesn't have different departments for things like loans or investments because every adviser sells all the different banking products. I'll learn about them during the next two and a half years.

I'm trying not to spend too much on my car at the moment so I can save part of my salary to fly over to see you next summer. Maybe you can make a trip to Germany before then? That would be great.

Take care,
Robert

**a** Find expressions in the e-mail which mean the following.

1 *Hauptstelle/Zentrale*
2 *Filiale/Zweigstelle*
3 *Privatkunden*
4 *Firmenkunden/Geschäftskunden*
5 *Abteilung*
6 *Berater/-in*
7 *Darlehen/Kredite*
8 *Geldanlage*
9 *Schalter*
10 *Gehalt*

**b** Compare Robert's bank, branch and traineeship with your own. What are the similarities and differences?

**c** Write an e-mail to an English-speaking friend about your work.

## 3 Inside the branch

When Justine comes to Germany, Robert shows her round his branch.

2

**a** Listen and say what each of the points 1–10 on the floor plan is.

ROBERT: … so you can use your bank card to get into this lobby even when the bank is shut. Here on the left we've got two cash machines …
JUSTINE: Cash machines? Is that what you guys call ATMs?
ROBERT: ATMs?
JUSTINE: Automatic teller machines for taking money out of your account.
ROBERT: That's right. And opposite them on the right there's the statement printer near the door and the self-service terminal is beside it on the left.
JUSTINE: I can see cameras everywhere. Security is a big thing in the US.
ROBERT: Same here. Let's go inside. See that desk straight ahead? That's our welcome point.
JUSTINE: Don't tell me – the person who works there has to say "Hi" to everybody who comes in?
ROBERT: You mean a meeter-greeter?
JUSTINE: That's it.
ROBERT: Well, Anna, that's her name, has to do a bit more than that. Some customers just say they have an appointment so she offers them a seat and rings through to their adviser who comes and collects them, but she deals with general enquiries as well.
JUSTINE: Why are all those folks standing in line on the left of the welcome point?
ROBERT: They're queuing at the tills. Both of them are open but we're always busy on Fridays.
JUSTINE: Then why don't they go to the ATMs?
ROBERT: They probably want to pay money in or withdraw large amounts, or maybe just talk to the cashier …
JUSTINE: We call them tellers in the States. Would you like to be a teller?
ROBERT: A cashier? I'm not sure, I think it's really hard work …
JUSTINE: Hey, where do those steps go?

ROBERT: Down to the basement. That's where we have the strongroom.
JUSTINE: Wow! Where all the money is! Can I go and have a look?
ROBERT: Only if you rent a safe. Even then you can't go alone.
JUSTINE: Hmm, pity. Where do you work? That's what I want to see.
ROBERT: Over there, behind the welcome point. It's called the service desk. There are four of us on it. We each have a PC and there's a till there because we pay out small sums in cash. We deal with all sorts of things – you would come to us if you'd lost your credit card or forgotten your PIN …
JUSTINE: Could you open an account for me or give me a loan?
ROBERT: Not if I'm on the service desk, no. People always come to us first, but when we see that they need advice – say, if they want to borrow money or invest some capital, we make an appointment for them with one of our personal banking managers or financial advisers.
JUSTINE: I suppose they all have their offices hidden away upstairs?
ROBERT: No, they don't actually. The branch is open plan. Their desks are over there on the right. The private banking department for wealthy customers is on the first floor and corporate clients are served at our head office.
JUSTINE: If you'll excuse me, I'm just going to pop into that little room next to the elevator …
ROBERT: No, hang on, don't go in there! That's the manager's office! The toilets are downstairs. I'll show you where they are, then afterwards we're going for lunch with some of my colleagues …

**b** Look at points 2, 5, 6, 7 and 8 on the plan. In each case, describe the job of the person who works there.

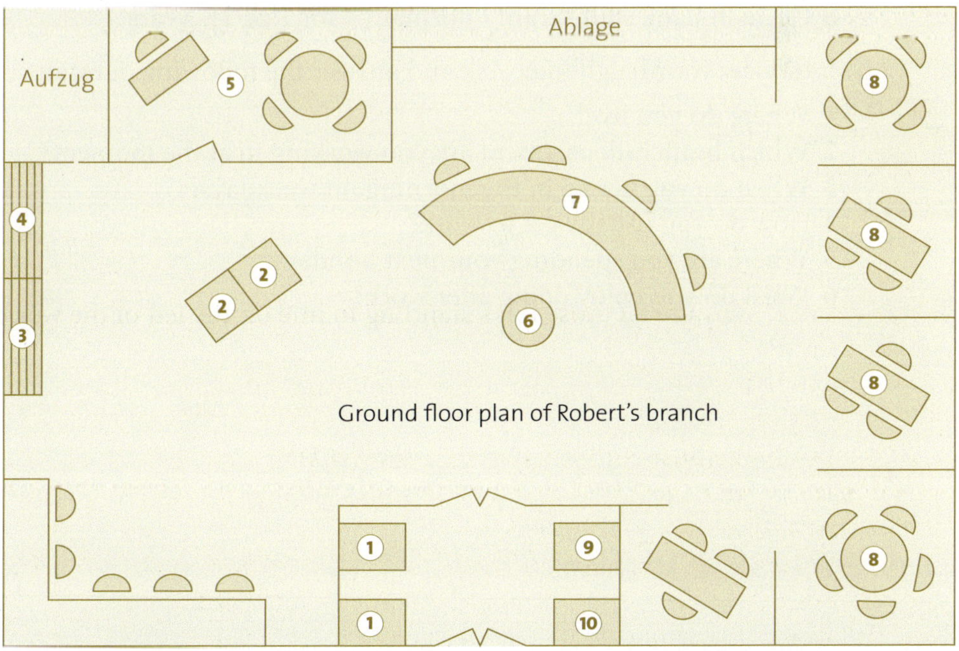


Ground floor plan of Robert's branch

**GRAMMAR** **Simple present and present continuous**

1 At the service desk we pay out small sums in cash.
2 She (Anna) deals with general enquiries as well.
3 We call them tellers in the States.
4 They're queuing at the tills.
5 We're going for lunch with some of my colleagues.

- The simple present is used for actions which happen regularly (1) or which are generally true (2, 3). It is formed using the infinitive of the verb (1) but in the third person singular *(he/she/it)* *s* or *es* is added (2).
- The present continuous is used for actions which are happening at the moment (4) or which are planned for the future (5). The present continuous also describes actions which take place over a limited period of time (4). It is formed using the present tense of the verb *be* and the present participle (4, 5).

## 4 Practice: the present

**a** Use the simple present or present continuous to make complete sentences.

1 Robert / in English / often / customers / serve
2 Wealthy people / into the branch / come / sometimes
3 Most people / a salary / earn / every month
4 I / to buy a car / at the moment / save
5 Robert / fly / next year / to America
6 The branch / at 9 a.m. / open / and / at 4 p.m. / close
7 I / with my bank / train / for 2 years
8 German bank staff / train / normally / for 2 or 2½ years

**b** Interview your neighbour. Ask and answer the following questions.

1 Where do you live?
2 Which branch/department are you working in at the moment?
3 When do you get up in the morning on weekdays?
4 How do you usually get to work?
5 Where are you spending your next holiday?
6 What do you enjoy doing after work?

## 5 Partner work

Draw a simple plan of the branch or bank where you work. Use it to tell your partner where to find the different services. Use expressions from the language box below.

**Example** If you want to print a statement, you can use the statement printer. It's in the lobby on the left when you come in.

**LANGUAGE** How to give directions

| | |
|---|---|
| It's | in the lobby / basement.<br>on the ground floor / first floor. |
| It's | opposite / in front of / behind the …<br>beside / next to / near to the …<br>straight ahead /on the left / on the right.<br>upstairs / downstairs. |
| Just take the lift (BE) / elevator (AE) / the stairs.<br>Then turn left / right.<br>It's the first / second door on your left / right. | |

## 6 Work with words

**a** Find expressions used in this unit so far to complete these sentences.

1 Cash machines are usually called … in America.
2 Most banks have one regional head office and many …
3 Companies or firms which are customers of a bank are its …
4 A person who borrows a fixed sum from a bank gets a …
5 If you wish to invest capital, you should speak to an …
6 The money that a person receives for his work every month is a …
7 The safes in the bank are kept in the basement in the …
8 The place where the cashier works is called the …
9 If you want to use the bank's services, you will have to open an …
10 If you want to check payments made this month, you can print a …

**b** Choose the correct prepositions.

1 Would you like to speak (at/to) one of our advisers?
2 The investment department is (at/in/on) the second floor.
3 The cash machines are in the lobby (at/on) the right.
4 I started working here (at/on) September 1st.
5 The branch opens (at/on) 9 a.m. and stays open (by/until) 4 p.m.
6 Student customers have to spend their money (for/on) books.

## 7 Banking products

Look at the customers shown in the photos below and say which products you would offer them and why. Remember to cross-sell.

loan | current account | savings account | credit card | debit card | overdraft
building society policy | insurance policy | foreign currency | securities

a)

d)

b)

e)

c)

f)

### CULTURE Forms of address

In the UK, the USA and many other parts of the world with an "American" business climate, colleagues on all levels call each other by their first names. Trainees, however, should call more senior members of staff by their surname until asked to use their first name. Bank staff call customers by their surnames but usually introduce themselves or a colleague using first names, e. g. "Good morning, I'm John. This is Kate, our investment adviser." Some customers then offer their first names, e. g. "Do call me Peter."
When using surnames, use Mr for a man and Ms for a woman. Use Mrs only if you are sure she is married.

## 8 At the service desk

3 Robert serves three English-speaking customers. (N.B. Transcripts are printed in the teacher's book.)

**a** Listen to each dialogue once and say why the customer has come to the branch.

**b** Listen to each dialogue again and take notes to answer these questions in detail.

1. What information does the customer give?
2. How does Robert pass the customer on to a colleague?

**LANGUAGE How to arrange for a customer to see a colleague**

If your colleague has time, you can say:

| | | |
|---|---|---|
| I'll just call | our adviser, Mr … | He will be able to help you. |
| | my colleague, Ms … | She will be able to advise you. |

Would you please go over to the till? / come this way please?

One moment please. I'll ring through and tell her/him you're here.
Mr/Ms … will be here in a minute. Would you like to take a seat?
May I offer you a cup of coffee or a glass of water while you're waiting?

If your colleague is busy, you can say:
I'm afraid Mr/Ms … is in a meeting / not available at the moment.
Would you like to speak to one of our other advisers?
Would you like to have an appointment with …?
Would … o'clock on Friday be convenient?
If you don't mind waiting, Mr/Ms … will be free in about … minutes.

## 9 Over to you

Working with a partner, do six short role-plays. Use expressions from the language box above. One of you is a customer who comes into the branch. The other person serves the customer at the service desk as follows:

- Greet the customer.
- Find out what the customer wants.
- Serve him or her as far as possible yourself.
- If necessary, arrange for the customer to see an adviser, either at once if a colleague is free or make an appointment for a later date.

Each partner plays the role of the customer three times. One partner uses role cards 1 and 2 printed on page 116. The other partner uses role cards 3 and 4 printed on page 118. For the third role-play, make up a role of your own.

## 10 Keep it simple

A customer does not understand the words underlined.
Find a way to say them simply.

1 Can I offer you an appointment with one of our advisers?
2 I'm afraid Mrs Schröder is not available right now.
3 Would 3 o'clock on Monday be convenient?
4 You will not be allowed to overdraw this account.
5 You can withdraw up to €1,000 a day.
6 You can use the self-service terminal to transfer money.

## 11 Lifestyle banking?

Read this text and then do the tasks below.

### McBanking

ING Direct, an international bank, was following one of the latest megatrends in retail banking when it opened its New York café in 2003. The bright orange-coloured branch offered everything from cappuccinos and blueberry muffins to savings accounts and loans. Everyone frothing the coffee was a bank adviser who could whip you up a new portfolio of funds before you could say "two lattes and a chocolate chip cookie, please".

In Japan, Suraga Bank has joined with Starbucks to run coffee shops on its premises while in the UK, the bank and building society Abbey National cooperates with Costa Coffee. The Bank of Yokohama has gone one step further with McDonald's hamburgers on sale next to its ATMs, but do customers actually say "a double cheeseburger and a mortgage, please"? And what about all those poor customers who are on a diet?

Your bank is thinking of joining in this banking trend. The non-financial products suggested are: snacks, mobile phones, sushi, package holidays.

**a** Split your class into four groups. Each group should write down the pros and cons of one suggestion. Each group then chooses a representative who presents the group's conclusions.

**b** After listening to the presentations, discuss which products, if any, should/could be put on sale in German banks.

**LEARNING** **Mediation**

Mediation bedeutet die Vermittlung des Inhalts eines Textes oder Gesprächs zwischen zwei Sprachen. Folgendes ist zu beachten:

- Markieren Sie unbekannte Wörter und schlagen Sie diese im Wörterbuch nach.
- Notieren Sie die Kernaussagen bzw. Fakten.
- Versuchen Sie nicht wörtlich zu übersetzen.
- Fassen Sie den Text zusammen und bauen Sie die Kernaussagen ein.

# Internet banking

## 12 Online banking

What are the advantages and disadvantages of internet banking?

**a** Working alone or with a partner, examine this question from both the customers' and the bank's point of view and write each of your ideas on a separate card. Then collect your cards on two wall charts with those of your fellow students.

**b** In class, look at the chart with the advantages. Discuss what the consequences are for bank branches. Then look at the chart with the disadvantages. Suggest how they can be overcome.

## 13 Phishing

The bank where you work has decided to print a flyer in English to increase customer awareness of the risks of internet banking and encourage them to take the necessary security precautions.
You have been asked to write a text (80–100 words) for the flyer using the following information. Use the learning box opposite to help you.

**DATENKLAU 23 PROZENT PLUS**

### Online-Banking: Betrug nimmt zu

Immer mehr Verbraucher werden beim Online-Banking Opfer von Betrügern. Die Zahl der Internet-Nutzer, deren Konten mit geklauten Passwörtern geplündert worden seien, sei im vergangenen Jahr bundesweit um 23 Prozent gestiegen, berichtete der IT-Verband BITKOM in Berlin. Insgesamt seien in 3250 Fällen 13 Millionen Euro von Konten der Opfer gestohlen worden.

Ein Grund für die steigende Zahl der Phishing-Opfer seien raffinierte Betrugsmethoden. Experten zufolge entstehen nur noch zehn Prozent der Schäden durch E-Mail-Links zu gefälschten Bank-Seiten, auf denen die Opfer eigenhändig ihre Kontodaten eingeben. In den meisten Fällen schicken Kriminelle per Mail ein Trojanisches Pferd. Dies ist ein Programm, das die Daten heimlich ausspäht und weitergibt. Andere Programme leiten die Nutzer beim Online-Banking im Hintergrund auf gefälschte Seiten weiter. „Deshalb ist es wichtig, die jeweils neuesten Schutzmethoden zu nutzen", meinte Bonn. Hier bemühten sich die Banken um bessere Gegenmaßnahmen. Transaktionsnummern (TANs) seien oft nicht mehr beliebig einsetzbar, sondern an weitere Sicherheitshürden gekoppelt. Würden Sicherheitsregeln eingehalten, sei das von 20 Millionen Deutschen genutzte Online-Banking durchaus sicher.

Um „Phishing" zu vermeiden, rät der Verband zu gesundem Misstrauen gegen E-Mails von Banken, denn die Bitte um Auskunft zu vertraulichen Daten sei unüblich. Verdächtige Dateien solle man keinesfalls öffnen, auch dann nicht, wenn mit einer Kontensperrung gedroht werde. Zudem rät BITKOM, die Anti-Viren-Programme und die Firewall auf dem neuesten Stand zu halten.

Falls man dennoch zum „Phishing-Opfer" werde, solle man sofort die Bank alarmieren, die häufig Überweisungen noch rückgängig machen könne.

(Source: Abridged from *Hamburger Abendblatt* 30.08.07)

# Personal Customers

## 1 Warm-up

**a** A survey carried out in Britain showed that, when passing a bank branch, most people start to walk faster! What do you conclude from this?

**b** What annoys customers about banks? This cartoon will give you some ideas.

**c** Do you think that banks in Germany generally get a good press? Why / Why not?

**d** How can banks increase customer satisfaction? List your suggestions and compare them with those of your fellow students.

**CULTURE** **Banks in the public eye**

In Britain, banks generally have a bad press. The media are keen to report on cases in which people are not satisfied with their bank, especially regarding high fees and charges. It is impossible for most personal customers to phone their bank branch; instead they will be connected to a call centre. On the other hand, they can be called into the bank to review their accounts, and some of them go there with the same feeling as when going to the dentist!
Banks even avoid using the word 'bank' in their marketing. Instead they use abbreviations, e.g. HSBC (= Hongkong Shanghai Banking Corporation), Lloyds TSB (= Trustee Savings Bank), NatWest (= National Westminster Bank) or simply Barclays instead of Barclays Bank.

## 2 Getting in touch

Claudia Wolff is at the service desk in her bank branch when the phone rings.

4 Listen and write down the following details:

- the caller's name, telephone number and e-mail address
- who the call is for and what action he/she should take
- the general subject of the call

**LANGUAGE** **Telephoning**

Starting a call:
This is John Smith / John Smith calling.
I'm calling about … / from …
Could I speak to …? / I'd like to speak to …

Putting the caller through to a colleague:
One moment please. / Hold the line, please. / Would you hold on, please?
I'll put you through.

If the line is busy:
I'm afraid the number is engaged / the line is busy.
May I take a message? / Would you like to leave a message?
Could he/she call you back? / Would you like him/her to call you back?
Could you give me your name and number / your e-mail address, please?

Finishing a call:
Thanks for calling.
I'll tell him/her. He/She will call you back as soon as possible.
I'll pass your message on to him/her.
I look forward to hearing from you / to your call.

## 3 Back to back

Write down a non-German name, telephone number and e-mail address. Sit back to back with a partner and play the roles below. Then swap roles. Use the tips from the box below and the learning box on page 14.

**Bankangestellte(r):** | **Kunde/in:**

- Bankangestellte(r): Melden Sie sich am Telefon.
- Kunde/in: Bitten Sie, Herrn Schneider zu sprechen.
- Bankangestellte(r): Fragen Sie den Anrufer nach seinem Namen.
- Kunde/in: Nennen Sie Ihren Namen.
- Bankangestellte(r): Versuchen Sie, den Anrufer durchzustellen. Die Leitung ist besetzt.
- Kunde/in: Bitten Sie, dass Herr Schneider Sie zurück ruft / Ihnen eine Mail schickt.
- Bankangestellte(r): Fragen Sie nach der Nummer/ Adresse.
- Kunde/in: Nennen Sie Ihre Telefonnummer und/oder Ihre E-mail Adresse.
- Bankangestellte(r): Beenden Sie das Gespräch.

### LANGUAGE Understanding phone calls

- Make sure you know who the caller is. Check the spelling of names.
- Write phone, fax and account numbers and addresses carefully. Then repeat them slowly. With numbers, say each digit separately except for double digits, e.g. 66 = double six. In the UK 0 is pronounced oh, in the USA and Canada, people say *zero*. For e-mail addresses and websites, note:

| | | | |
|---|---|---|---|
| - = hyphen | / = forward slash | . = dot | abc = in lower case |
| _ = underscore | \ = backward slash | @ = at | ABC = in capitals |

- If you do not understand, stop the speaker by politely saying, e.g.
“I'm sorry I didn't catch/get that.” “Could you repeat that, please?”
“Would you spell that, please?”
- Focus on the key facts and write them down as soon as you hear them. If you are uncertain, check by repeating the information.
- If you take a message for someone, make sure that you understand it yourself. Then write the message out again clearly, add the date and time of the call and sign it.

## 4 A new customer

Claudia Wolff is on the phone to another customer.

5 Listen and note the formalities for opening an account.

MARIE: My name is Marie Dubois. I'd like to open an account. Will I need an appointment?

CLAUDIA: That would be best, but I'm afraid we're closing shortly. Would ten o'clock tomorrow morning be convenient?

MARIE: Could you make that half past?

CLAUDIA: Certainly, Ms Dubois. Would you bring some proof of identity with you, please?

MARIE: I'm from France, so would my identity card do?

CLAUDIA: Of course. And do you have a permanent address in Germany?

MARIE: Yes. I moved here last week.

CLAUDIA: Have you got a certificate from the residents' registration office yet?

MARIE: I got it today. I'll bring that as well. Can I make the application in English?

CLAUDIA: I'm afraid not, but our adviser will help you fill in your personal details on our application form. Then all you'll have to do is sign the SCHUFA declaration and …

MARIE: Excuse me. What did you just say?

CLAUDIA: Sorry, I should have explained. The SCHUFA is the credit reference agency for the banks in Germany. We have to check with them before we open an account. It's standard procedure, part of our security regulations.

MARIE: I see. Is that all I have to do?

CLAUDIA: You will also be asked to give a specimen signature …

MARIE: What exactly is a specimen signature?

CLAUDIA: It's for comparison. Every time we receive a transfer form or any other order from you, we can examine the signature to be sure it's genuine. It's for your own protection. And if you grant a third party mandate to anybody, they'll have to give a specimen signature as well.

MARIE: Er, third party what?

CLAUDIA: A third party mandate. That means that you allow someone else to use your account: make withdrawals or transfer money, for example, or even overdraw the account.

MARIE: Does that person become an account holder, too?

CLAUDIA: No, you're the sole account holder. You're the only person who can close the account or grant a third party mandate to anyone else. An account with two or more account holders who have equal rights is called a joint account. Husbands and wives often open one together.

MARIE: Did you say "husband"? No thanks! I've left him in Paris!

## 5 Explaining formalities

Use expressions from the dialogue in Exercise 4 to deal with these customers.

1 Mr A is late for his appointment and arrives just before closing.
2 Ms B does not know how to prove that she has a permanent address in Germany.
3 Mr C asks why he has to sign the SCHUFA declaration.
4 Mrs D does not see how a specimen signature will protect her.
5 Ms E is not sure what rights her partner will have if she grants him a third party mandate.
6 Mr and Mrs F want an account they can both use.

### GRAMMAR Question forms

1 **Do** you **have** a permanent address in Germany?
2 **Does** that person **become** an account holder too?
3 What **did** you just **say**?
4 **Will** that person **become** an account holder too?
5 **Have** you **got** a certificate from the residents' registration office yet?

- Questions in the simple present are formed using *do* (1), except for the third person singular which uses *does* (2).
- Questions in the simple past are formed using *did* (3).
- In sentences with auxiliary verbs, questions are formed by reversing the subject and the auxiliary. This is the case with all other tenses, for example the *will*-future (4) and the verb *have got* (5).

## 6 Practice: questions

When Marie Dubois comes into the branch the next day to open an account, you have to take over.

Ask Ms Dubois questions about these points:

1 … proof of identity?
2 … permanent address? / registration certificate?
3 … the application form? / personal details?
4 … SCHUFA declaration?
5 … a third party mandate? / joint account?
6 … specimen signature?

## 7 Proof of identity

Look at this passport and do the tasks below.

**a** Compare the UK passport with a German identity card. What details do they both show? Are there any differences?

**b** Write a list of German expressions used on the identity card with their English translations.

Example Geburtsdatum = date of birth

## 8 The application form

Look at the application form on page 125. Find expressions on the form which mean the following:

1 *Antragsteller/in*
2 *Legitimationsbeweis*
3 *geschieden*
4 *unterhaltspflichtige Kinder*
5 *selbstständig tätig*
6 *Beruf*
7 *Jahreseinkommen vor Steuern und Abzügen*
8 *monatliche Ausgaben*
9 *betriebliche Rente*
10 *Mieter/in*

**LEARNING Vokabeln lernen mit Wort-Feldern**

Eine sinnvolle Methode, neue Wörter zu einem bestimmten Themenbereich zu lernen, besteht darin, sie um den jeweiligen Obergriff in Form eines Mindmap zu schreiben. Oft prägen sich die Wörter durch die grafische Ordnung leichter ein, da der Zusammenhang der Begriffe im Vordergrund steht, nicht das isolierte Wort.

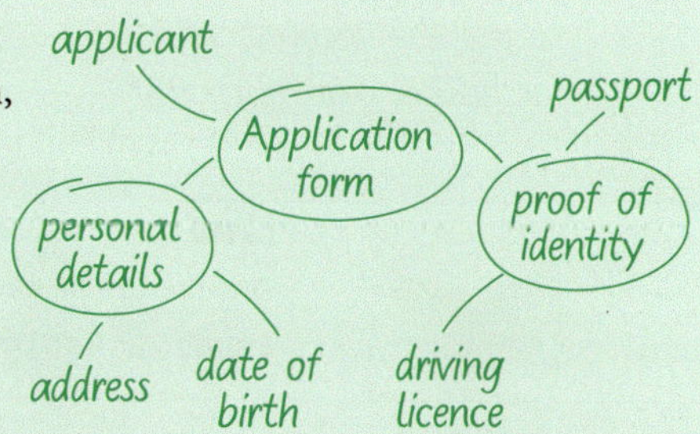

## 9 Work with words

Make nouns from the verbs in the box and use them to fill the gaps below.

| advise \| apply \| compare \| declare \| inform \| overdraw \| prove \| withdraw |
|---|

1 You will need a PIN to make a … at the ATM.
2 When opening an account, customers have to complete the … form.
3 Most people need specialist … on investment.
4 A passport can serve as … of identity when opening an account.
5 The customer has to sign the SCHUFA …
6 Here are the files on both funds for … so you can decide which is best.
7 Customers who have a regular income may be allowed an …
8 For further … on our products, please visit our website.

## 10 Opening an account

A trainee is going to open an account for the first time. He has written the steps on separate cards but he is so nervous that he has dropped them and they are all in the wrong order.
In a group, discuss what order to put them in. (There is more than one correct order.)

Offer help in future, say goodbye

See certificate from registration office

Check proof of identity

Find out personal details for application form

Get acceptance of bank's general business conditions

Explain SCHUFA declaration

Ask about third party mandate

Congratulate customer on opening account

Ask for specimen signature

Ask if applicant is going to use the account solely for his/her own purposes*

Greet customer, make small talk

Hand over a folder for the customer with brochure, copies of forms, etc.

* This information is required under the German Money Laundering Act.

**LANGUAGE** Asking politely

To ask politely, avoid expressions like "I need" / "I want" / "you have to" / "you must". Do not give orders, e.g. "Sign here!" Instead use expressions like:
Can/Could/Would you bring your passport, please?
May I see your certificate from the registration office, please?
Would you mind **asking** your wife to come in sometime next week?

Use expressions like "just" and "all you have to do is …":
Just sign here, please.
All you have to do is fill in this form.

Often it is more polite to say "Could you tell me …" instead of asking directly.
"Could you tell me your address, please?" is more polite than "What is your address?"
"Would you like … ?" sounds better than "Do you want … ?"
"Would you like to grant anyone a third party mandate?"

## 11 Over to you

Working with a partner who plays the customer's role, follow the steps from Exercise 10 to open an account using a German application form from your bank. Use expressions for asking politely from the box above.

## 12 Attracting new customers

**a** Look at these two advertisements. How do these banks hope to attract new customers?

**b** Think of more ways in which banks try to attract new customers. List some different methods and decide what type of person each method on your list would attract.

## 13 Celebrity endorsement

Read this magazine article and do the tasks below.

### Bank goes to Bollywood

*Star kicks off new bank role by saying he's so rich, he doesn't care about finance.*

During his first engagement as the face of one of India's leading banks, Bollywood superstar Sharukh Khan claimed in Mumbai yesterday that he was so rich that he didn't have to worry about financial matters.

Representing ICICI Bank, Sharuhk – who is paid two million dollars a film – said that he didn't care what level of interest banks gave him on his money. "Honestly, I don't really worry too much about interest rates. I am too rich to worry about money," the actor and ICICI's global brand ambassador said at a press conference in the Grand Hyatt hotel.

The multi-millionaire, known as "King Khan", added that he was happy that ICICI had chosen him to be the face of the bank. The bank stated yesterday that Sharuhk's energy and innovation coupled with his popularity in both India and abroad made him an ideal choice to endorse the bank.

"The films I have acted in reached a global audience and I am glad the bank thinks I can represent them globally," said Sharuhk. However the 41-year-old star admitted that he does not know much about banking but says he is trying to learn more about it."I don't know too much banking terminology, but I am trying to learn and will give it my best shot."

Sharuhk, who started his career in a TV soap opera in the 1980s, has starred in 37 films. "King Khan" is also known for his regular donations to charity and recently funded a children's ward at the Nanavati Hospital in Mumbai. He also contributed generously to the Indian Prime Minister's Tsunami Relief Fund in 2005.

(Source: 7 Days, U. A. E., March 2006)

**a** State the reasons why ICICI chose Khan to be "the face of the bank".

**b** Give your opinion: would a German bank use a celebrity who says "I am too rich to worry about money" to endorse its products?

**c** Name some persons that German banks use for product endorsement. Say why each is suitable.

# Premier customers

## 13 Premier service

**a** What can Premier customers expect from their bank? Read this advertising letter and find out which added services Premier customers can enjoy.

**b** Give your opinion on the way your bank treats affluent customers.

**HSBC PREMIER**

Dear

**It's time to get more out of the world**

We've spent the past year listening to customers to find out what they need from HSBC Premier. This has driven the development of a range of new and improved benefits – which are now ready for you to explore.

**At your service**

Increasingly, customers have been telling us that they are looking for expert wealth management advice to help them take advantage of the world's rich financial opportunities. So we've created the world's first globally linked-up banking service – one that gives access to funds that are invested around the world, not just the UK.

**Support when and where you need it**

We know many customers value the personal touch, and we've now extended this worldwide.

Your HSBC Premier status will now be recognised at over 6,000 HSBC branches worldwide. And at over 250 HSBC Premier Centres in key locations around the world you will be greeted by an English-speaking Relationship Manager who will offer the same level of personal service, support and advice you enjoy at home.

**The offshore advantage**

As part of the new worldwide reach of HSBC Premier we can now offer you support and advice if you are living and working abroad through HSBC's specialist offshore provider, HSBC Bank International.

This free, award-winning offshore service recognises that your needs are different and can provide you with some useful guidance on the tax implications of banking offshore. We could also offer you an offshore account which gives you a central and convenient place to manage your money.

**Explore your new benefits before you explore the world**

You can find full details of the new service in the enclosed pack so please take a moment to reacquaint yourself with the world of HSBC Premier. Since its launch in 2000, HSBC Premier has been offered for free to those who meet certain eligibility criteria. From 1 November 2007, we are changing the criteria and we will review your account with you annually to ensure you continue to meet them.

Please see overleaf for details of the new eligibility criteria and other important information.

If you'd like to arrange an Individual Review to help you get the most out of HSBC Premier, you can contact your Relationship Manager directly on the number listed below. We look forward to being of service now and in the future.

Yours sincerely,

Chris Pitt, Head of Customer Communications

# Current Accounts

## 1 Warm-up

This is the cover of a brochure about the current accounts offered by the UK-based bank Lloyds TSB.

**a** Describe the picture on the brochure cover.

**b** Give your opinion on these questions. The expressions in the box below will be helpful.

1 What could be "the things that matter"?
2 How can a current account give the account holder "time"?

**LANGUAGE** How to express your opinion

Avoid starting sentences with 'I think … '. Here are some alternatives:

In my opinion, one of the things that matters is …
The way I see it, a current account gives you time because …
In my view …
From my point of view …
I would say (that) …
I believe (that) …

## 2 The cash account

One of the range of accounts offered by Lloyds TSB is the Cash Account. Read the brochure extract and do the tasks below.

### What you can do with your Cash account...

Here's a quick look at what you get with your Cash account. You can find out more about these features further on in the brochure.

**Withdrawing your cash**
Convenient ways for you to withdraw your cash, when you want it take out up to a maximum of £200 each day.

**Paying in cheques and cash**
Pay in cheques & cash with your personalised paying-in book at any of our **deposit**points or at any Lloyds TSB or Post Office® branch.

**Keeping up to date with your account**
Check your balance or account statement online, on the phone or in branch. You can also get a mini statement at any Lloyds TSB Cashpoint machine, which will list up to the last 7 transactions.

**Making regular payments**
You can set up, change or cancel your standing orders and view and cancel most Direct Debits online, over the phone or in branch.

**Mobile phone top ups**
Top up your mobile phone at our Cashpoint machines - for no extra charge.

Open a Lloyds TSB Cash account today | Ask our friendly staff in your local branch

### What's not included in your Lloyds TSB Cash account...

Our Cash account is free for your everyday banking and offers straightforward account services which are easy to use.

As a result, there are some products and services which this account doesn't offer. Here are some of the features you won't find with the Cash account:

- Overdrafts and loans
- Cheque books
- Credit interest
- Being able to use your Cashpoint card at cash machines that do not belong to Lloyds TSB.

Please check carefully to make sure the Cash account suits your needs. We have a wide range of accounts, so please talk to a member of our staff if you haven't found the account that's right for you.

about saving | Just come into your local Lloyds TSB branch

**a** Find expressions in the above brochure which mean the following:

1 the sum of money in an account balance
2 taking money out of an account, e.g. at a cash machine withdrawing
3 payments into and out of an account that are shown on the statement transactions
4 the fee that the customer pays for a service charge
5 interest paid on money that is in an account
6 the account feature which allows a customer to overdraw overdraft
7 the system in which the account holder allows another person/company to collect payments from the account
8 fixed payments which the bank transfers regularly on an agreed date

**b** In your opinion, what sort of people will open a Cash Account? Why?

**c** Does your bank offer an account similar to this? If so, describe it.

## 3 Additional benefits

Current accounts can include additional benefits, often at an extra charge. Holders of Royalties accounts at the Royal Bank of Scotland can enjoy the following:

RBS Make it happen — The Royal Bank of Scotland

Contact RBS | Accessibility | Site Map | Search:

Digital Banking

Personal banking | Private banking | Business banking | Corporate banking | LOG IN ▸ | ▸ Tel

Home | ▾ Current accounts | Credit cards | Mortgages | Loans | Savings & investments | Insurance | Trav

Extra benefit current accounts

Royalties current accounts are designed to save you money.

| Key features | ▸ Royalties £6.95 per month | ▸ Royalties Gold £12.95 per month |
|---|---|---|
| **Mobile phone insurance** - great cover for your mobile phone. (up to 2 phones with Royalties Gold) | ✓ One phone | ✓ Two phones for joint accounts |
| **Backup your mobile** - backup and restore your numbers | ✓ | ✓ |
| **Worldwide travel insurance** - multi-trip cover for you and your family, with a 5-star Defaqto rating | | ✓ |
| **Car breakdown cover** - built-in with Royalties Gold or with Royalties when you buy Royalties Motor Insurance | ✓ | ✓ Includes home assistance |
| **Home emergency cover** - up to £500 to help with repair costs, lines open 24 hours a day | | ✓ |
| **Home insurance** - save 25% in your first year | ✓ | ✓ |
| **Extended warranty** - additional cover for domestic electrical goods | | ✓ |
| **Identity theft protection** - defend and restore your credit status after fraud | | ✓ |
| **Credit cards** - tailored rate | ✓ | ✓ |
| **Royalties Saver Account** - an instant access savings account offering preferential rates | | ✓ |
| **Savings** - earn a bonus on our Instant Access Savings Account | ✓ | |
| **Mobile phone banking and text alerts** - balances and mini statements, wherever you are | ✓ | ✓ |
| **Many, many more features...** | ✓ | ✓ |
| **Potential Annual Saving** | £245 | £896 |
| | View & Apply ▶ | View & Apply ▶ |

**a** Choose one of the features listed opposite to match each of these pictures. Then explain where the benefit for the customer lies.

**b** Describe some additional features of your bank's current accounts.

1

2

3

4

## 4 A bank statement

**a** Match the points numbered 1–10 on this statement with the explanations a–j below.

| | | | |
|---|---|---|---|
| Privatgirokonto 123456 / Stadtsparkasse München | 1 | BLZ 701 500 00 / UST-ID DE129272684 | 2 Kontoauszug 8 / Blatt 1 |
| Datum Erläuterungen | | | Betrag |
| Kontostand in EUR am 05. 0.2007, Auszug Nr. 7 | | | 3 2.500,00+ |
| 12.10 Gehaltsüberweisung Musterfirma | | Wert: 15.10.2007 | 1.750,00+ |
| 12.10 Bareinzahlung | 4 | Wert: 12.10.2007 | 5 1.000,00+ |
| 12.10 Einzugsauftrag Beitrag Fitnessstudio | | Wert: 12.10.2007 | 50,00- |
| Kontostand in EUR am 13.10.2007, 15.00 Uhr | 6 | | 5.200,00+ |
| Ihr Dispositionskredit | 5.000,00 EUR | 7 | |
| verfügbar | +10.200,00 EUR | 8 | |
| Aktuelle Wertstellung | +3.450,00 EUR | 9 | |
| Herr / Mustermann Mario / Mustermannstraße 15 / 80331 München | | 10 | Int. Bank Account Number: DE26 7015 0000 0908 1142 83 / SWIFT-BIC.: SSKMDEMM |

a current balance with the date and time
b previous balance with the date of the last statement
c overdraft facility
d current account number and bank sort code
e international bank account number (IBAN) and SWIFT bank identification code
f transaction details
g entries (two credits and one debit)
h statement number and page number
i total sum available, including the overdraft facility
j sum currently available without interest charges

**b** Use expressions from the box below to explain the three entries on the statement to a customer.

### LANGUAGE How to describe entries to accounts

When money is taken out of an account, the bank debits the account with the sum.

When money is paid into an account, the bank credits the account with the sum.

Often the passive is used:
the account was / is / will be debited.
the sum was / is / will be credited.

The entries shown on a bank statement are debits or credits. At the end of the statement, customers can see their balance. This is sometimes called a debit balance ('in the red') or a credit balance ('in the black').

## 5 Selling a current account

6

Chris Hanley, a teacher from the USA on a two-year exchange programme, is asking Ina Braun, an adviser at a German bank, about current accounts.

**a** Before you listen to their conversation, say which account services you think Chris Hanley will need.

**b** Listen to the dialogue and see if you were right.

**c** Say how you think the conversation ended.

**d** Listen again or read the text and list what the Classic Account offers.

**e** Use your notes to write a text for a brochure in English about this account.

CHRIS: … so I'll be teaching American Studies here for the next two years.
INA: How interesting. I hope you enjoy it. How can I help you?
CHRIS: Well, I'm gonna need a checking account while I'm here.
INA: Of course. Is your salary going to be paid into this account?
CHRIS: That's right. And I'm gonna have a lot of bills to pay as well.
INA: Then I'd suggest our Classic Account. It offers you a wide range of services free of charge.
CHRIS: Sounds great. Will I get a check book with it?
INA: We don't often use checks in Germany. In fact you won't need any at all.
CHRIS: Really? I didn't know that. In the States folks write checks all the time.
INA: In this country you can make standing orders for regular payments like the rent or insurance and arrange direct debits to pay utility bills or …
CHRIS: Sure, but those are all regular payments. What if I just want to pay once? Like … say, a medical bill or at the supermarket?
INA: In shops it's best to pay with your bank card. For other payments we have a credit transfer system – you just fill in a form, online if you like, and we'll transfer the sum for you.
CHRIS: Will I be able to do all my banking online?
INA: Yes. The Classic Account includes free online and phone banking.
CHRIS: That bank card you mentioned, is it a credit card?
INA: No, it isn't a credit card, it's a debit card. You can use it in shops, at the statement printer and at cash machines. I'm afraid this account doesn't include a free credit card, but you can have a Mastercard for an annual charge of 20 euros.
CHRIS: Okay. But can't I just open a line of credit if I need extra cash?
INA: Yes, as soon as your salary is paid in, we can arrange an overdraft facility for you. Then you can overdraw the account up to an agreed limit.
CHRIS: I see. And do you pay interest on the money in the account?
INA: I'm afraid not. We have other accounts that pay credit interest and include a free credit card but we charge a basic monthly fee for them.
CHRIS: Well in that case …

### GRAMMAR Negative forms

1 This account doesn't include a free credit card.
2 We don't often use cheques in Germany.
3 I didn't know that.
4 You won't need any cheques at all.
5 It isn't a credit card.
6 Can't I just open a line of credit if I need extra cash?

- The verb *do* + *not* is used to make a negative sentence in the simple present (1, 2) and the simple past (3).
- The verb *do* is **not** used with other tenses, e. g. the future (4), with verbs *be* (5) and *have got* and with modal verbs (6).
- The negative form *must not* means 'It is wrong to …' = *nicht dürfen.*
The negative form *need not* means 'It is not necessary to …' = *nicht müssen.*

The customer **needn't** open the account right away. He can do it later.
The adviser **mustn't** open an account without seeing the customer's passport.

## 6 Practice: 'must not' and 'need not'

Complete the following sentences with 'must not', or 'need not'.

1 Students … pay fees for current accounts.
2 In Germany you can pay bills by credit transfer so you … write cheques.
3 US checking account holders … overdraw unless they have a line of credit.
4 If you have a debit or credit card with a PIN, you … queue at the till to make withdrawals. But don't forget you … write your PIN on the card!
5 Customers who use online banking … pay fees for transferring money. They also … visit their branch so often.
6 If you have an overdraft facility, you … ask for permission to overdraw your account but you … exceed the agreed limit.

## 7 Practice: negative forms

Complete these sentences with negative verb forms. Note: there may be more than one correct answer.

1 Shops in Germany … accept cheques nowadays.
2 Customers … smoke in the branch.
3 Mr Brown … make any withdrawals last week.
4 Account holders who use the ATM … queue at the till.
5 Americans … normally use a credit transfer system to pay their bills.
6 If you pay the rent by standing order, you … miss a payment.
7 If you arrange a direct debit, you … remember to transfer the sum.
8 The bank … pay any credit interest on free current accounts.

**LANGUAGE** **Saying yes and no**

Native speakers of English rarely answer a question simply with 'Yes' or 'No'. To them this sounds impolite. They normally repeat the verb, e. g. 'Yes, I do / Yes, we can'. Alternatively they often say, e. g. 'Yes, that would be fine/good/nice' or use words like 'certainly', 'definitely', 'all right' or 'of course' instead of simply 'yes'.
When saying 'no', native speakers often start a sentence with 'I'm afraid' or 'I'm sorry', e. g. 'Do you pay any interest?' – 'I'm afraid we don't / I'm afraid not' sounds more polite than 'No, we don't'.
The word 'unfortunately' is not used as widely as the German word *leider* to express regret. 'Unfortunately' is used only if something negative happens, e. g. 'Unfortunately the computer crashed and we lost the data.'

## 8 Answering questions

Follow the guidelines from the language box above to answer these customers' questions without using the words 'yes' or 'no'.

**Example** Can I speak to the branch manager, please? (No) … (but … our deputy branch manager)

Answer: I'm afraid she isn't available, but our deputy branch manager is free at the moment. Would you like to speak to him?

| | |
|---|---|
| 1 Does the bank stay open till 6 p. m. today? | (No) … (but … on Thursdays) |
| 2 Are there any parking spaces outside the branch? | (No) … (but … our underground car park) |
| 3 Will I get a PIN for my debit card? | (Yes) … (by post in the next two weeks) |
| 4 Can I open an account right now? | (Yes) … (your passport with you) |
| 5 Is Mr Schmidt in today? | (No) … (but … one of our other advisers) |
| 6 Do you offer special accounts for students? | (Yes) … (free of charge) |
| 7 Will I get a cheque book? | (No) … (but … efficient transfer system) |
| 8 Does the account include a credit card? | (No) … (but … 20 euros a year) |
| 9 May my wife use the account? | (Yes) … (joint account … both names) |
| 10 Have you got a brochure in English? | (No) … (but … our website) |

## 9 Over to you

**a** Working with a partner who plays the customer using role card 5 on page 116, explain the details of this account.

### Ihr UltraBank StudentenKonto

Rufen Sie regelmäßig Ihre Eltern an, weil Ihnen das Geld ausgegangen ist?

Kommt Ihnen die Entschuldigung „Sorry, ich bin zur Zeit nicht so flüssig“ bekannt vor?

Wir bei der UltraBank verstehen, dass Geld nicht auf der Straße liegt. Und dass Sie Unterstützung brauchen, wenn etwas schiefgeht. Daher sind unsere Mitarbeiter jederzeit für Sie erreichbar, um Sie professionell und kostenlos zu beraten.

Bei der UltraBank stehen Sie und Ihre Bedürfnisse als Student im Mittelpunkt. Die Vorteile des UltraBank Studentenkontos sprechen für sich:

- Kostenlose Kontoführung mit unserer neuen UltraBank Card und 650 € Dispokredit. Mit der UltraBank Card können Sie Ihr Bargeld jederzeit und weltweit abheben.
- Die ersten sechs Monate kostenlose Nutzung der UltraBank Kreditkarte – für einfaches bargeldloses Zahlen. Jetzt auch mit Unfallversicherung auf Reisen, wenn z. B. Hotel oder Flug mit der Kreditkarte bezahlt wurde.
- Unser bequemer Online-Banking Service. So können Sie u. a. Daueraufträge von zu Hause einrichten, damit keine Rechnung auf der Strecke bleibt.
- Die UltraBank-SparCard, falls Sie etwas auf die hohe Kante legen möchten – Ihre Ersparnisse bleiben trotzdem kostenlos verfügbar.

***UltraBank – Wir schaffen das zusammen.***

**b** Change roles. The customer now uses role card 6 on page 118. The account can be a product offered by your bank.

### CULTURE Current accounts in Britain and the USA

In the UK, debit cards and credit cards (or cash) are used in shops. Though people still have cheque books for making occasional single payments, online transfers are increasingly used. Standing orders and direct debits are used for regular transfers.

In the USA current accounts are called 'checking accounts'. Salaries and pensions are paid by cheque (US: check) or by Direct Deposit (= transferred directly into a person's bank account). Debit cards and credit cards are used in shops.

## 10 At the cash machine

Say which of the statements below are true, false or not in the text.

# BRISTOL EVENING NEWS

ISSUE 08/20 • 70p

### Cashpoint Gang Strikes Again

Thirty-five-year-old hairdresser Jane Turner* left the salon where she works in Bristol for a couple of minutes to take £50 out of a nearby cash machine. It was Friday and she was looking forward to the weekend. But just two days later, when she tried to withdraw more cash from a different machine, she got a nasty shock: her card was refused. On checking her balance, she saw to her horror that her current account had been practically cleared. On Monday morning she was first at the counter when her bank opened, where she was told that that £270 had been withdrawn at 8.30 a.m. on Saturday, leaving her with only £5 in her account. She had become the latest victim of the Cashpoint Gang.

"I'm furious," she said. "How could this happen? I can't afford to lose the money. I'm saving up for a holiday. On Saturday morning I was at home with my partner. We were doing the gardening and didn't go near any cash machines at all."

Jane Turner is not the only victim. Police are investigating reports that over £10,000 has been illegally withdrawn from 25 separate current accounts during the past month. In each case card holders visited the same cash machine in Bristol before noticing that money was missing from their accounts.

It was a quick-thinking police officer who finally solved the mystery. On Saturday morning PC Dan Wilde* was passing the cash machine on his beat when something unusual caught his eye. "The slot where you insert your card seemed to have a strip of plastic stuck across it. When I ran my hand over it, it fell off. There was an electronic panel behind it, which appeared to be where people's card data were being saved. A hidden camera was probably also used to film people entering their PINs."

Police believe that the gang in Bristol may target other banks elsewhere in Britain and have issued a warning: "If you notice anything unusual on a cash machine, do not touch it but report the matter to the bank at once. Gangs behind this sort of crime can be extremely dangerous and could cause serious harm to anyone they see damaging their illegal equipment."

A bank spokesperson said that all customers who had lost money from their accounts would be fully reimbursed. And Jane Turner? She is looking forward to her holiday even more after all of this bank stress! (406 words)

* Names in this article have been changed

1 25 illegal withdrawals were made at one cash machine.
2 Jane Turner could not book her holiday.
3 The money was stolen from Jane Turner's account on Saturday morning.
4 The cash machine refused Jane Turner's card on Sunday.
5 In all, Jane Turner lost £265.
6 Jane Turner is furious that she will not get the money back.
7 The gang used stolen card data and probably also illegal film material to rob people's accounts.
8 Police are telling customers to remove any unusual equipment they see.
9 Jane Turner's bank has ATMs all over Britain.
10 More crimes like this are expected in other areas.

## 11 Mediation

A new customer asks you about safety precautions for using cash machines in Germany.

Use the English prompts below and write down how you would communicate the points below. Read the learning box on page 14 to help you.

**So können Sie sich gegen Kartenmissbrauch schützen:**

- Achten Sie auf ungewöhnliche Aufbauten am Karteneinzug und an der Tastatur des Bankautomaten!

- Verdecken Sie die Eingabe der Geheimnummer mit der Hand!
- Händigen Sie die Karte beim Bezahlen nie anderen Personen aus!
- Teilen Sie anderen Personen niemals Ihre Geheimnummer mit!
- Bewahren Sie die Karte sorgfältig auf!
- Lassen Sie die Karte bei Verlust oder Diebstahl sofort sperren!
- Kontrollieren Sie regelmäßig Ihre Kontoauszüge!

To protect yourself from card misuse:

1 Watch out for any unusual devices on …
2 Always hide the keypad with your hand, when …
3 When paying by card, never …
4 Never tell …
5 Always look after …
6 Ask the bank to cancel your card if …
7 Make sure you check …

**LEARNING** **Wie kann ich mein Hörverständnis verbessern?**

- Machen Sie sich vor dem Zuhören klar, um was es beim Hörtext gehen wird. (Welche Thematik? Worauf lässt der Titel schließen?)
- Versuchen Sie beim ersten Zuhören, den Text sinngemäß zu erfassen, und verzichten Sie auf das Verstehen von Details.
- Wenn Sie sich einen Text zum zweiten Mal anhören, können Sie auf Einzelheiten achten.
- Bleiben Sie nicht an Einzelwörtern hängen, sondern versuchen Sie, die Gesamtaussage zu erfassen.

## 12 Group project

As a class, identify some customer target groups like those in the caricatures below. Then get into small groups. Each one chooses a target group and creates a new current account for it, working as follows:

1 Analyze the lifestyle of the type of customer in your target group.
2 Decide what this type of customer will need and expect from a current account.
3 Create an account with attractive features for this target group and give it a suitable name.
4 Write a short text for a brochure about the new account.
5 Imagine that your fellow students are your colleagues who will be selling the account that you have created. Present it to them, using visual aids such as Powerpoint, flip charts, pin boards, overhead projectors, handouts, etc. Use expressions from the box below.

**LANGUAGE** **How to present a product**

**At the start of your presentation:**
I'd like to begin by giving you an overview of the structure of our presentation.
First I'm going to talk about …
Then my colleague, *(name)*, will give you an insight into …
After that we are planning to take a (closer) look at …
*(Name)* will take over and examine in detail …

**In the main section of your presentation:**
Now let me move on to …
Next I'm going to turn to …
At this point I'd like to add / comment on …
At this stage I'll hand over to … *(name)* who will give you details about …

**At the end:**
Finally, I'd like to summarize the main points.
To sum up I'm going to review the main aspects of …
Let's see what conclusions we can draw from …
I'd like to close by inviting you to ask questions.
Thank you for listening!

# Banking in Britain

## 13 Inside a UK bank branch

Compare the interior of this UK bank branch with the bank where you work. Point out the advantages and disadvantages in each case.

## 14 Speaking personally

7 Two employees of UK banks are talking to *Money Matters* about their work.

1 Donna describes job training and qualifications.
2 Harry gives his views on uniform and opening hours.

Listen and take notes on each of these topics. (See page 35 for some hints on improving your listening skills.) Then compare their experiences of banking with your own. What are the similarities and differences?

Unit 4

# Payments

## 1 Warm-up

**a** Could these be the contents of your bag or pockets? Identify the items shown above. Say what they tell you about their owner.

**b** Decide which of the following means of payment the owner probably uses, saying what each one may be used for.

| |
|---|
| cash \| credit card \| credit transfer \| debit card \| direct debit \| standing order |

## 2 Online transfers

Look at this form and do the tasks below.

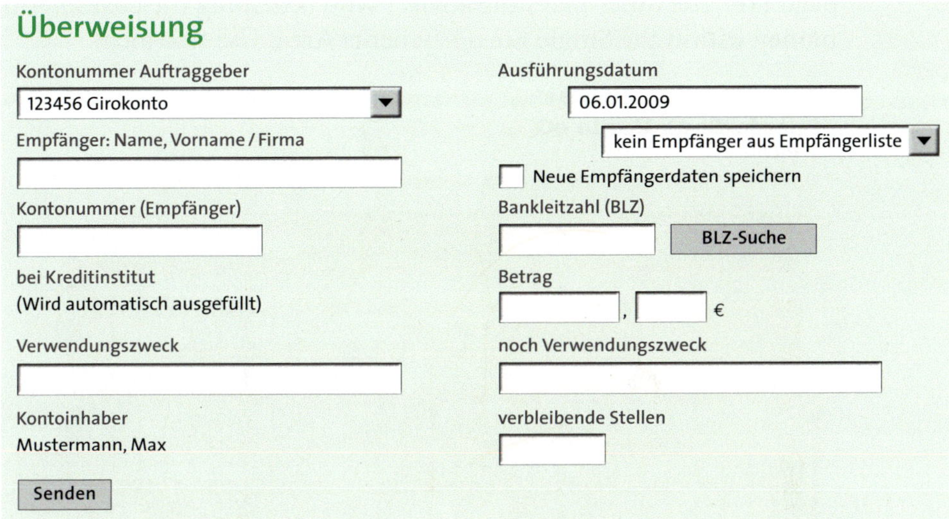

Überweisung

Kontonummer Auftraggeber

123456 Girokonto

Ausführungsdatum

06.01.2009

kein Empfänger aus Empfängerliste

Empfänger: Name, Vorname / Firma

Neue Empfängerdaten speichern

Kontonummer (Empfänger)

Bankleitzahl (BLZ)

BLZ-Suche

bei Kreditinstitut
(Wird automatisch ausgefüllt)

Betrag

, €

Verwendungszweck

noch Verwendungszweck

Kontoinhaber
Mustermann, Max

verbleibende Stellen

Senden

**a** A customer wants to know how to access the form above via online banking. Explain what to do.

**b** Describe where to fill in the following points on the above form. Use expressions from the language box below.

1 the payee's name
2 the payee's account number
3 the sort code of the payee's bank
4 the sum in euros and cents
5 the purpose of the transfer

**c** Explain to the customer what he/she needs to do after entering the details above, in order to authorize the payment.

**d** Say how long the transfer will take after pressing the Confirm button. Use the words "debited" and "credited" in your explanation. (See Language Box Unit 3, page 29.)

### LANGUAGE Using forms

| | | |
|---|---|---|
| Please | fill in | your name |
| Just | write | the payee's name |
| | put | the sum / amount |
| | enter | the details |
| | sign | |

on the front
on the back

on the top line / at the top
underneath/below/on the next line
on the left
in this space / in this box
on the right
on the bottom line / at the bottom

## 3 Euro transfers

**a** Work with a partner. One of you plays the customer using role card 7 on page 116. The other plays the adviser who is helping the customer transfer money within the Single Euro Payments Area. Use this form.

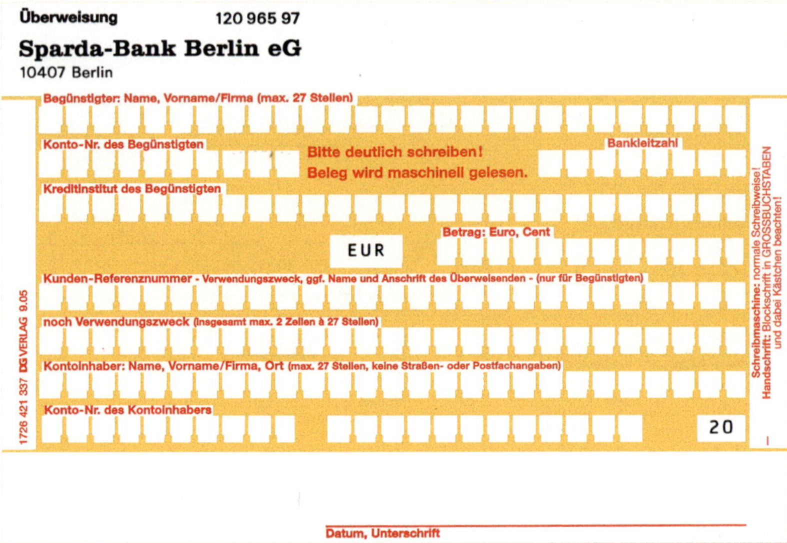
Überweisung 120 965 97
Sparda-Bank Berlin eG
10407 Berlin
Begünstigter: Name, Vorname/Firma (max. 27 Stellen)
Konto-Nr. des Begünstigten
Bitte deutlich schreiben!
Beleg wird maschinell gelesen.
Bankleitzahl
Kreditinstitut des Begünstigten
Betrag: Euro, Cent
EUR
Kunden-Referenznummer - Verwendungszweck, ggf. Name und Anschrift des Überweisenden - (nur für Begünstigten)
noch Verwendungszweck (insgesamt max. 2 Zeilen à 27 Stellen)
Kontoinhaber: Name, Vorname/Firma, Ort (max. 27 Stellen, keine Straßen- oder Postfachangaben)
Konto-Nr. des Kontoinhabers
20
Datum, Unterschrift
Schreibmaschine: normale Schreibweise!
Handschrift: Blockschrift in GROSSBUCHSTABEN und dabei Kästchen beachten!
1726 421 337 DG VERLAG 9.05

**b** Change roles. If you are playing the customer this time, use role card 8 on page 118. If you are playing the adviser, use a euro transfer form from your bank.

## 4 Standing orders

8

Julius Frank serves two customers on the phone.

**a** Copy this chart. Then fill it in in German while you are listening.

| | 1. Kunde | 2. Kunde |
|---|---|---|
| Dauerauftrag[1]: | | |
| Name des Auftraggebers: | | |
| Konto-Nr. des Auftraggebers: | | |
| Name des Empfängers: | | |
| Konto-Nr. des Empfängers: | | |
| Bankleitzahl: | | |
| Verwendungszweck: | | |
| Betrag: | | |
| Ausführung[2]: | | |
| Erste Ausführung am: | | |
| Letzte Ausfürung am: | | |

1 Einrichtung / Änderung / Löschung
2 monatlich / vierteljährlich / halbjährlich / jährlich

**b** What are the security precautions for account enquiries or transactions over the phone in the two dialogues? Compare them with the procedure at the bank where you work.

## 5 Direct debits

An American customer comes into your bank branch with the direct debit form below.

Working with a partner who takes the role of this customer, do the tasks below using the words in the box below. Then swap roles.

**Funsport Fitness-Studio GmbH**

**Einzugsermächtigung**

Hiermit ermächtige ich die Funsport GmbH, den Mitgliedsbeitrag für

Name des Mitglieds: ..........

Mitgliedsnummer: ..........

monatlich ☐ vierteljährlich ☐ halbjährlich ☐ jährlich* ☐

bei Fälligkeit von meinem nachstehenden Konto durch Lastschrift einzuziehen.

Name des Kontoinhabers: ..........

Anschrift: ..........

Bank / Sparkasse: ..........

Kontonummer: .......... BLZ: ..........

Unterschrift des Kontoinhabers: ..........

Ort, Datum: ..........

* Gewünschtes bitte ankreuzen

**a** Explain the points on the form to help the customer fill it in.

**b** Ask and answer questions on these points.

1 He/She does not know what to do with the form after filling it in.
2 He/She is worried that the health club may claim too much money from his/her account.
3 He/She wants to know how much direct debiting will cost.

*bei Fälligkeit* – on the due dates
*einziehen* – to claim
*ermächtigen* – to authorize
*Ermächtigung* – authorization
*Mitgliedsbeitrag* – membership fee
*widerrufen* – to revoke

## 6 Standing orders and direct debits

**a** Copy this table and complete it to compare the two means of payment.

| With standing orders: | With direct debits: |
|---|---|
| 1 the sum has to be fixed.<br>2 the dates … | 1 the payee can vary the sums. |

**b** Match each of these payments with its definition.

| | |
|---|---|
| loan instalments | regular transfers to savings accounts or funds |
| hire purchase payments | payments due for electricity, gas, water, etc. |
| savings or investment plans | repayments of money borrowed from a bank |
| newspaper subscriptions | amounts saved with a building society |
| season tickets | partial payments for goods bought on credit |
| insurance premiums | payments for regular delivery of a newspaper |
| building society payments | regular payments for insurance |
| utility bills | annual tickets for public transport, etc. |

## 7 Debit cards

Look at this brochure about debit cards.

Say which facts in the text support the picture.

### Your new Chip and PIN Debit Card

**Did you know that …**

one in three people in the UK has been affected by card fraud?

most fraud losses are used to fund organized crime?

That is why Chip and PIN technology has been developed!

**Chip …**

- The gold chip is harder to copy or alter than a magnetic strip.
- The chip contains encrypted data for increased security.

**PIN …**

- Entering your four-digit PIN when making a purchase at a point of sale is far more secure than a signature. Unlike your signature, your PIN cannot be forged.
- Do not worry about entering your PIN: it will not be logged or recorded in any way.
- You have three consecutive chances to enter your PIN correctly. Your PIN will be blocked after three failed attempts.

**GRAMMAR** The passive

1 Most fraud losses **are used** to fund organized crime.
2 Your PIN **will be blocked** after three failed attempts.
3 One in three people **has been affected** by card fraud.
4 Your PIN **can't be forged**.

- The passive is formed using a form of the verb *be* and the past participle. The passive can be used with all tenses of the verb *be* (1–3) and with modal verbs (4).
- The passive is often used in sentences in which the person or thing taking the action is not as important as the action itself.
- The word *by* is used if the agent is mentioned (3).

## 8 Practice: the passive

Your bank is preparing a leaflet to explain to its English-speaking customers how to use their debit card.

Re-write the text by putting the verbs underlined into the passive. Leave out the words in brackets.

Example 1 First, your card can be inserted …

Enclosed you will find your new bank card. It has several functions which we are sure you will find useful and convenient.

First, (you) <u>can insert</u>[1] your card at any of our statement printers whenever you want to see your latest bank statement of account. In addition, (you) <u>may use</u>[2] it at ATMs to check your balance or to withdraw cash. (The machine) <u>will ask</u>[3] you to enter your PIN* and choose the amount that you wish to withdraw. For security reasons, (we) <u>limit</u>[4] withdrawals at cash machines to €1000 a day.

But that's not all. (You) <u>can use</u>[5] it as a debit card to pay for goods and services at any point of sale where (they) <u>display</u>[6] the Electronic Cash or Maestro symbol. Just hand over your card to the salesperson who will put it into a reader. (The reader) <u>will show</u>[7] the sum that you have to pay on the screen. If this is correct, enter your four-digit PIN and press the green Confirm button. (We) <u>will then debit</u>[8] your account and <u>transfer</u>[9] the sum to the payee.

If (you) <u>have lost</u>[10] your card or (someone) <u>has stolen</u>[11] it, please contact us on our emergency 24-hour hotline immediately.

* (We) <u>will send</u>[12] your PIN (= Personal Identification Number) to you separately by post within the next few days.

## 9 Selling a credit card

9

Julius Frank is advising Bob Hewitt, an Australian customer, about credit cards.

**a** Listen to the dialogue and answer these questions.

1 What are Mr Hewitt's plans at the beginning of the dialogue?
2 Has he changed his plans by the end of the dialogue? If so, why?

**b** Listen again and write down the advantages of credit cards that are mentioned.

JULIUS: Good morning, Mr Hewitt. Nice to see you again.

BOB: Not exactly a good morning, is it? All this rain! Well, my wife and I are heading down under soon. Get a bit of sunshine. We're going to need a few traveller's cheques and some Australian dollars in cash.

JULIUS: I'll order the currency, but I'm afraid we don't sell traveller's cheques.

BOB: Really? Why on earth not?

JULIUS: Most people use credit cards these days. They're accepted nearly all over the world.

BOB: But so are traveller's cheques too, aren't they?

JULIUS: In theory, yes, but traveller's cheques have fixed denominations. That's why hotels, shops and restaurants usually prefer credit cards. They're so easy to use: you just show your card, sign the bill and that's that!

BOB: Too easy I reckon! Anybody who gets hold of your card can pay with it!

JULIUS: Don't worry about that. In case of loss or theft, notify us and we'll stop payment on the card at once. Then you won't have to bear any losses if it's misused.

BOB: Great! Then there I am, stuck in the middle of Australia, with no card!

JULIUS: That wouldn't be a problem either. We could arrange for you to get a replacement card within 24 hours.

BOB: And how much would all this cost me?

JULIUS: Our standard card costs 30 euros a year. That includes a free partner card as well.

BOB: What do you mean "standard card"?

JULIUS: We also offer gold cards with additional services like baggage insurance, accident cover, everything you'd need in an emergency, really.

BOB: Sounds a lot safer to stay at home! Look, let's say I have a card and use it to pay for things. What happens then?

JULIUS: With most cards your current account will be debited automatically once a month. So you have a period of interest-free credit until that happens. You'll get a monthly statement and you can check your entries online as well.

BOB: That reminds me. Do you know, I wanted to order something on the web recently but they wouldn't send me a bill. They asked for a credit card number.

JULIUS: Yes, lots of online payments are made by credit card.
BOB: Surely that's risky. I mean, entering your credit card number on the computer! You don't even have to give a signature!
JULIUS: There are highly developed security systems. You enter your name, your card number, its expiry date and a three-digit security number as well.
BOB: Yeah, but there's always a risk ...
JULIUS: Cash is the riskiest means of payment there is, and we use that all the time!
BOB: True. I'm still going to take some traveller's cheques but I'd better have a credit card as well. Can I get one now?
JULIUS: Of course. We can make the application right away ...

**c** Now read the dialogue and see if you have missed any advantages. Can you think of any more to add to the list?

**d** Decide which of the arguments for having a credit card are the strongest ones and rewrite your list with the points in that order. Use the passive where suitable.

Example 1 Credit cards are accepted nearly all over the world.
2 They can be used ...

## CULTURE Credit cards in the UK and the USA

Credit cards are more widely used in the UK and the USA than in Germany. One reason for this is that UK and US credit card issuers often undertake aggressive marketing campaigns to persuade people to take out more credit. Unsolicited mail offers and advertising in the media encourage even people who are already in debt to apply for further cards. Also, all UK and US credit cards only require the holder to repay a minimum sum each month. Interest will then be charged on the remaining debit balance. Since interest rates are variable and can be as high as 20% per annum or more, holders of several credit cards can easily get deeply into debt.
In contrast, under the Eurocard/Mastercard system in Germany, money is automatically transferred from the current account to cover the credit card debt each month.

## 10 Over to you

Take over Julius Frank's role.

**a** Using this information from the Sparda Bank, explain to Mr Hewitt how this credit card works.

**b** Tell Mr Hewitt about the advantages of this credit card.

**Sparda-Bank**
*freundlich & fair*

**Ihre neue Flexibilität mit dem MasterCard FlexKredit:**

- Flexible Ratenzahlung der monatlichen MasterCard-Abrechnung ab 2% bis 50%, mindestens 50,00 Euro monatlich
- Jederzeitige Komplettrückzahlung zum nächsten Abrechnungstag
- Änderungen der Ratenzahlungen jederzeit per Telefon, in der Filiale oder via Internet unter www.spare-cent.de im Sparda-Onlinebanking unter Service/Aufträge
- Beenden des FlexKredites jeweils zum nächsten Abrechnungstag (100% Rückzahlung) ohne Einhaltung von Kündigungsfristen – ebenfalls per Telefonbanking, via Internet oder einfach in Ihrer Filiale
- Keine Bearbeitungsgebühren!

☐ **Ja, ich möchte für meine MasterCard die FlexKredit-Funktion. Bitte stellen Sie mit Wirkung zum nächsten Abrechnungstag die o.g. Kreditkarte auf eine Teilrückzahlung um in Höhe von:**

☐ **2%** ☐ **5%** ☐ **10%** ☐ **20%**

☐ **30%** ☐ **40%** ☐ **50%**

**Die monatliche Mindestzahlung beträgt 50,00 Euro.**

### LEARNING Wie man Sprache für den Berufsalltag lernt

Neue Ausdrücke lassen sich auf verschiedene Arten lernen, etwa indem man die einzelnen Wörter „paukt“ oder sich die entsprechende Grammatik aneignet. Manchmal hilft es jedoch, nicht auf einzelne Vokabeln und Regeln zu achten, sondern sich gebräuchliche Wendungen als ganze einzuprägen.

Denken Sie an diese Methode, wenn Sie eine Fremdsprache für Ihren Beruf lernen. Dort sind feste Wendungen, die man immer und immer wieder braucht, besonders wichtig. Etwa beim Telefonieren: Der Erfolg stellt sich schneller ein, wenn man eine Frage wie ‘Would you like to leave a message?’ nicht aus einzelnen Vokabeln und den grammatischen Frageformen zusammenbaut, sondern sie sich direkt vollständig einprägt.

## 11 Combi-cards

Read the text and speech bubbles that follow. Then answer the questions below.

### London Launch of Combination Card

Just as mobile phones are no longer limited to telephoning, today's credit cards are also taking on an increasing variety of additional services. The new age began recently in London with the launch of Barclaycard OnePulse.

A Barclaycard spokesperson announced OnePulse as a step forward for the whole credit card industry. The major difference between a OnePulse card and any normal credit card is the Pay-Wave function: to pay for a purchase, the holder simply passes the card over a vending machine and no signature or PIN is required. The OnePulse card has been developed by Barclays in collaboration with Visa and London Transport. Many retailers that handle small sums of cash, such as cafés, newsagents and other businesses, have signed up for the scheme. They have installed vending machines with built-in readers that decipher the encrypted data on the OnePulse card and deduct the correct amount of money from it.

Barclaycard emphasizes that the new 3-in-1 card has benefits not only for retailers but also for consumers because it improves the usability and convenience of credit cards.

I love using my combi-card to pay for little bits of shopping, but I sometimes worry that it makes it a bit TOO easy to spend money! Sometimes I spend far more on chocolate and magazines than I can afford.
**Jaya, 26, Ickenham**

As a retailer, I think the Pay-Wave function is a great idea. Customers often come in without much cash, wanting to make small purchases. Now that I've installed the new vending machine, they can make a quick cashless payment instead.
**Simon, 39, Brixton**

When I'm carrying the combi-card, I always take some spare cash in case I lose the card. I have a friend who lost his combi-card on the way to work once and he got really frustrated that he didn't have any cash with him to pay for his train ticket home.
**Meera, 45, Camden**

I always used to forget to top up my pay-as-you-go balance. I'd have to queue up to pay for it and that would make me late. But now I've set up the auto top-up service, my card credit never runs out – it gets automatically topped up via Visa.
**Richard, 22, Lewisham**

**a** Explain why OnePulse is a combi-card?

**b** Point out the benefits and drawbacks of this combi-card for card holders, retailers and credit card companies.

**c** Describe any combi-cards that you know about.

## 12 Work with words

Find expressions used in this unit which match the clues below.

1 If you regularly read a newspaper, you will save money if you have one of these.
2 If you join a club or society, you will have to pay these regularly.
3 This means the reason why a credit transfer or standing order is made.
4 This is the form you have to sign to allow direct debiting.
5 If a direct debit is incorrect, you can do this to get your money back.
6 This word means "every three months".
7 If you want to stop paying by standing order, you have to do this.
8 If your debit or credit card is lost or stolen, you must ask the bank to do this.

## 13 Mediation

A German colleague asks you about the text below. Read it and then answer the questions underneath in German.

### Digital Detectives

Today, not all detectives are human. Software is increasingly being used to search through financial transactions and find out which of them are fraudulent – far more quickly and efficiently than any human being could. Just like a real detective, the software analyzes patterns in the ways people normally behave, then compares new data with those patterns to discover which do not correspond. This method is now being used in the field of credit card misuse. Retailers in Britain who have introduced detection software have cut their losses from fraud by up to 50%. So how does it work?

The software evaluates the details of every payment made by credit card: the item purchased (from the bar code), the time, the place, etc. and gives each transaction a risk-score based on the way similar transactions stored in the data bank have proved to be correct or fraudulent. A transaction that reaches a certain score will either be stopped or queried. Here are some examples.

Paying for petrol by credit card seems to be fairly normal, but filling up the tank at night instead of during the day (when the pump attendant may be present) gives a higher score. Buying an expensive watch after the visit to the filling station raises the score again. Purchases in big cities count more than those in small towns. A card holder's buying pattern is also stored: if someone regularly buys return train tickets from Berlin to Frankfurt, the software may stop the payment of a plane ticket from Moscow to Las Vegas for a flight leaving in three hours.

The single pieces of information are simple, combined they can bring spectacular results. As Sherlock Holmes said, "I'm glad of all details, whether they seem to you to be relevant or not."

(Source: Adapted from *The Economist*)

**a** Was soll mit der neuen Software erreicht werden?

**b** Gibt es bereits Erfolge?

**c** Wie funktioniert das System?

**d** Welches Kaufverhalten ist verdächtig? (Nennen Sie Beispiele.)

# Marketing credit cards

## 14 Two marketing strategies

Here are two marketing strategies for VISA cards: one is a postcard sent to customers and the other is a leaflet for branches about earning reward points.

Describe the advertising material in each case. Then answer the questions.

a How does each company try to persuade the reader to apply for a credit card?

b What are the target groups of the postcard and the leaflet?

c Which advertising strategy do you find more effective? Give reasons.

# Savings

## 1 Warm-up

Here are three ways in which people save money.

**a** Examine the advantages and disadvantages of these three ways of saving.

**b** Describe the difference between saving and investing. Give examples to explain why people save and why people invest.

**c** Banks in the UK no longer sell piggy banks like the one shown above. Suggest why.

**LANGUAGE** Long numbers and decimals

In English-speaking countries commas and dots are not used in the same way as they are in Germany:

| | | | |
|---|---|---|---|
| German: | 5.000,00 Euro | English: | 5,000.00 euros |
| | 1.500.000 Einwohner | | 1,500,000 inhabitants |
| | 2,25 % | | 2.25% = two point two five per cent |

eine Milliarde = US: one billion, UK: one thousand million
eine Billion = US: one trillion, UK: one billion or one million million

When saying long numbers, the word "and" follows the word "hundred":
1,257,364 = one million, two hundred and fifty-seven thousand, three hundred and sixty-four

## 2 Wealth distribution in Germany

Look at these two charts and answer the questions below.

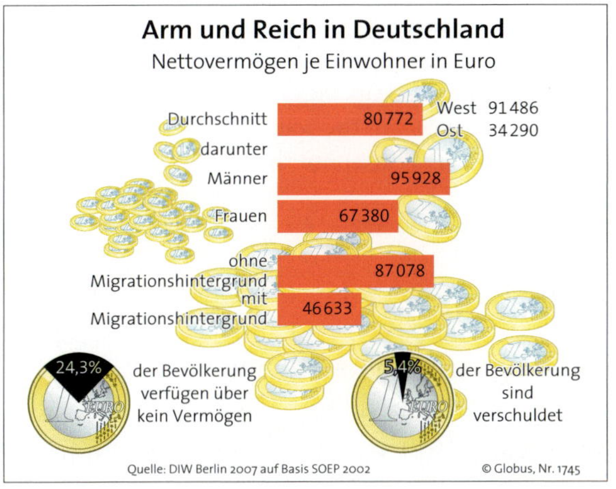

**a** How much does the average person in Germany hold in net assets?

**b** What is the difference between the assets of people living in the west and the east of Germany?

**c** How do the assets held by men compare with those held by women?

**d** Is there a connection between a person's ethnic background and his or her assets?

**e** What percentage of the population of Germany has no assets at all?

**f** What percentage of the population of Germany is in debt?

**g** How is wealth distributed in Germany?

## 3 Discussion

**a** Working with a partner, prepare for the discussion by doing the following four tasks. Write down the conclusions you reach.

1 Find reasons for the unequal distribution of wealth in Germany
- between East and West
- between men and women
- between people with and without an immigrant background.

2 Look at other factors that can play a role in the distribution of wealth.

3 Will the gap between rich and poor increase or decrease in future? Say why.

4 Point out ways in which banks can react to these changes.

**b** In class, discuss the questions raised in points 1–4 above. Use expressions from the box on the next page to express agreement or disagreement with your fellow students' ideas.

**LANGUAGE** **How to express agreement or disagreement**

| If you agree: | If you disagree: |
| --- | --- |
| I (totally/absolutely) agree. | I wouldn't go so far as to say that. |
| That's (absolutely) true. | I take your point, but on the other hand … |
| I couldn't agree more. | I agree up to a point, but … |
| I take your point. | I see things differently. |
| That's exactly the way I see it. | That's not the way I see it. |
| Absolutely! | That's (just) not the case. |
| Definitely! | |

## 4 Talking about saving (Part 1)

10

Jane Hyatt is making a radio programme about saving money. She is interviewing Liam Bonner, who works for a large UK bank.

**a** Before you listen, say what you would ask Liam Bonner if you had to make the programme.

**b** Now listen to the first part of Jane's interview and then answer the questions below.

JANE: Thank you for coming in to talk to us today, Mr Bonner.

LIAM: Not at all. My pleasure.

JANE: Saving is an important topic for many of our listeners today, though only a few years ago everyone was buying shares on the stock exchange instead of putting money in the bank. Savings accounts were just something for children to put their pocket money in …

LIAM: Yes, I couldn't agree more. But things have changed a lot. People are not as willing to take risks as they used to be.

JANE: Why is that?

LIAM: The economic climate has got worse. Life is more uncertain nowadays. In times of recession and unemployment people think twice about what they do with their hard-earned cash.

JANE: So the good old savings account has come back to life again?

LIAM: I wouldn't go so far as to say that. Banks are really in competition to get people's money, so they've developed a much wider range of products for savers.

JANE: You mean there's more on offer than just a savings account?

LIAM: Definitely! There are many different ways to save nowadays, so most customers need advice to find the right product to suit their needs.

JANE: What should you look at when choosing a savings product?

LIAM: Two main things. Clearly, first of all, the interest rate – you'll want to get the highest possible rate – but it can be just as important that you have access to your savings …

JANE: You mean that I can get my money out if I need it?

LIAM: That's right. Without paying a penalty fee or losing interest if you do.
JANE: So the second thing you have to look at is how long your money is blocked?
LIAM: Absolutely. You'll get a higher rate of interest if you deposit it for a longer period.
JANE: So what should I tell my bank adviser if I'm planning to save?
LIAM: Your adviser is going to ask you three main questions. The first one is how long you want to save your money for. A second is how you want to save: do you want to save smaller sums regularly or have you got a lump sum to invest? And the third question your adviser is going to ask you is, of course, how much do you want to save?
JANE: Because the amount that you save affects the rate of interest?
LIAM: That's correct. Generally, the more you save, the higher the interest rate will be.
JANE: And I suppose it's important to have a fixed interest rate?
LIAM: That's not the way I see it. If interest rates rise, it can be better to have a product with a variable rate …
JANE: I take your point. Perhaps you could give our listeners an overview of some of the products for savers on the market?
LIAM: Certainly, let's take a look at the main ones …

1 Why have people become more careful with their money?
2 Why do bank customers need advice on saving?
3 What two things should a customer look at when choosing a savings product?
4 What three questions will the bank adviser ask before advising a customer?

**c** Read this part of the interview and find expressions from the last box.

## GRAMMAR Comparative and superlative forms

1 Banks have developed a much **wider** range of products for savers.
2 Life is **more uncertain** nowadays.
3 There's **more** on offer **than** just a simple savings account.
4 Today people are **not as** willing to take risks **as** they used to be.
5 … it can be **better** to have a product with a variable interest rate.
6 The economic climate has got **worse**.

- Words of one syllable and some words of two syllables make comparisons with *-er/-est* (1).
- Most words with two syllables and all words of three or more syllables make comparisons with *more/most* (2).
- The comparative form + *than* (= als) is used in comparisons (3).
- *as … as* (= so … wie) is used to show if two things are equal or not (4).
- Some adjectives have irregular comparative and superlative forms (3, 5, 6).

## 5 Practice: comparatives and superlatives

Complete these comparisons using the correct form of the word in brackets.

1 Interest rates are … (low) now than they have been for a long time.
2 Banking has become a lot … (competitive) than it was ten years ago.
3 As banks offer a far … (wide) range of products nowadays, advice has become … (important) than ever before.
4 It is not as … (easy) as it used to be to find the …(suitable) product.
5 Generally speaking, the … (much) you save, the … (high) the interest rate will be.
6 If the ECB raises the base rate, people will borrow … (little) and saving will become … (attractive).
7 Investing on the stock exchange is … (risky) than putting your money into a savings account, but it can be … (profitable).
8 It is hard to say which method of saving is the … (good), but the … (bad) thing you can do is to hide your savings under your mattress.

## 6 Talking about saving (Part 2)

11

In the second part of the interview, Liam Bonner is telling Jane Hyatt about savings products that his bank offers.

These expressions will be of help:
notice account = an account in which money is deposited for a fixed period
give notice = *kündigen*
observe a period of notice = *eine Kündigungsfrist einhalten*

**a** Working with a partner, read the text below and use these expressions to fill the gaps.

1 choose the term that suits you best
2 park money before deciding how to invest it
3 withdraw at ATMs with your savings card
4 pay a penalty fee
5 observe a three months' period of notice
6 cash it in before the end of the term
7 need the money for two years

LIAM: Let's take a look at some savings products we have on offer. I'd like to mention four popular ones. The first is an account called "The Instant Access Savings Account" …

JANE: Does "Instant Access" mean you can withdraw your money whenever you need it?

LIAM: That's right, there's no period of notice for withdrawals. The only condition is that you have to have a current account with us. There's no minimum sum to save and you can …[A]

JANE: But I suppose the interest rate is fairly low?

LIAM: Lower than on other savings products, yes, and the rate is variable.

JANE: Mmm, what if I want to save regularly but get more interest?

LIAM: In that case, we come to our second possibility, which is to open a notice account. You can use it to save regularly or pay sums in whenever you like.

JANE: A notice account? That means I have to give notice if I want to make a withdrawal?

LIAM: Exactly. Just to give you an example, if you have a Three Months Notice Account, you'll have to …[B] before you can take any money out.

JANE: And if I need the money sooner than that?

LIAM: In that case, I'm afraid you'll have to …[C], but the interest rate on a notice account is higher than on an Instant Access Account. Here too, the rate is variable. And the larger the sum you save, the higher it will be.

JANE: What if I have a lump sum and know that I'm not going to …[D], should I put it into a Two-Year Notice Account?

LIAM: No, if you want to save a lump sum for a longer term, there is a third possibility: you can buy a deposit bond. Deposit bonds are available for sums from £2,000 upwards and the interest rate is fixed. We offer six-month, one-year, two-year and three-year bonds so you can …[E]

JANE: But again, the money is blocked, isn't it?

LIAM: Yes, you'll lose 2% of the value of the bond if you …[F]

JANE: One last question. You've told us about three popular ways of saving so far, but what about money market accounts? Are they a good alternative?

LIAM: Well, in times when no one knows which direction the economy is going to take, lots of people like to …[G]. As the name says, the interest rate depends on the money market so it varies daily. Money market accounts are flexible because you can withdraw your money on demand but at our bank they are only available for sums of £50,000 or more.

**b** Now listen to this part of the interview and see if you have filled the gaps correctly.

**c** Four savings products are mentioned. What are they called in German?

**d** Compare the four savings products with the ones offered at your bank.

**CULTURE** **State subsidies for savers**

The UK government encourages people to save in the form of ISAs = Individual Savings Accounts. Savings in an ISA (pronounced "eye-sa" ) are tax-free.
In Germany, on the other hand, the state encourages people to save with the *Arbeitnehmer-Sparzulage* for *vermögenswirksame Leistungen.* As no equivalent system exists in the English-speaking world, there are no single expressions to translate these terms. The *Arbeitnehmer-Sparzulage* can be explained as a state subsidy for payments that employers make towards certain savings or investments of their employees. *Vermögenswirksame Leistungen* are these asset-building savings or investments.

## 7 Assistance for regular savers

People from abroad who are employed in Germany can benefit from the *Arbeitnehmer-Sparzulage*. Tell an English-speaking customer the following information.

### Vermögenswirksame Leistungen

- Für die vermögenswirksamen Leistungen sind u. a. folgende Anlageformen zulässig:
  - Bausparvertrag
  - Lebensversicherung
  - Investmentfonds
  - Banksparplan
- Der Arbeitnehmer kann die Art der Anlage und das Unternehmen oder Institut, bei dem sie erfolgen soll, frei wählen.
- Die Einkünfte aus nichtselbstständiger Arbeit dürfen bestimmte Einkommensgrenzen nach Abzug von Steuern nicht überschreiten.
- Die Arbeitnehmer-Sparzulage wird vom Arbeitgeber bezahlt. Sie ist steuerfrei und nicht Bestandteil des Gehalts.

## 8 Over to you

Work with a partner who takes the role of a customer of your bank.

Find out your customer's needs and offer a suitable savings product. If appropriate, tell your customer about the *Arbeitnehmer-Sparzulage*. Then change the roles. One partner takes role cards 9 and 10 on page 117, the other partner takes role cards 11 and 12 on page 119.

## 9 Marketing a money market account

Here is some advertising material produced by ING DiBa. Which points should persuade the reader to open the "Extra" account? Write a list of these points in English. (Do not translate word for word.)

### Das Extra-Konto macht mehr aus Ihrem Geld:

Der eindeutige Zinsvorteil mit dem Extra-Konto rechnet sich!

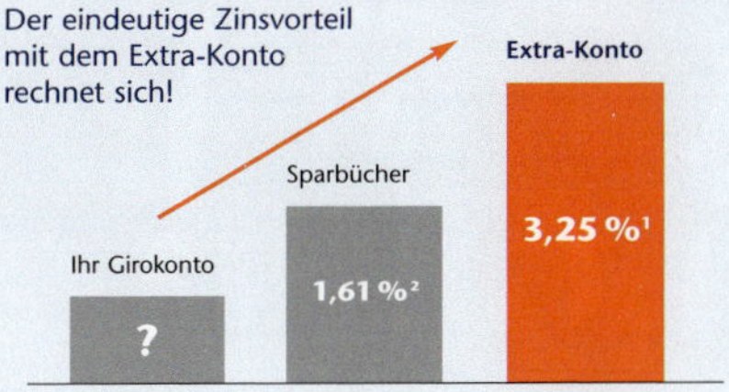


**Auf dem Extra-Konto vermehrt sich Ihr Geld sicher und zinsstark: Bei den aktuellen Konditionen werden so aus 10.000 Euro in nur 5 Jahren stolze 11.734 Euro!**

**Gleich ausfüllen und einsenden –**

**und Ihr Geld bringt sofort hohe Zinsen ab dem ersten Euro!**

- **Genau so muss Sparen sein: Flexibel, renditestark und sicher**

Egal wie oft, wie viel oder für wie lange Sie sparen, jeder Euro wird mit 3,25 %[1] p. a. verzinst. Beim Extra-Konto sind Sie an keine Laufzeiten, Mindestbeträge oder Kündigungsfristen gebunden. Sie können sich jederzeit Geld auf Ihr Girokonto (Referenzkonto) auszahlen lassen – telefonisch, per Internet oder Brief.

- **Einmal eröffnet, immer hohe Zinsen!**

- **Schnell sein lohnt sich!**

Eröffnen Sie Ihr Extra-Konto **bis XX.XX.XXXX** mit beiliegendem Vertrag. Dann sichern Sie sich nicht nur hohe Zinsen, sondern auch unser Dankeschön:

**25 Euro Gutschrift**
ab 2.500 Euro Einmalanlage

**50 Euro Gutschrift**
ab 5.000 Euro Einmalanlage

## 10 Designing a money market account

Work in pairs. Your head of department has asked you to use your experience of selling money market accounts to design a new money market account to be offered by your bank.

As the marketing consultant for the new account is American, your head of department has asked you to outline your ideas for the new account in English. Make sure you include information on the following points:

- interest rate
- conditions (e.g. amount, term, etc.)
- Unique Selling Points (USPs) for customers
- ideas for marketing the account

## 11 A bank in trouble

**a** Look at the photo and say what you think is happening.

**b** Now read this article and see if you are right. (For some useful guidelines on reading difficult texts see the learning box on page 60.)

### Bank's customers take no chances with savings

LONDON: Hundreds of customers across Britain crowded into branches of mortgage bank Northern Rock on Friday to pull out their savings. The news that the Bank of England had granted Northern Rock an emergency loan triggered fears that Northern Rock might default. Northern Rock has been short of funds since the cost of borrowing between banks rose in the credit crisis.

The Financial Services Compensation Scheme protects customers' deposits of up to £31,700 should a bank default.

The Bank of England said Northern Rock was solvent and only in need of short-term help, but many customers were not taking any chances.

"I've spun all my savings into another bank," said customer John Duncan on his way out of a London branch. "You read the headlines in the paper: 'Northern Rock, Cash SOS!' If you had money in there, what would you do?"

"It's scary," said Peter Pye, 60, standing in line with about 30 people outside his branch. "I have my life's savings in Northern Rock." He said he would withdraw a "six-figure" sum and leave £5,000 in the account.

Some customers were satisfied by Northern Rock's reassurances. "Our savings are all right, they said, so we are just going to take their word," said Robert Butler, 26. "People are overreacting."

Northern Rock's website closed down after frustrated customers wanting to withdraw money froze the system. "I've been on the pc trying to get my savings out since 7 this morning," Andrew Murphy, 27, complained.

Meanwhile Northern Rock's chief executive officer, Adam Applegarth, asked customers to be patient and said it was "business as normal". "You don't get better than being backed by the Bank of England," he added, in reference to the emergency loan.

"I don't think the bank's going to go bust, because the Bank of England won't let that happen," said customer Paul Delamere, 46, though he added that he was "more comfortable" with reducing his account.

Not everyone was so optimistic. "Why leave money in a bank that has problems?" asked Michael Ribotham, 74. "I'm not young and I won't have the chance to get it back if I lose money now."

(Source: Abridged from *International Herald Tribune*, 2007)

**c** Say which customer in the article

1 … wanted to withdraw more than £99,999.
2 … decided to leave all his money in Northern Rock.
3 … tried to withdraw his money online.
4 … thought he was too old to start saving again.
5 … trusted in the Bank of England.
6 … transferred all his savings to another bank.

**d** Give the German expression for "Financial Services Compensation Scheme" (line 10).

## 12 "How safe are my savings?"

Use information in this article to answer the customers' questions below.

### So ist Ihr Geld geschützt

Die Einschläge kommen näher. Wenn nun bereits die Briten panikartig ihr Erspartes in Sicherheit bringen wollen, da wird es auch so manchem deutschen Verbraucher mulmig zumute. Doch hierzulande muss niemand zum Geldautomaten oder in die Bankfiliale stürmen, um sein Konto zu räumen. Bei den großen Privatbanken springt im Ernstfall der Einlagensicherungsfonds ein. Für den einzelnen Kunden gilt: Seine Einlagen sind bis zu einer Höhe geschützt, die 30 Prozent des haftenden Eigenkapitals* des jeweiligen Instituts entsprechen. Bei der Deutschen Bank wären das beispielsweise 7,6 Mrd. Euro, sprich: jeder Kunde bekommt im Zweifelsfall Einlagen bis 7,6 Mrd. Euro vom Sicherungsfonds ersetzt. Bei der HVB beträgt die Summe 4,4 Mrd. Euro, bei der Commerzbank 3,9 Mrd. Euro, bei der Dresdner Bank 2,9 und bei der Postbank 1,25 Mrd. Euro.

Bei den Sparkassen sowie den Volks- und Raiffeisenbanken stehen die Geldhäuser füreinander ein. Es gilt das Prinzip der Institutssicherung. Im Klartext: Gerät ein Institut in Schieflage, eilen die anderen zu Hilfe. Damit sind auch die Kundengelder geschützt – in unendlicher Höhe.

Aufpassen müssen Kunden bei Kredithäusern außerhalb des Einlagensicherungsfonds und der Institutssicherung. Hier greift lediglich der gesetzliche Schutz in Höhe von 20.000 Euro.

Source: *Die Welt*, 2007

* Note: *haftendes Eigenkapital* (line 11) = equity capital

1 The Financial Services Compensation Scheme in Britain pays up to £31,700 if a bank defaults. Is it the same in Germany?
2 What's the maximum compensation I would get if, for example, the *Commerzbank* got into trouble?
3 Why are the sums different?
4 How much would I get if I had my savings at a *Volksbank* or *Raiffeisenbank?*
5 Where would that money come from?
6 What should I look at when choosing a bank to put my savings in? Why?

## 13 Work with words

**a** Find expressions used in this unit which mean the following:

1 a savings account which has an agreed period of notice for withdrawals
2 the charge that an account holder has to pay if a period of notice is not observed
3 a savings account which allows withdrawals on demand
4 an investment that offers a fixed rate of interest on a fixed sum for a fixed term
5 the scheme that protects savers if a bank gets into financial trouble
6 financial help that is given by the state

**b** Choose one of these pairs of words to fill the gaps in these sentences.

safe / save

1 It is important to … a part of your salary every month.
2 Your money will be … if you … it in a bank account.
3 Customers can … tax on their interest income.

raise / rise

4 The Central Bank is expected to … interest rates soon.
5 If interest rates …, saving becomes more attractive.
6 Employees will want their employers to … their salaries if prices … any higher.

advice / advise

7 We can … you how to invest your money.
8 If you follow our …, you will receive a guaranteed income.

economic / economical

9 The … climate is not as good as it was ten years ago.
10 It is not … to keep your savings under your mattress.

**LEARNING** **Wie lese ich einen schwierigen Text?**

Wenn Sie schwierige Texte lesen, ist es wichtig zu wissen, worauf Sie Wert legen: auf ein allgemeines Textverständnis oder auf ein detailliertes Verständnis.

1 Vergegenwärtigen Sie, was Sie bereits zur Thematik wissen.
2 Verschaffen Sie sich einen ersten Eindruck vom Text, indem Sie sich zunächst die Überschrift, evtl. auch Bilder ansehen und dann den Text rasch überfliegen.
3 Suchen Sie den Text nun nur auf die Gesichtspunkte oder Fakten ab, die Sie interessieren.
4 Sie können Texte visualisieren (d. h. wesentliche Textstellen durch Markierung hervorheben) und strukturieren (z. B. mit Hilfe einer Mindmap).
5 Schlagen Sie nur dann unbekannte Wörter im Wörterbuch nach, wenn das Wort aus dem Satzzusammenhang nicht erschlossen werden kann und für das Textverständnis unabdingbar ist.

# Offshore savings

## 14 Going offshore

A customer from another EU member state now living in Germany plans to transfer his savings to an account in his home country to receive gross interest.

Use this text and the diagrams below to tell him whether or not this will be tax-efficient and why.

### The European Savings Directive (ESD)

The ESD is an agreement between the member states of the European Union to collect and automatically exchange information about individuals who earn savings income in one EU member state but are resident in another. It aims to counter cross-border tax evasion. Savings income is essentially interest earned on bank deposits, interest from and proceeds on the sale or redemption of certain bonds and income from certain types of investment funds, for example open-ended money market retail funds. Most other types of income, such as dividends on shares, salaries and pensions, are outside the scope of this agreement.

While the automatic exchange of information is the ultimate objective of the ESD, certain EU members (in 2008 Austria, Belgium and Luxemberg) have elected to apply the withholding tax option, whereby tax may be deducted at source from income earned on savings. The payee may, however, request that withholding tax is not levied either by allowing the paying agent to report information to the tax authority in his or her state of residence or by giving the paying agent a certificate of exemption from an authorized tax authority.

Countries which have elected to use the automatic exchange of information do not offer a withholding tax option. The tax authority of the country where the paying agent is based will automatically supply details of the payee's identity and residence, the paying agent, the level of savings income and the period to which it relates to the local tax authority in the payee's country of residence. This information may then be compared with the payee's tax returns.

**Witholding tax**

Client has bank account in another ESD country.

→ Paying agent (bank) pays interest with tax deducted and pays all tax witheld to tax authority in the paying agent's country.

→ Tax authority in the paying agent's country pays 75% of this tax to the tax authority in the client's country of residence and keeps 25%.

**Information exchange**

Client has bank account in another ESD country.

→ Paying agent (bank) pays interest to the client's account and makes an annual report to local tax authority in the paying agent's country.

→ The tax authority in the paying agent's country annually exchanges details with the tax authority in the client's country of residence. These details can then be compared with the client's tax returns.

# Investment

## 1 Warm-up

Life as a pensioner is very different for different people …

company pension
contribute to / pay contributions to
provide for the future /
make provision for the future
private pension (plan)
state pension (fund)

**a** Decide which factors determine how much a person has to live on after retirement. Use words from the box above.

**b** Describe the development shown in this chart. Then point out the consequences for young people and the opportunities for banks. Use expressions from the language box opposite.

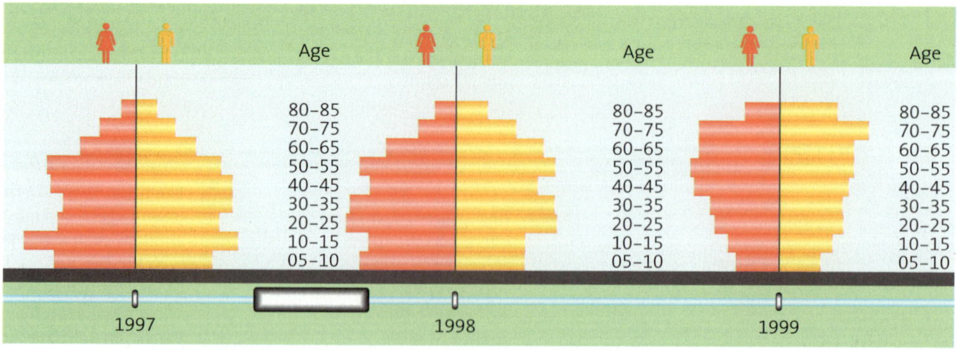


(Source: www.provincial.com)

**LANGUAGE** **Describing trends**

Verbs to describe a rise / an upturn: climb – increase – leap* – jump* – rise – soar*
Verbs to describe a fall / a downturn: decline – decrease – drop – slump – plunge*
* Use these verbs if the rise or fall is dramatic.

Adverbs to describe trends more precisely:

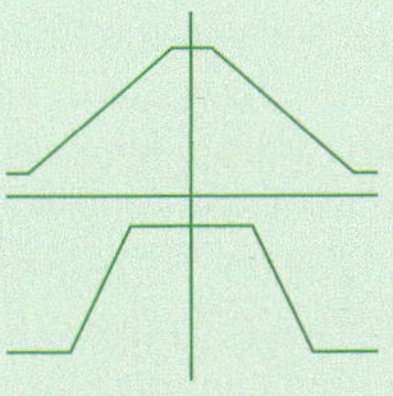


| | |
|---|---|
| rise/fall | gradually<br>slightly<br>steadily |
| rise/fall | abruptly<br>rapidly<br>sharply |

- If prices frequently rise and fall: be volatile – fluctuate – vary
- If prices fall and then rise again: rally – rebound – recover
- If prices do not change: remain constant/stable/unchanged

## 2 Describing charts

Match each of these three texts with one of the charts (a–d) shown below. Then write a fourth text to describe the remaining chart.

The four charts show how markets performed in the year November 2007 to October 2008 in the turbulences triggered by the US credit crisis.

1 It remained fairly stable until February when it rose sharply, but in July a rapid decline began. Despite a brief rally in September, it continued to fall dramatically.

2 After an upturn in December it dropped abruptly in January and again in March. A rebound followed, but in May it started to fall gradually and plunged drastically in October.

3 In December it began to increase, soaring to its highest point in March. It then fluctuated until July when it suddenly fell. It recovered briefly, but in October dropped sharply again.

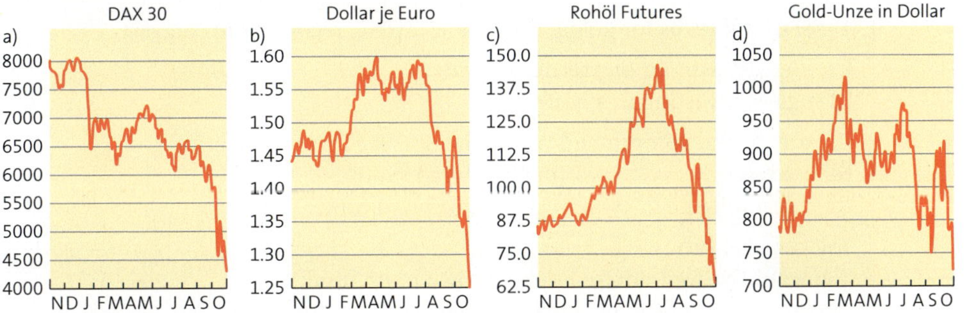


Source: Hamburger Abendblatt/Frank Hasse, 25th/26th October 2008

## 3 Shares

Read this newspaper report and do the tasks below.

### Apple Sales Soar

San Francisco: Apple CEO* Steve Jobs has increased Macintosh computer sales since incorporating faster chips from Intel in 2006. Last September Jobs also introduced the new version of Nano and the iPod Touch, which uses the same widescreen display as the iPhone. As a result of these innovations, Apple yesterday announced the biggest gains among U.S. personal computer makers for the fourth quarter of 2007. Computer shipments rose 28%, more than double the 9.6% increase for market leader Hewlett Packard. Net income grew to $1.58 bn from $1 bn a year earlier and sales soared 35% to $9.61 billion, beating analysts' expectations of sales of $9.43 billion. Apple forecast that sales in the first quarter of the current year will decrease to $6.8 billion. The shares reacted by dropping 3.5% to close at $155.64 on Wall Street, a slump of 23% since a record high of $202.96 in December 2007. "Fears that a slowdown in the U.S. economy may reduce consumer spending on electronics have led Apple shares to fall along with the rest of the technology sector," said Shaw Wu, an analyst with American Technology Research.

* chief executive officer

(Source: Abridged from *The International Herald Tribune*, 23rd January 2008)

**a** Say whether the following statements are true, false or not in the text.

1. Apple increased sales in the last quarter of 2007.
2. In the fourth quarter of 2007 Apple sold more computers than Hewlett Packard.
3. Analysts had not expected such good results.
4. Apple said that sales would continue to increase in 2008.
5. Apple shares fell by 23% on the stock exchange in December.
6. The technology sector as a whole is under pressure because of fears of a US recession.

**b** Explain why Apple shares fell although its sales and income had increased.

**c** What general advice would you give a customer about investing in shares?

### LANGUAGE Giving advice

Three useful verbs for giving advice are: advise, recommend, suggest

Use suggest with an *-ing* form (gerund):
I'd suggest investing in a bond fund.

Use advise and recommend with either an *-ing* form or an infinitive:

| | | |
|---|---|---|
| I'd | advise | investing in a bond fund. |
| | recommend | you to invest in a bond fund. |

You can also say:
You would be well-advised to invest in a bond fund.
In your case, it would be advisable to invest in a bond fund.

## 4 Bonds

Working with a partner, look at the table below and do the following tasks. The table shows the details of an issue of German government bonds.

| Zins | Laufzeit | Zins-termin | 26.2.08 Schluss | 27.2.08 15.41 | 27.2.08 Rendite |
|---|---|---|---|---|---|
| 4 | 06/16 | 4.7. | 100,06 | 100,21 | 3,9648 |

(Source: *Frankfurter Allgemeine Zeitung*, 27th February 2008)

**a** A customer asks you about these German government bonds. Answer his/her questions.

1 "How much interest will I get?"
2 "What is the latest market price?"
3 "When were the bonds issued?"
4 "When is the redemption date?"
5 "How much is the yield?"
6 "Why is the yield lower than the coupon?"

**b** The bonds below were traded on the same day as the ones above. Compare the two bonds and explain any differences.

| Zins | Laufzeit | Zins-termin | 26.2.08 Schluss | 27.2.08 15.41 | 27.2.08 Rendite |
|---|---|---|---|---|---|
| 4 | 05/37 | 4.1. | 90,53 | 90,72 | 4,5848 |

**c** Government bonds are generally seen as a safer investment than shares. Say why.

**d** Look at these high-yield government and corporate bonds. Explain the different ratings and yields.

| Issuer | Redemption date (m./yr.) | Coupon | Ratings* S | M | F | Bid price | Bid yield |
|---|---|---|---|---|---|---|---|
| Daimler Chrysler | 01/31 | 8.50 | BBB+ | A3 | A– | 125.41 | 6.38 |
| Gen Motors | 03/32 | 8.00 | BB+ | B1 | BB+ | 106.00 | 7.46 |
| Argentina | 12/33 | 8.28 | B+ | – | – | 92.10 | 9.08 |
| Ecuador | 08/30 | 10.00 | B– | Caa2 | CCC | 96.00 | 10.52 |

* S = Standard and Poor's, M = Moody's, F = Fitch
US$ denominated bonds, NY close. Source: Reuters

(Source: *The Financial Times*, 7th February 2008)

## 5 Funds (Part 1)

12

Listen to the following conversation and describe the customer's problem.

Phil Hoby from Canada has made an appointment with Britta Engel, the investment adviser at his bank.

BRITTA: Good Morning, Mr Hoby.

PHIL: Hi, nice to meet you.

BRITTA: Do take a seat. ... My colleague told me you're interested in some form of investment.

PHIL: Yeah, I really need your help. You see, I work for SAP and so I know a bit about the computer sector – at least I thought I did! When I read about the great profits Apple were making, I went and put all my money – 15,000 euros – into Apple shares. I don't know what got into me! I must have been crazy! Have you seen where they are now?

BRITTA: They haven't performed well recently, have they? Though of course all shares are down at the moment and the technology sector as a whole is very volatile ...

PHIL: Yes, but it's not just that! Look what's happened to the dollar!

BRITTA: Mmm, it's fallen quite drastically against the euro, hasn't it?

PHIL: You can say that again! D'you know, the currency risk never even crossed my mind! After that I thought I'd better get some professional advice, so – here I am!

BRITTA: I'd be glad to help. I understand you're looking for a long-term investment?

PHIL: That's right. I turned thirty last week so I guess it's time I started thinking about my future. I could afford to invest two hundred euros a month. I don't want to lose any money on shares again, so I wondered what else you'd advise.

BRITTA: Well, shares are not necessarily a bad investment. In fact, over the years, shares have yielded far better returns than bonds or real estate ...

PHIL: That may be, but how can I know which shares to buy and when to sell them? I'm more interested in the sports section of my newspaper than the financial pages!

BRITTA: I can understand that. Watching the stock markets isn't most people's idea of fun. Have you considered investing in a fund instead?

PHIL: I've heard of funds, but I'm not too clear on what they do. Will a fund buy shares for me?

BRITTA: Basically yes, but you won't hold the actual shares. The fund managers pool your capital with that of other investors and so you hold a number of units that represent your part of all the assets that are in the fund. This has a lot of advantages for you ...

## 6 Funds (Part 2)

13 Britta Engel goes on to tell Phil Hoby about the advantages of funds. Do tasks a–c.

**a** Britta mentions seven advantages of funds. Listen and note at least four.

PHIL: … so if I invest in a share fund, the managers will do the work for me?
BRITTA: Exactly. They have specialist knowledge and access to information that you don't have. They take the decisions and trade on your behalf.
PHIL: And is this service included in the price?
BRITTA: I'm afraid not. There's usually an initial charge of between two and five per cent, plus a management fee of one to two per cent a year.
PHIL: And what about all the money the fund makes? Will it be paid out?
BRITTA: With most funds the profits are automatically reinvested for you in new units. So you don't have to bother about that.
PHIL: Hmm. Would I have to pay in a lump sum or could I invest regularly?
BRITTA: You can pay money in whenever you like, but funds are an ideal way of investing on a regular basis. The more you save, the more units you'll have.
PHIL: I see. But I suppose these units go up and down in price like shares do?
BRITTA: Yes, but the fluctuations aren't as great because there are many different investments in the fund. You see, the aim of a fund is to spread the risk over a large number of securities but to obtain good yields at the same time. If you wanted to do that on your own, you'd need a huge amount of capital to have such a diversified portfolio.
PHIL: Will €200 a month be enough then?
BRITTA: Certainly. You can invest in funds with €50 a month or even less.
PHIL: What if I want to get my money out, or perhaps just part of it?
BRITTA: You can return your units to the fund at any time, though I'd advise you to see funds as a medium to long-term form of investment, because of the initial charge.
PHIL: Sounds good so far. The only problem is that, after what happened with those Apple shares, I'm not particularly keen on shares any more.
BRITTA: Well, we offer a wide range of other funds. Some invest in bonds, real estate or a mix of securities; some invest only in a particular sector, like energy, or a particular region, like the emerging markets. Or you can invest in a fund of funds to spread the risk even more. I've printed out a selection which have good prospects for growth …

**b** Read the dialogue and find the other advantages of a fund.

**c** Find expressions in the dialogue which mean the following:

1 *Agio*
2 *Aktienfonds*
3 *breitgestreutes Depot*
4 *Dachfonds*
5 *Erträge*
6 *Schwellenländer*
7 *Verwaltungsgebühr*
8 *Wachstumsaussichten*

**GRAMMAR** Adjectives and adverbs

1 Could I invest **regularly**?
2 The profits are **automatically** reinvested for you.
3 I'm not **particularly** keen on shares any more.
4 Funds are an ideal way of investing on a **regular** basis.
5 (That) sounds **good** so far.

- Adverbs describe verbs (1, 2) or adjectives (3).
- Adjectives describe nouns (4) or pronouns.
- The verbs *be, look, sound* (5) and *seem* are followed by an adjective.
- Adverbs are formed by adding *-ly* (1+3) or *-ally* (2), but there are exceptions:

| | |
|---|---|
| Many customers speak good English. | They speak English **well**. |
| Jane is a hard worker. | She works **hard**. (hardly = *kaum*) |
| The development was fast. | It developed **fast**. |
| I was late for work. | I arrived **late**. (lately = *neulich*) |
| My colleague is friendly. | She behaves **in a friendly way**. |

## 7 Practice: adjectives and adverbs

**a** Use adjectives or adverbs in these sentences.

1 Many people cannot … (easy) understand financial news.
2 A fund is … (ideal) for investing small sums …(regular).
3 Most funds pay profits … (annual) and reinvest them … (automatic).
4 Technology shares performed … (good), but the forecast is … (poor).
5 The new CEO speaks … (fluent) Spanish and his Russian seems … (excellent) too.
6 In emerging markets share prices can rise … (fast) but fall just as … (rapid).
7 Units of new energy funds have risen … (steep) in price because of the … (strong) demand for eco-friendly investments.
8 The company's sales figures were announced too … (late) for the European markets but Wall Street reacted … (immediate) and the shares plunged … (dramatic).

**b** Rewrite the following sentences using adverbs instead of adjectives.

Example It is hard to make the correct decision. (to decide)
It is hard to decide correctly.

1 The company had a good performance in the first quarter. (to perform)
2 Energy prices saw a sharp rise. (to rise)
3 There was a drastic fall in the demand for cars. (to fall)
4 There will be an abrupt decline in the yields on bonds. (to decline)
5 Growth in the automobile sector is slow. (to grow)
6 That fund of funds has very active managers. (to be managed)

## 8 Talking about a fund

Tell an investor the main facts about this fund.

(Source: www.allianzglobalinvestors.de)

### CULTURE Small talk

Small talk is an essential part of any business meeting or phone call. It breaks the ice and shows clients that they are getting personal treatment.
While small talk in Germany can be limited ("Did you find a parking space all right?"), English-speaking bank staff try to show an interest in their customers by chatting about their own families, holidays, homes, hobbies, etc. They create a link between themselves and the customer by speaking personally, e. g. "My son goes to that school as well" or "I love Mallorca, too", but, as in Germany, religion and politics are taboo.

## 9 Assessing risk tolerance

CD 14

Listen to the CD and do the tasks below.

Three customers come to ask Britta Engel for advice on investment. You will hear the beginning of each consultation.

**a** Listen and take notes about each potential investor. Then use your notes to assess how risk-tolerant each one is on this scale:

| 1 | 2 | 3 | 4 | 5 | 6 | 7 | 8 | 9 | 10 |
|---|---|---|---|---|---|---|---|---|---|
| conservative | | cautious | | balanced | | venturesome | | speculative | |

**b** Recommend a suitable type of investment in each case, giving reasons. Use expressions from the box on page 64.

## 10 Work with words

Form nouns from the verbs in the box. Then complete the following text with the nouns.

suggest | recommend | yield | grow | select | retire
mature | provide | decide | intend | solve | consult

As state pensions will not always be as large as they are today, it is important for young people to make …[1] for the future, even if, at present, …[2] seems a long way off. There is, however, such a large …[3] of securities on the market that it is hard for the inexperienced investor to make the right …[4] on which ones to buy. The best …[5] to this problem is to make an appointment for a …[6] in the investment department at the bank.

Before an adviser can make a suitable …[7], it is important to find out what the customer's …[8] is. Some investors are willing to tolerate a high degree of risk in order to obtain the greatest possible …[9]; in this case, the adviser may suggest a fund containing shares with good prospects for …[10] in the long term. Other investors are more cautious; in their case a fund containing bonds with different coupons and …[11] dates should be less volatile. An alternative …[12] could be a fund containing a mix of equities and bonds or a fund of funds to combine the advantages of both investment strategies.

John and Jane had different investment strategies.

## 11 Tax on investment earnings

Mediate in this conversation.

A colleague, who does not speak English, wants to tell a customer about tax on earnings from investments and the saver's tax-free allowance.

| The customer | You | Your colleague |
|---|---|---|
| How much is the tax-free allowance for savers in Germany? | ... 1 | |
| | | Momentan 801 Euro pro Person, wenn Sie einen Freistellungs-auftrag bei uns stellen*. |
| | ... 2 | |
| And if I earn more than 801 euros? | ... 3 | |
| | | Auf Einkünften aus Geldanlagen, die diesen Betrag übersteigen, müssen Sie Abgeltungssteuer zahlen. |
| | ... 4 | |
| What sorts of invest-ment are affected? | ... 5 | |
| | | Das sind alle Gewinne aus Aktien, Fonds, Zertifikaten, Dividenden und Zinsen. |
| | ... 6 | |
| Even the interest on my savings account? | ... 7 | |
| | | Ja, Zinsen aller Art werden besteuert, z. B. aus Sparbüchern, Termingeldern, Anleihen oder Bausparverträgen. |
| | ... 8 | |
| But what about my private pension plan? | ... 9 | |
| | | Formen der Altersvorsorge wie Gold, selbstbewohnte Immobilien und Lebensversicherungen unterliegen der Abgeltungssteuer nicht. |
| | ... 10 | |
| How much is this investment tax? | ... 11 | |
| | | 25 %, plus Solidaritätszuschlag und Kirchensteuer, also insgesamt rund 28 %. Sie wird direkt von der Bank abgezogen und an das Finanzamt weitergereicht. |
| | ... 12 | |
| Thank you. | | |

Abgeltungssteuer: Stand 2009

* *einen Freistellungsantrag stellen* = to make an application for tax exemption

**LEARNING** Feedback

**Wenn Sie Feedback geben:**
1 Äußern Sie sich konkret. Vage Formulierungen helfen nicht.
2 Bleiben Sie sachlich. Meiden Sie Bewertungen oder gar Beleidigungen.
3 Seien Sie konstruktiv, niemals destruktiv. Bieten Sie Perspektive.
4 Formulieren Sie subjektiv: Sie können nur Ihre eigenen Eindrücke mitteilen.
5 Betten Sie negative Kritik zwischen zwei positiven Bemerkungen. („Sandwich-Theorie")

**Wenn Sie Feedback annehmen:**
1 Lassen Sie den anderen ausreden.
2 Nehmen Sie die Meinung des anderen als solche hin. Er beschreibt, wie Sie auf ihn wirken, nicht wie Sie sind. Deshalb versuchen Sie nicht, sich zu rechtfertigen.
3 Stellen Sie Verständnisfragen, wenn Sie nicht sicher sind, was der andere meint.
4 Bedanken Sie sich. Feedback hilft Ihnen, Ihre Wirkung auf andere zu kennen und dadurch kompetenter und sicherer aufzutreten.
5 Denken Sie über das Feedback nach. Gegebenenfalls lernen Sie daraus.

## 12 Over to you

Work with your fellow students to do the following tasks.

**a** Divide your class into groups of four.

- one person takes the role of a wealthy customer.
- one person plays the customer relationship manager.
- two people play the roles of investment advisers in the private banking department.

Then prepare the role play in pairs using the role cards below.

**The customer and the relationship manager**
- Create an investor profile for the customer (personal details, assets, investment aims, etc.).
- Work out what information each of you will give during the consultation.
- Decide what questions the customer should ask, e.g. about risks, charges, tax, etc.

**The two investment advisers**
- Note the questions you must ask to get a complete investor profile and to assess the customer's risk tolerance.
- Decide which products from your bank(s) you can recommend for different risk levels.
- Work out how you will open and close the consultation.

**b** Do the role play. The three bank employees should work as a team, equally sharing tasks (greeting the customer, making small talk, giving or asking for information, making recommendations, closing the consultation).

**c** Each group member gives feedback on how he/she found the consultation. Using the feedback, practise the role play again.

**d** Perform the consultation in front of your fellow students. Ask for their feedback.

# Ethical investment

## 13 Brainstorming

In a group, decide what you understand by 'ethical investment'. Then consider which companies ethical investors might prefer or refuse to invest in.

## 14 Green investments

You want to tell an ethically-minded customer about the main facts in this text. In preparation for your meeting, write down the main points in German.

### Is going green really worth it?

In the face of the tremendous problems threatening our environment, most of us, given the size of our portfolios, tend to think that we would make a more positive impact by planting a tree in our garden than by investing ethically. The feeling is also widespread that ethical investment is nice – if you can afford it. In both cases, the opposite is true. Ethical issues are changing the way we live and invest. Research has shown that interest in ethical funds is growing at the rate of 18% a year, and small investors are increasingly seeing them as a great way of improving both their finances and the health of the planet.

Socially responsible investments (SRIs) are ecologically and socially oriented funds that are concerned with human, animal and environmental welfare; climate funds deal only with the environmental footprint we leave on the planet. The latter can be divided into three groups: first, clean technology funds invest only in companies that work towards a cleaner environment, secondly there are funds which exclude companies that pollute the environment, such as oil producers, and the third type includes companies that profit from climate change, even if they pollute the environment themselves, such as car manufacturers.

SRIs may sound simple, but investors have to decide where their ethical priorities lie. Some funds screen out arms producers and companies that exploit people in developing countries or use animal testing. Others may decide to include pharmaceutical enterprises which use animals only for medical purposes. Some ask questions like: what are the conditions like for the workers in Bangladesh who supply the eco-friendly cotton clothing? Should the grain needed to make the eco-friendly bio-fuel be used to feed the starving millions instead? The greener the fund, the stricter its ethics are.

Choosing an ethical investment does not mean sacrificing profit for morality. Ethical funds are repeatedly listed among the top 150 fund performers. Nearly all funds operate within certain parameters, a geographic region, a particular sector or size of company, ethical funds are no exception. Given the current focus within the EU and G8 countries on environmental concerns, future legislation could benefit ecologically and socially responsible companies. Ex-UN General Secretary Kofi Annan predicted that the most important investment trend in the 21st century will be the concept of sustainable growth. He may be right.

## 15 Present a product

Recommend an ethical investment product offered by your bank. Describe it in detail. Point out its opportunities and risks.

Unit 7

# Personal Borrowing

## 1 Warm-up

**a** Would you borrow money to pay for any of these items? Or would you save up until you could afford them? Or would you prefer to do without? Give reasons for your answers.

**b** What should you think about before borrowing money?

**c** Why must banks be careful when lending money to personal customers?

**CULTURE** Credit reference agencies in the USA and UK

There is no central agency like the SCHUFA in the USA or the UK.
For personal customers in the USA there are four national credit bureaus: Experian, Equifax, TransUnion and Innovis, but lots of small agencies exist as well. In the UK there are three credit reference agencies: Experian, Equifax and Callcredit.
These agencies are profit-making organizations and in competition. Consumers are advised to check their credit reports once a year to make sure they are accurate.

## 2 A personal loan

Read this text from a brochure about bank loans and then do the tasks below.

### A personal loan – borrowing made simple

Isn't it time to buy that new car? Carry out those home improvements? Have the holiday of a lifetime?
Or would you like to consolidate some debts and repay in fixed instalments you can afford?

Whatever the purpose, a personal loan could be the answer!

- Borrow any round sum from £5,000 to £20,000. The loan amount will be paid directly into your current account as soon as your application has been approved.
- Choose a repayment plan with set monthly instalments that are tailored to suit you.
- Take advantage of our competitive interest rates which are fixed for the full term, so you will know right from the start how much you will have to pay. The APR* includes the arrangement fee, so there are no other charges. (There may be extra fees for borrowers asked to provide security for loans of £15,000 and over.)
- Enjoy peace of mind with our loan protection plan. For a small extra premium, your repayments will be covered by loan insurance if you cannot work as a result of accident or illness, if you become unemployed through no fault of your own or if you pass away.

If you are aged 18 or over and seeking to borrow, call in at any of our branches, fill in the loan application form at the back of this brochure or visit our website.

* annual percentage rate of interest

**a** Find expressions in the text that mean the following:

1 *effektiver Jahreszinssatz*
2 *Disagio / einmaliges Bearbeitungsentgelt*
3 *Kreditantrag*
4 *Kreditbetrag*
5 *Kreditnehmer*
6 *Kreditversicherung*
7 *Laufzeit*
8 *monatliche Raten*
9 *Sicherheiten*
10 *Versicherungsbeitrag*

**b** Translate these expressions into German:

1 carry out those home improvements (line 1)
2 consolidate some debts (line 3)
3 your application has been approved (line 7)
4 instalments that are tailored to suit you (line 8)
5 enjoy peace of mind (line 13)
6 through no fault of your own (line 15)

**c** Summarize the terms and conditions of this personal loan.

**d** In what ways does the text try to sell this loan? Say whether you find it effective and why.

## 3 Loan or overdraft?

15

Barbara Schmitt is working on the counter when Lee Wang comes in.

**a** Listen to the dialogue and say how the bank can help Mr Wang.

**b** Listen again and note the information given about loans.

BARBARA: Hi Mr Wang. How are you today?

LEE: Fine thanks. And how are you?

BARBARA: I'm fine too thanks. And what can I do for you?

LEE: I'd like to have a higher overdraft limit on my account. It's 500 euros at the moment, but I need 3,000. You see, I want to buy a motor bike.

BARBARA: Let me just check your account details … yes, here we are. We could extend your overdraft facility, but have you thought about a personal loan instead?

LEE: A loan? Why? Wouldn't a loan be more expensive?

BARBARA: No, in fact it could even work out cheaper for you. The APR for a loan is much lower than the interest rate we charge on overdrafts.

LEE: Er … AP what?

BARBARA: Sorry. APR stands for "annual percentage rate of interest". It's the true interest rate you pay because it includes the arrangement fee as well.

LEE: But with an overdraft, I won't have to pay any arrangement fee, will I?

BARBARA: That's true, but with an overdraft the interest rate can vary, depending on rates on the money market. If you took out a loan, you'd have a fixed interest rate for the full term.

LEE: But I still think I'd be a lot more flexible if I had an overdraft because I could repay it whenever I liked.

BARBARA: That's true, but our loans are flexible too. If you tell us your average monthly expenditure, we can arrange set monthly instalments.

LEE: Hmm … but don't banks want to have security for loans?

BARBARA: Sometimes yes, but I think in your case we would ask you to take out some loan insurance instead. Then if you can't repay the loan for any reason, the insurance pays it for you.

LEE: Would I really have to have that?

BARBARA: Why not talk it over with our loan adviser, Mr Reimer. He's free right now and he'd be glad to tell you more about it …

**c** Read the dialogue and find differences between loans and overdrafts. Make a chart like this one to compare the two. Then add ideas of your own.

| Personal Loans | Overdrafts |
|---|---|
| 1 The borrower has to pay an arrangement fee. | 1 There is no ... |
| 2 The interest rate is ... | 2 ... |

## GRAMMAR *If*-sentences

1 If I have an overdraft, I won't have to pay any arrangement fee.
2 If you took out a loan, you would have a fixed interest rate.
3 I'd be a lot more flexible if I had an overdraft.
4 If Mr Wang had had enough money, he would not have needed a loan.
5 If you can't repay the loan for any reason, the insurance pays it for you.

- Note the tenses used in the above sentences:

| ***if*-clause** | **main clause** |
|---|---|
| simple present | will + infinitive (future) (1) |
| simple past | would + infinitive (conditional) (2, 3) |
| past perfect | would + have + past participle (conditional perfect) (4) |

- In general statements that are always true, both clauses can be in the present (5).

## 4 Practice: *if*-sentences

**a** Make meaningful sentences from the table below.

| | | | | | |
|---|---|---|---|---|---|
| If you | have<br>had<br>take<br>took | a loan,<br>an overdraft, | you | will<br>won't<br>would<br>wouldn't | have to pay an arrangement fee.<br>have a fixed APR.<br>borrow for an agreed term.<br>repay in set instalments.<br>need loan insurance.<br>have to sign an agreement. |

**b** Put the verbs in brackets into the correct tenses.

1 If you … (need) money, we could increase your overdraft facility.
2 Your overdraft will cost you more if the interest rate … (rise).
3 If you borrow for a longer term, your instalments … (be) lower.
4 A loan protection plan … (cover) your loan if you were unable to repay it.
5 If interest rates fall, borrowing generally … (become) cheaper.
6 If we arranged a loan, the instalments … (be fixed) for the full term and so you … (know) exactly how much the loan … (cost) you.

## 5 A line of credit

Read this information about lines of credit at a US bank. Then do the tasks below.

### Dynabank Choice Line of Credit

**The flexible way to pay.**

If you want to go on vacation, make a major purchase or just pay off your high-interest loans and credit cards, Dynabank Choice is the line of credit you can use for anything. You decide how much you pay each month by choosing the right term for you.

**Apply for a Dynabank Choice Line of Credit**

#### Advantages of Dynabank Choice

**Freedom to spend on whatever you want**

With Dynabank Choice, you choose your own repayment term from 12 to 60 months[1] – and you can adjust this whenever you like. If you want to reduce your monthly payment, simply extend the term. Alternatively, repay faster by increasing your monthly payment. It's up to you.

You can use your Dynabank Choice Line of Credit for whatever you want. For instance, you can consolidate your debt or pay off balances from high-interest loans by taking advantage of our significant credit lines.[2]

**Competitive rates**

11.53% variable APR,[3] with flexible monthly payments[4]

**No fees or penalties**

We won't charge you for opening or maintaining the account, and there are no prepayment penalties.

**Key features**

- The repayment term on your Dynabank Choice Line of Credit is initially set to 48 months. Change the term to reflect your needs by calling your personal customer adviser.
- When you sign up with Dynabank Choice, you'll receive 3 checks, which you can write to access your credit line. To order more checks, just call your personal customer adviser.
- Every month we'll send you a statement showing all transactions on your line of credit.

1 When you first use your Dynabank Choice Line of Credit, the repayment term is automatically set to 48 months.

2 Subject to credit approval.

3 Your APRs may vary each billing period. The APR equals the Prime Rate + 5.49%.

4 The transaction term or monthly payment may increase if the prime rate increases.

1 An American who has a Dynabank line of credit wants to know if an overdraft at your bank is the same. Point out two differences.

2 Of the four points in the small print at the bottom:
   a Which two contain a warning? What is it?
   b Which one means “Bonität vorausgesetzt”?

3 Write a similar text for a leaflet in English about overdrafts at your bank.

## 6 Mediation

Read this information about the Commerzbank's Flexicard and do the tasks below.

A British customer, Tim Fisher, wants to find out about a German Flexicard.

### FLEXICARD

Günstige Gelegenheiten, die man nutzen möchte, gibt es immer wieder – doch reicht Ihr finanzieller Spielraum auf Ihrem Girokonto dann dafür aus?

Mit der **FlexiCard** auf jeden Fall! Denn mit ihr erweitern Sie Ihren finanziellen Spielraum – ganz einfach und überraschend günstig. Sie bietet die Möglichkeit, alle günstigen Gelegenheiten zu nützen, und Sie genießen **die Freiheit, immer spontan „ja" sagen zu können.**

**FlexiCard:**

- Verfügungsrahmen von 2.000 bis 4.000 Euro
- unbefristete Laufzeit
- individueller Zinssatz – nur auf die genutzten Beträge
- jederzeit direkte Inanspruchnahme über ec-Maestro Karte am Geldautomaten, Online Banking oder Überweisung möglich
- Rückzahlung nur 3 % des genutzten Betrages oder mind. 99 Euro pro Monat
- kein Bearbeitungsentgelt
- schnelle und unkomplizierte Kreditentscheidung in nur 20 Minuten

**spontan „ja" sagen können**

Erweitern Sie mit der Commerzbank FlexiCard Ihren finanziellen Spielraum und genießen Sie die Freiheit, immer spontan „ja" sagen zu können.

(Source: Commerzbank)

**a** Use the information above to answer Mr Fisher's questions:

1 "Can I borrow the money only once?"
2 "Will you charge interest on the whole sum for the full term, whether I use it or not?
3 "How long can I have the money for?"
4 "How much will I have to repay every month?"
5 "What about handling charges?"
6 "I'd like to have a Flexicard. How long will it take to get one?"

**b** There are two important points that Mr Fisher has not asked about. Say what they are and tell him about them.

## 7 Comparing loan terms

**a** Give an English expression for the title of each column.

| Sofortkredit | Details zum Kreditanbieter | Laufzeit in Monaten | Effektiver Jahreszins | Mindest-kredit-summe | Maximale Kredit-summe | Kredit Besonderheiten | Kredit Zusage |
|---|---|---|---|---|---|---|---|
| Postbank | Postbank Privatkredit | 12–84 | **ab 4,44 %** | 3.001 Euro | 50.000 Euro | Zinsvorteil beim Onlinekredit | sofort |
| GE Money Bank | GE Money Sofortkredit | 12–120 | **ab 4,29 %** | **1.000 Euro** | 50.000 Euro | Best-Zins-Garantie | sofort |
| citibank | Citibank Kredit | 12–72 | **ab 3,99 %** | 1.500 Euro | 50.000 Euro | 89 Tage bis zur ersten Ratenzahlung | sofort |
| credit4me | Fortis Kredit Credit4me | 12–84 | ab 4,49 % | 1.000 Euro | 50.000 Euro | **Kostenlos** einmal jährlich mit der Rate aussetzen | sofort |
| smava Kredite von Mensch zu Mensch | Smava Kredit | 36 | ab 4,25 % | **500 Euro** | 10.000 Euro | Kredit auch für **Selbständige und Freiberufler** | sofort |
| BON | Bon Kredit Onlinekredit | 12–120 | ab 4,9 % | 3.000 Euro | 100.000 Euro | **Kredit ohne Schufa** | online |
| SWKBank | SWK Bank | 12–84 | ab 3,90 % | **1.000 Euro** | 50.000 Euro | Sofortzusage in 30 Sekunden | sofort |
| DKB Deutsche Kreditbank AG | Deutsche Kreditbank AG | 12–84 | ab 5,45 % | 1.000 Euro | 50.000 Euro | Kredit für freie Berufe | sofort |
| creditX | CreditX Sofortkredit | 12–84 | ab 3,75 % | 1.500 Euro | 50.000 Euro | Fix-Zins und Raten ab 25 Euro im Monat | sofort |

(Source: www.kreditklick.com)

**b** Choose the most suitable loan in the table for each of these customers:
1. Mr A wants the loan with the lowest APR.
2. Ms B would like to repay over as long a term as possible.
3. Mr C has a poor credit history after defaulting on a previous loan.
4. Mr and Mrs D want to take a break from their monthly repayments once a year.
5. Ms E works freelance as a website designer.
6. Mr F can only afford monthly instalments of €25 – he is a trainee.

**c** In a group, work out the advantages and disadvantages of online loans for borrowers and lenders.

## 8 Credit-scoring

**a** One of these statements is not correct. Which one is it?
1. Credit-scoring compares data about a potential borrower with statistics on how persons in similar situations have paid their debts.
2. A credit score shows how likely it is that a loan applicant may default.
3. In Germany credit-scoring is only done by the SCHUFA.
4. Credit-scoring helps banks assess the risk of lending.

**b** Working in a small group, discuss the following questions and write each point made in the discussion on a separate card.
1. What personal or financial information affects a person's credit score?
2. Which conditions of a loan can be influenced by a person's credit score?

**c** In class, set up two pin boards, one for each question. After each group has pinned its cards on to them, discuss which of the points are the most important. Give reasons and examples where suitable.

**LANGUAGE** Talking about sums of money

When adding up sums of money, you can say:

| | | |
|---|---|---|
| Your joint income | comes to | 3,000 euros. |
| Your average expenditure | amounts to | |
| | totals | |

If you cannot give an exact figure, you can say:

| | | | |
|---|---|---|---|
| My expenditure | is | roughly | 1,000 euros. |
| | | approximately | |
| | | about | |
| My income | averages 2,000 euros a month. | | |
| | is 2,000 a month on average. | | |

*ein hoher Betrag* = a large sum/amount
*die Höhe der Raten* = the amount of the instalments
a loan **of** five thousand euros / a five thousand-euro loan

## 9 Assessing creditworthiness

16

Listen to the two dialogues and do the following tasks.
Loan adviser Max Reimer has two conversations with prospective borrowers.

**a** Copy the chart below and fill it in while you are listening.

| | 1. Kunde | 2. Kunde |
|---|---|---|
| **Gewünschter Kreditbetrag:** | | |
| **Einnahmen/Ausgaben:** | | |
| Nettoeinkommen (Gehalt/Rente/Pension): | | |
| Einkünfte aus selbstständiger Tätigkeit: | | |
| Sonstige regelmäßige Einkünfte: | | |
| Miete / Belastungen Eigentum: | | |
| Lebenshaltungskosten: | | |
| Versicherungsbeiträge: | | |
| Sparverträge: | | |
| Bestehende Kredite / Ratenzahlungen: | | |
| Unterhaltszahlungen: | | |
| Sonstige regelmäßige Verpflichtungen: | | |
| **Verfügbares monatliches Einkommen:** | | |

**b** Working with a partner, use your chart to assess each customer's creditworthiness. Apply the criteria from Exercise 8c to decide whether a loan might be granted in each case, and, if so, what conditions there might be.

**c** In class, compare your results with those of your fellow students. Discuss any differences of opinion.

**LEARNING** Tandem-Lernen

Falls Sie einen *Native-speaker* treffen, der Deutsch lernen möchte, verabreden Sie sich zum Tandem-Lernen. Die Regeln sind einfach:
- Sie treffen sich regelmäßig in entspannter Atmosphäre, z. B. in einem Café.
- Für jede Sprache wird gleichviel Zeit aufgewendet.
- Die Sprachen werden nicht gemischt.
- Jeder bemüht sich, den Anderen zu unterstützen und sorgt dafür, dass beide gleichermaßen vom Tandem-Lernen profitieren.
- Neben der Sprache versucht jeder auch mehr über die Kultur des Partners zu lernen.

… und vergessen Sie nicht: Tandem-Lernen soll Spaß machen!

## 10 Tandem work

Practise tandem learning by doing the tasks below.

**a** Your class should split into two groups, A and B. Work with a partner in your group to create a profile of a loan applicant who wants to borrow €10,000 (Group A) or €15,000 (Group B). The applicant is not German and must be creditworthy for the sum he or she needs. Decide on all the other personal and financial details relevant for a loan consultation.

**b** Form a new partnership (tandem) with a student from the other group. Play the role of the person that you have created, while your new partner takes the role of the loan adviser who has to check your creditworthiness before offering you a loan. Then swap roles. Use the loan terms on page 117 or offer a suitable loan product from your bank instead.

## 11 Work with words

Choose the correct term for each sentence.

1. Why do you need a (credit / loan)?
2. How much would you like to (borrow / lend) to buy the car?
3. The interest (are / is) included in the monthly instalments.
4. The interest rate is (variable / varying).
5. For (high / large) loans you will be asked to provide security.
6. For loans under 15,000 euros no security (are / is) necessary.
7. The bank has to estimate your (disposable / free disposable) income.
8. Your application for a loan has been (accepted / approved).
9. The bank will grant you a loan (about / of / over ) 7,000 euros.
10. You can dispose (of / over) the sum immediately.

## 12 Security for loans

Match these terms with the definitions below.

an assignment | an assignment by bill of sale | a guarantee/guaranty | a land charge | a mortgage | a pledge/lien

1 This is given by a person or an institution that is liable to repay the loan if the borrower defaults.
2 This allows the borrower the right to use an item, e. g. machinery, during the term of the loan, but the bank is the owner of the item.
3 This is given if valuable articles, e.g. jewellery, are offered as security. It is also used with the title documents to goods on a ship or in a warehouse.
4 This transfers rights to the bank, e.g. to an insurance policy or savings.
5 This secures a loan with a property until that loan has been repaid.
6 This may be used again, e.g. to finance another property, after a loan has been repaid.

## 13 Group work

Split your class into groups. Each group should do the following tasks:

1 Choose one of the cases below and work out the advantages/disadvantages of the two types of security named.
2 Decide which type of security the bank would prefer, giving reasons.
3 Present your case study to your fellow students.

| Case One | Case Two |
|---|---|
| Franco and Sophia Rossi are the owners of a profitable Italian restaurant. They need a loan of €70,000 to build an extension for smokers. As security the bank could<br>a) register a land charge on the restaurant premises, valued at €280,000, or<br>b) take a guaranty from Mrs Rossi's father, who runs a successful take-away pizza business. | Jeremy Little owns a house in London but spends a lot of time in Germany on business. He has applied for a loan of €100,000 to buy a flat in Berlin. As security the bank could<br>a) register a land charge on the flat which is valued at €190,000, or<br>b) arrange a mortgage on Mr Little's London home, worth £750,000. |

| Case Three | Case Four |
|---|---|
| Vivienne Wilde from Canada has an art gallery. She needs a loan of €75,000 for renovations and, as security, she could<br>a) pledge a painting valued at €140,000, or<br>b) assign her life assurance policy worth €90,000 to the bank. | Abdul Al Hassan trades in Arabian antiques. To modernize his shop and install a security system, he has applied for a loan of €35,000 which he could secure by<br>a) an assignment by bill of sale of his new car, a Mercedes worth €85,000, or<br>b) an assignment of his German government bonds, currently valued at €48,000. |

## 14 Work with pictures

These cartoons should warn people about the dangers of unwise borrowing. Match each of the captions in the box with one of the cartoons. Then describe each picture and explain what the danger for the borrower is.

**1** Beware of 'cheap' loans. | **2** Think twice before you co-sign for a loan.
**3** Repayment holidays are expensive. | **4** Pay the mortgage before other bills.
**5** Always check the true APR. | **6** Budget to keep up your instalments.

# The debt trap

## 15 Group activity

**a** Borrowing can end in disaster. Using these case studies, suggest why.

**1 Marco and Gina,** 31 and 29, took out a mortgage and bought furniture on hire purchase. Gina gave up work when their baby was born. When Marco, a sales assistant, was made redundant, the couple started using their credit cards more and stopped opening bills and bank statements. Now they owe €175,000.

**2 Marie,** 27, is a single parent with three small children. She lives on state benefits and her ex-partner does not pay her any maintenance. She has overdrawn her account and is in arrears with the rent, utility payments, etc. She owes over €11,000.

**3 Selma,** 48, grew up in a rich family and never learned to budget. During her marriage she let her husband deal with their finances and co-signed for a loan to set up a business that went bankrupt. After divorce, Selma has debts totalling €85,000.

**4 Faruk,** 39, borrowed from a money-lender to open a fast-food bar. The business broke even until he became ill and had to take on an employee. Faruk owes €29,000 in rent, debts to suppliers and taxes in addition to the original loan of €15,000 plus accrued interest.

**b** Are some people more at risk of getting into debt than others? Use the graph and map to find out. Suggest explanations.

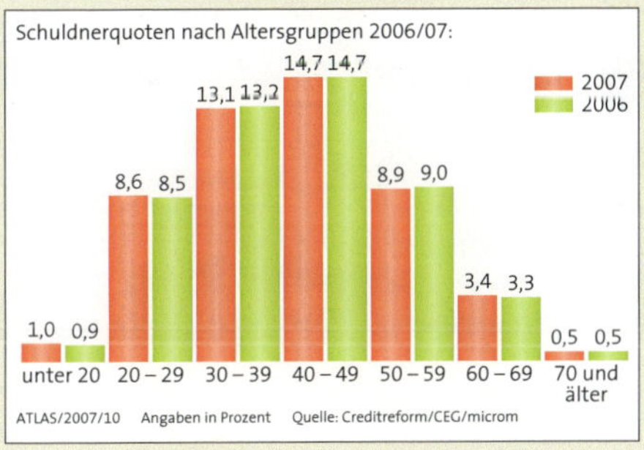


Source: Der Spiegel

Source: www.privatschuldung.de

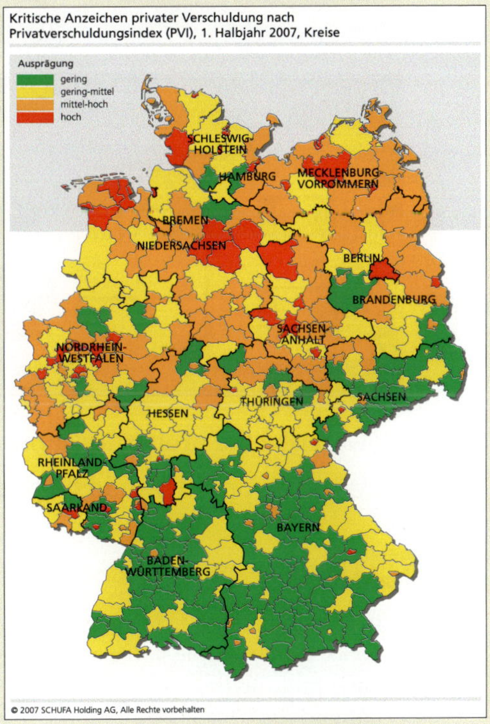


**c** What can or should be done to prevent people from getting hopelessly into debt? Discuss this question from the point of view of the following:

1 banks. 2 society as a whole.

Unit 8

# Financing Property

## 1 Warm-up

**a** Describe the properties shown in these pictures.

**b** Which property would be your dream home? Say why.

### CULTURE Home ownership

In Britain and the USA nearly 70% of people own their home (in Germany about 42%). While people in Germany generally see buying a property (US: realty) as a once-in-a-lifetime purchase and rent a home while they save up, many people in the UK and the US get a foot on the property ladder as soon as they can and later move home several times.
The size of a property is usually measured by the number of bedrooms: a three-bedroomed flat (US: apartment) or house has four main rooms.

## 2 Rent or buy?

Working in a group, look at this poster and answer the questions below.

**a** What is the message of this poster?

**b** Do you agree with the message? Find arguments for and against. See if everyone in your group comes to the same conclusion.

## 3 Work with words

Match these German words about building societies (US: savings and loan associations) with their English translations.

| | |
|---|---|
| *Bauspardarlehen* | redemption, repayment |
| *Bauparguthaben* | extra repayments |
| *Bausparsumme* | granting of the loan and release of deposits |
| *Bewertungszahl* | policy sum / target sum |
| *monatlicher Beitrag* | building society loan |
| *Sonderzahlungen* | building society deposits |
| *Tilgung* | premium |
| *Zuteilung* | number of valuation points |

## 4 Saving with a building society

Read this brochure extract and do the tasks below.

LBS
Bausparkasse der Sparkassen

**LBS-Bausparen – Ihre Vorteile auf einen Blick**

- Sie sparen so schnell und grundsätzlich so viel Sie möchten.
- Sie profitieren von Anfang an von den staatlichen Förderungen. (Es gelten Einkommensgrenzen.)
- Die Finanzierungskosten Ihrer Immobilie bleiben kalkulierbar, denn die LBS garantiert Ihnen ein günstiges Bauspardarlehen mit festen, niedrigen Zinsen.
- Sie können jederzeit über Ihr Guthaben verfügen.
- Nach sieben Jahren behalten Sie die Prämien und Sparzulagen auf jeden Fall – unabhängig davon, ob Sie bauen oder nicht.

**a** Daniel Oldfield from Britain wants to know more about building society policies in Germany. Use the information above to answer his questions:

**b** The bank where you work is planning a welcome brochure to give new English-speaking customers an overview of its services. One page will be about having a building society policy. Write a short text for this page using information from the building society that cooperates with your bank. Use the culture box opposite for background information.

## 5 Selling a building society policy

17 Daniel Oldfield has an appointment with his adviser Joanna Witt to open a building society policy. Do the following tasks.

**a** Before you listen, work with a partner and write down what you think they will discuss about the policy.

**b** Now listen to the dialogue. Write down the terms they agree on.

## 6 Over to you

Tell a partner, who takes the customer's role, about the building society policies offered by your bank. Talk about:

1 the purpose of a building society policy
2 the granting of a loan and release of deposits
3 interest rates on deposits and loans
4 loan repayment

### LANGUAGE The adjective 'own'

The adjective 'own' is never used after the definite or indefinite article:

| | |
|---|---|
| *Er hat eine eigene Wohnung.* | He has **his** own flat. / a flat of **his** own. |
| *Das Haus hat eine eigene Garage.* | The house has got **its** own garage. |
| *Jeder träumt vom eigenen Haus.* | Everyone dreams of having a house of **their** own. |

The word *eigen-* is not always translated.

| | |
|---|---|
| *Eigenheim* | home / house (which is owned by the occupant) |
| *Eigentumswohnung* | flat / apartment (which is owned by the occupant) |
| *Eigenkapital (von Personen)* | capital / savings |
| *Eigenkapital (eines Unternehmens)* | equity / equity capital |

## 7 Preparing an appointment

Adviser Joanna Witt is expecting a British couple who want to finance a property. Look at her notes, translate the headings and say what questions she is going to ask them.

### CULTURE Building societies in the UK

In Britain building societies compete with banks and offer the same products: current and savings accounts, loans, debit cards, credit cards, investments, etc. In fact people use UK building society accounts like bank accounts. This is why British people may need help in understanding that building societies in Germany offer saving and lending services only.

## 8 A golden rule for financing property

At Joanna Witt's bank this rule is seen as an ideal way to finance a property. Describe it in English.

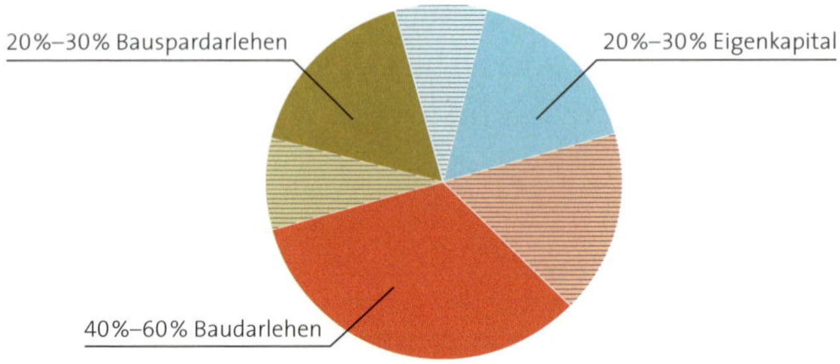


## 9 Financing a property

18

Joanna Witt is advising the Andersons.

**a** Listen to the consultation. Take notes in English about the Andersons' financial plan under the headings listed in Exercise 7. Then say whether the Anderson's financial plan fits the golden rule from Exercise 8.

**b** Read the text of the consultation and decide whether the bank may grant this couple a loan of 107,000 euros. Give reasons for your opinion.

KEVIN: … and this brochure shows the plan of the flat we'd like to buy …

CLAIRE: We've been looking for months but this is exactly what we want: it's new, on the ground floor, with three bedrooms and in a very nice area.

KEVIN: It's not cheap of course. 210,000 euros is a lot of money, but we think it's worth it.

JOANNA: It looks very nice indeed. So the total sum you need to finance the property will be …

KEVIN: 232,000 euros, that's 210,000 for the purchase price plus another 22,000 euros to cover the solicitor's fee, the commission for the estate agent and the land transfer tax.

JOANNA: Yes, that makes sense. So 232,000 euros all together. Do you have a property to sell?

CLAIRE: No, unfortunately not. We've lived in a rented flat since coming to Germany, but we'll both be fifty next year, so it's time we had a home of our own.

JOANNA: Of course. Have you got any capital or savings you could use as a deposit?

KEVIN: Yes, we've got 10,000 euros in a savings account and 15,000 euros in a term deposit account that's due this month.

JOANNA: Let's get a few figures down on paper. … 10,000 savings, 15,000 deposit account – that comes to 25,000 euros. Do you have a building society policy as well?

CLAIRE: Yes, we've been saving with the building society for seven years …
KEVIN: And they've just told us that we're eligible for a loan. We have already saved 40% of the sum and got the full number of valuation points.
JOANNA: How much is the policy for?
KEVIN: 100,000 euros. We've paid 40,000 in so they'd grant us a building society loan of 60,000 euros.
JOANNA: And do you have any other funds available that you could use to finance the property? Any life insurance or other investments perhaps?
KEVIN: Claire has some life assurance and I've got about 42,000 euros in a private pension plan but we'll need all that money for our retirement so we'd prefer not to cash either of those in.
JOANNA: That shouldn't be necessary. Let's see what alternative there is. Your file shows that you both earn a regular salary. Do you have any debts, bank loans or other commitments?
CLAIRE: None at all, do we Kevin?
KEVIN: No, that's why we'd like to apply for a loan of 107,000 euros …
CLAIRE: Yes, to cover the remaining sum.
JOANNA: Well, from what you've just told me …

**LANGUAGE** **Insurance or assurance?**

In the UK the word 'assurance' is generally used with 'life', i.e. life assurance. In other cases, the word 'insurance' is used, e.g. *Haftpflichtversicherung* = liability insurance. The USA and other English-speaking countries only use the word 'insurance'. Both words are uncountable, e.g. she has **some** insurance / **an** insurance policy.

**GRAMMAR** The present perfect

1 We **have lived** in a rented flat since coming to Germany.
2 We'**ve been saving** with the building society for seven years.
3 We **have already saved** 40% of the sum.
4 They'**ve just told** us that we're eligible for a loan.

- If an action began in the past and continues up to the moment of speaking, we use the present perfect (1, 2).
- For the German word "seit", *since* and *for* are used: *since* = from a point in time (1), *for* = over a period of time (2).
- The present perfect is also used when no particular time is mentioned but when there is a connection to the present, especially with words like *already* (3), *just* (4), *often, never, sometimes* and *yet.*
- The present perfect progressive may be used when an action has been happening without interruption or repeatedly until the moment of speaking (2).

## 10 Practice: the present perfect

**a** Answer these questions using the present perfect.

Example Have you seen the report yet? – Yes/I/read it/already
Yes, I've already read it.

1 Have the Andersons come for their appointment? – Yes/they/arrive/just
2 Have you posted the letter yet? – Yes/I/send it/already
3 Has Joe served at the till before? – Yes/he/work there/since Easter
4 Have you ever traded securities online? – Yes/I/buy shares/often
5 Have property prices stopped rising? – Yes/they/fall/for some time
6 Has the manager already gone to Head Office? – No/she/not leave/yet

**b** Use the present perfect and 'since' or 'for' to complete these sentences.

1 The Andersons … (live) in a rented flat (since/for) many years.
2 Claire … (have) a life assurance policy (since/for) 2001.
3 Kevin … (pay) into a pension scheme (since/for) the same period.
4 Both customers (earn) a regular salary (since/for) arriving in Germany.
5 They (be) customers of their branch (since/for) last year.
6 Joanna Witt (know) the Andersons (since/for) the last year.

**LEARNING** Wie kann ich Grammatik lernen?

1 Suchen Sie sich eine Grammatik, die zu Ihrem Kenntnisstand passt.
2 Lernen Sie die wichtigsten Begriffe.
3 Machen Sie sich Ihr grammatikalisches Problem klar.
4 Suchen Sie sich die Informationen dazu im Grammatikbuch.
5 Achten Sie beim Lesen englischer Texte besonders auf diese Form.

## 11 Property loans

19

Do the tasks below the dialogue.

Joanna Witt is telling the Andersons about loans for financing property.

JOANNA: Well ... There are basically two types of property loan. The first one is what we call a repayment loan. That means that you have a set instalment every month that pays the interest on the loan and ...[A]. During the term of the loan, the interest payments decrease and the loan repayments increase, but the instalments stay the same.

CLAIRE: I thought all loans were like that!

JOANNA: There's an alternative. It's called an interest-only loan. With this type of loan you make two monthly payments. The first one covers only the interest on the loan. The second payment could be made into an endowment assurance policy that would be paid out when the loan is due. The capital that you'd get from the endowment assurance ...[B].

CLAIRE: So will the monthly instalments for the loan be smaller then?

JOANNA: Yes, because you only pay interest. And interest-only loans ...[C].

KEVIN: But isn't it riskier than a repayment loan?

JOANNA: That's true. If the endowment assurance ...[D], you may not receive enough money to repay the loan.

CLAIRE: That would be awful. What would happen then?

JOANNA: You'd have to pay the difference yourself, I'm afraid, or extend the term of the loan.

KEVIN: And if we couldn't do that?

JOANNA: Well, the bank has got security for the loan. I believe that in Britain most borrowers take out a mortgage on the property. In Germany it's different: banks here prefer to register a land charge, but either way, if you can't repay the loan, the bank ...[E] –

CLAIRE: You mean, we might lose the flat?

JOANNA: In the worst case, yes. Your home could be at risk.

CLAIRE: Oh dear! Well we'd sleep better with the first option.

**a** Read the text and use these expressions to fill the gaps A–E.

1 have tax advantages as well
2 can take possession of the property
3 repays part of the borrowed money
4 does not yield as much as expected
5 would pay the loan back at the end of the term

**b** Listen to the discussion and see whether you have filled the gaps correctly.

**c** Give the German expressions for

1 a repayment loan
2 an interest-only loan
3 endowment assurance
4 a mortgage
5 a land charge

## 12 Shortfall

**a** What is a shortfall? What should you do if you are in danger of having one? Read this report and answer these two questions in German.

### If You Get a Red Letter …

In Britain, if you have taken out endowment assurance to repay an interest-only loan, your insurance company has to write to you every two years to inform you whether your investment is on track to meet your target sum. These letters are colour coded.

If you receive a green letter, your investment should repay your mortgage loan if it continues to grow by at least 6% a year. If you receive a yellow letter, there is a significant risk that your endowment policy will fall short, which means it will not yield enough at the end of the term to pay off your loan. If you receive a red letter, the risk of a shortfall is high! Experts warn people not to panic, even if they have received a red letter.

But what should you do? Most experts advise people to steer clear of increasing their payments on their existing policy or opening a new one. Mortgage broker David Hollingworth says this is "simply throwing good money after bad". He says the safest route is to change your mortgage into a part-repayment loan. This means that in addition to paying off the interest every month, you make extra payments to repay the loan. This will reduce the size of both the loan and any shortfall that there may be if the endowment assurance underperforms.

**b** What steps do banks in Germany take to protect themselves and their customers from shortfall? List your ideas in English.

## 13 Work with words

Use expressions from this unit to fill the gaps.

1 Nearly everyone wants to have a home of their ….
2 The flat has … own garden.
3 A … loan has set instalments that pay the interest and repay part of the sum each month.
4 If you have an interest-only loan, you can take out some … assurance to repay the loan at the end of the term.
5 If your assurance does not perform well, you may have a … when the loan is due.
6 You could open a building society policy with monthly … of €100.
7 The building society will grant you a loan … €20,000 to buy the flat.
8 If the building society loan is not enough, the bank will grant you a … loan.
9 In Britain a person who wants to buy a house usually takes out a … .
10 In Germany the bank would probably register a … as security.

# Life assurance

## 14 Life assurance products

Read this text and do the task below.

**There are three main types of life assurance:**

1 **Term assurance** provides life cover. The holder pays regular premiums and an agreed sum will be paid out to the beneficiary if the person whose life is insured dies during the term. There is no maturity benefit. If the policy is cashed in early, the surrender value is low.

2 **Endowment assurance** covers the policy holder's life but also guarantees a lump sum on maturity, which can be increased by bonus payments that accumulate during the term. On maturity, the holder may have the choice of turning the endowment policy into an annuity.

3 **Annuity assurance** provides a regular income for the holder, usually until death as part of a private pension plan. The deposits or premiums may be invested in funds. In this case the guaranteed sums are low but returns may be higher than with other types of life assurance.

A customer, who had read this information, asks you to explain the difference between these insurance terms:

1 the policy holder and the beneficiary
2 premiums and lump sum deposits
3 the guaranteed sum and the bonus payments
4 the surrender value and the maturity benefit
5 an endowment and an annuity

## 15 Group activity

Work in groups of 3 to do the following task.

Create profiles of 3 different customers, one suitable for each type of life assurance, and write the details on 3 separate cards. Then exchange cards with another group. Using the cards your group receives, do 3 role plays, taking turns to play the roles of:

- the customer who wants to find out about life assurance
- the account manager, who gives general information about life assurance
- the adviser, who offers a suitable insurance product sold at his or her bank

Unit 9

# Business Banking

## 1 Warm-up

Look at this flyer from Lloyds TSB Middle-East and discuss the questions below.

**a** What sort of business client might feel like a "small fish in a big sea"? Why?

**b** What problems do small businesses face, especially if working abroad?

**c** How can banks help to solve these problems?

**CULTURE** Dealing with Middle-Eastern clients

- Be patient: your client may arrive late or not at all if family business calls.
- Avoid touching and making eye contact with women. Ask them nothing personal.
- Always accept hospitality: eat and drink everything you are offered.
- In small talk, ask after the client's family but never mention his wife or daughter.
- Stay cool. If you are energetic, you may be seen as disorganized and incompetent.
- Do not feel you have to talk: silence is not embarrassing for Arabs.
- Let your client choose when to talk business. Then come to the point at once.
- Do a presentation "upside-down": start with the product you want to sell.

## 2 Business clients and corporate clients

20 *Money Matters* interviewed Alexandra Gandini, Communications Manager for Lloyds TSB Middle-East in Dubai.

**a** Listen to the dialogue and note three topics which Alex talks about.

**b** Listen again and use expressions from this box to fill the gaps in the text.

corporate hospitality | customized events | ex-pats | foreign exchange | negotiation | round-table discussions | syndicated loans | turnover

MM: Is there a difference between personal and business banking?

ALEX: In personal banking, products are standardized and rates are fixed by the bank, but in business banking, the products are more complex, there is room for …[1] of terms, fees and interest rates, and, especially with corporate clients, the relationship is very important.

MM: But aren't business clients and corporate clients the same?

ALEX: No, they aren't. Corporate clients are bigger companies, with a larger …[2]. They usually require specialized products.

MM: I see. What products does Lloyds TSB offer its corporate clients?

ALEX: We offer accounts in all major currencies and trade finance services like documentary credits for import-export business. We can also provide treasury services – that's everything to do with …[3] –

MM: You mean buying and selling foreign currencies?

ALEX: Yes, and transferring money as well – for example if a company had to pay a bill in yen in Japan in six months' time, we'd help them to do that.

MM: And I suppose lending is important too?

ALEX: Absolutely. We arrange simple business overdrafts and loans as well as what we call "structured finance." That includes …[4] when several banks join together to lend huge sums of money, as well as specialised financing for ships and trucks, or takeovers and mergers.

MM: And how do you market these bank products?

ALEX: In corporate banking we don't market products directly. We focus on improving our relationship with existing customers and meeting new ones. We use …[5], for example we give people tickets to sports events – say the Dubai Tennis Open, where we have a VIP tent, or we invite them onto our yacht to take part in a regatta. We also run …[6] –

MM: Those are events specially organized by the bank?

ALEX: Yes, like our Lloyds TSB Golf Day. Clients are invited to play, have lunch, get free gifts like Lloyds TSB golf bags, and maybe their photo in the press. There are serious events too, like …[7] on topics our clients are interested in.

MM: And are most of these clients Arabs?

ALEX: Some are, yes, but most are …[8] from all over the world who do business in the Gulf region. They all speak English, of course!

c Decide whether these statements are true or false. Correct the false ones.

1 Business clients have a larger turnover than corporate clients.
2 Terms are more flexible in business banking than in personal banking.
3 Syndicated loans are granted by more than one bank.
4 Foreign exchange services include dealing in foreign currencies.
5 The Dubai Tennis Open is a customized event.
6 A round-table discussion takes place between a client and an adviser in the bank.
7 Ex-pats are native speakers of English.

d What are your bank's communication strategies with corporate clients? What do you think of these strategies? What changes would you suggest?

## 3 A balance sheet

The balance sheet of a small, privately-owned manufacturing company could look like this. The figures have been omitted. Do the task below.

| ASSETS | LIABILITIES |
|---|---|
| **Non-current assets** | **Owners' capital** |
| Goodwill | Retained earnings |
| Fixed Assets | |
| Buildings and land | **Long-term liabilities** |
| Machinery | Loans |
| Vehicles | Mortgages |
| Tools and equipment | |
| **Current assets** | **Short-term liabilities** |
| Inventory | Overdrafts |
| Accounts receivable | Accounts payable |
| Cash equivalents | Interest payable on loans |
| Cash | Provisions for taxes |

Find items on the balance sheet that show the following. Then give the German equivalents.

1 the credit balance on its current account
2 the profits kept from the previous year
3 the value of its trucks
4 the total amount it owes to its suppliers
5 the value of its good reputation
6 the total sum owed by its creditors
7 the value of its computer hardware
8 the total value of raw materials, work-in-progress and finished products

## 4 Cash flow

Decide with a partner which of these statements is incorrect. Say why.

1 In simple terms, a company's cash flow shows how much cash it receives and pays out during a certain period.
2 The cash flow measures a company's liquidity.
3 A company can have a positive or negative cash flow.
4 Profitable companies have a positive cash flow at all times.

## 5 Cash flow problems

**a** Working in a group, imagine that you have a small business. What sort of situations could lead to cash flow problems? List as many as you can.

**b** Read this article and write down five pieces of advice you would give a client who is starting out in business.

### Cash is King

Barclays, the UK bank, estimates that 17% of all new businesses close after the first year, 37% after two years and 49% after three. One reason for closures is that the entrepreneur has run out of cash to pay the bills. This has influenced the way some entrepreneurs operate.

Take Claire Owen, aged 30. After she had lost her job when the company where she was working went into liquidation, Owen decided to set up her own business. In 1993, without using any borrowed capital, she founded Stop Gap Marketing – an agency that recruits staff for companies. She asked friends to lend her a desk, a computer and a telephone to keep her overheads low.

As the business expanded, Owen took on freelance staff. This meant making sure that her clients paid their bills in time for freelancers to receive their wages. Owen says that even if a client had not paid, she still paid the freelancer. "I would look at the cash and say that as long as I had enough for the next three months, that would be OK, I could sleep at night. Then as the business grew, I wanted six months in the bank. Then we got a year of cash in the bank and I stopped worrying. Now we can make our cash work for us by moving it around to profit from short-term interest."

Owen has always reinvested her profits in her business and resisted the temptation to expand too quickly. She employs an accountant but has never used a factoring firm because of the fees. She avoids bad debts. "When we started out we would take on any customer, but now we are more cautious. You can go bankrupt overnight if one big client fails to pay up."

This strategy has paid off: today Stop Gap Marketing has a turnover of £30 million with offices in the UK and Australia.

(Source: Abridged from *The Daily Telegraph*)

**LANGUAGE** Talking about a business

**Business** is the activity of making, buying, selling or supplying goods or services for money. A business is a commercial organization that does business.
A **company** is a legal business organization. It can be privately or publicly owned, e. g. ICI plc is one of the largest companies in the UK. (plc = public limited company)
The word **firm** is normally used for a small privately-owned company, e. g. Smith & Jones Ltd is a building firm. (Ltd = (private) limited company)

**GRAMMAR** The simple past and the past perfect

1 In 1993 she **founded** Stop Gap Marketing …
2 As the business expanded, Owen **took** on freelance staff.
3 After she **had lost** her job … Owen decided to set up her own business.
4 … the company where she **was working** went into liquidation …

- The simple past is used when an action was completed at a named (1) or known (2) time in the past. (cf. the use of the present perfect, p. 92)
- The past perfect is used when an action took place before the action that is expressed in the past (3).
- The simple past (4) and the past perfect may be used in the progressive form when the action took place without interruption or repeatedly.

## 6 Practice: expressing the past

Put the verbs in this text into the present perfect or the simple past or the past perfect.

### The Richard Branson Story

Sir Richard Branson …[1] (leave) school at 16 to set up his first successful business, Student magazine. After he …[2] (found) Virgin, a company that …[3] (sell) records by mail order, he …[4] (open) a record shop in London and a recording studio under the same name. Virgin's first record …[5] (become) a No. 1 hit. Since then, many famous artists including Phil Collins and The Rolling Stones …[6] (help) to make Virgin Music one of the top six record companies in the world.

The Virgin Group …[7] (expand) internationally in sectors like air and rail travel, healthcare, telecommunications, financial services, retail outlets, hotels and leisure facilities with around 200 companies in over 30 countries. In 2004 Branson …[8] (sign) the deal for Virgin Galactic, the first company to take paying passengers into space.

Branson's personal assets …[9] (be valued) at more than £4.4 billion, but he …[10] (not only make) a name for himself as an entrepreneur. He …[11] (help) to finance many charities and environmental projects and, since 1985, …[12] (become) famous for breaking world records, such as being the first person to cross the Atlantic by hot-air balloon.

## 7 Tandem work

Work with a partner.

**a** Together you run a small business that has a temporary cash flow problem and needs help from its bank. Decide on the following points and make your own role card.

1 the name of your company and the type of work it does
2 the reason for your cash flow problem (Exercise 5 will give you ideas.)
3 the amount and term of the money you need
4 how you plan to repay the money
5 your previous business and credit history
6 what documents you will take to your appointment in the bank
7 which part of your case each of you will present

**b** Join another pair who take the roles of two business banking advisers. Play the roles you have created and apply for credit. Then swap roles.

If you are the applicants:
- make your case clear.
- provide any documents required.
- give all the details needed.
- ask about the borrowing terms.

If you are the bank advisers:
- find out as much as possible.
- ask for relevant documents.
- decide whether you will need security.
- make the lending terms clear.

**c** In class, the bank advisers should imagine that their fellow students are colleagues in the bank and report to them. (One person describes the case and the other presents the lending terms offered.) Ask your colleagues for their feedback.

**LEARNING** **Wie man neue Vokabeln lernt**

Um das Lernen neuer Wörter zu erleichtern, lernen Sie nicht immer einzelne Vokabeln. Lernen Sie ein Verb zusammen mit seinem Prädikat, z. B. to do business, oder mit der dazugehörenden Präposition, z. B. to set up a company. Lernen Sie eine Vokabel zusammen mit ihrem Synonym, z. B. security = collateral oder mit ihrem Gegensatz, z. B. to accept ≠ to refuse. Merken Sie sich Besonderheiten: Wenn ein Substantiv auf deutsch Mehrzahl ist und auf englisch Einzahl, lernen Sie es zusammen mit einem passenden Verb, z. B. interest is paid.

## 8 Learning vocabulary

Say which of the above methods could help you to learn these words.

1 liabilities
2 syndicated
3 go into liquidation
4 publicly-owned
5 found
6 valued

## 9 A brochure

Read this brochure from the US bank Wells Fargo and do the tasks below.

To build a successful business, it takes hard work, creativity and, above all, capital.

Quick access to cash. It's an essential tool of the small business owner. It helps you seize opportunities when they arise. And get what you need when you need it.

That's what the BusinessLine® Line of Credit is all about. With a credit line of up to $100,000, it puts you in charge of your finances. You can access the amount you need, repay it over time at favorable rates and then reuse your credit as often as you like.

**Grow Your Business and Manage Your Finances with a BusinessLine® Line of Credit**

It's a fundamental fact of business. Having money on hand can help you earn more and save more in the long run. You can invest in your business when the time is right and keep your enterprise running smoothly regardless of the marketplaces ups and downs.

- **CONSOLIDATE DEBT** with a lower interest rate.
- **MAINTAIN CASH FLOW** during fluctuations in the business cycle.
- **SAVE MONEY** by buying in bulk or making special purchases.
- **KEEP YOUR GOOD CREDIT** by paying receivables promptly.
- **EXPAND WHEN THE TIME IS RIGHT** – with new offices, equipment, employees or product lines.
- **ACCESS CASH** when important opportunities arise.

(Source: Used with permission from Wells Fargo & Company)

**a** Explain what a BusinessLine Line of Credit is.

**b** Say how this line of credit can

1 help you save money.
2 protect your creditworthiness.

## 10 Work with words

Use words from the box opposite to fill these gaps.

1 Britain and Spain are the countries in Europe … property prices have fallen most.
2 Losses last year were … great … the company was forced into liquidation.
3 … the company made a profit, they are not paying any dividend this year.
4 The bank granted the company an overdraft … it could solve its cash flow problems.
5 … you can provide suitable security, the bank cannot grant you the loan.
6 The company has … a large turnover … it will need new premises.
7 He joined the business … he was a trainee.
8 … profits have increased, the company's shares have risen in value.

**LANGUAGE** **How to link sentences**

If two sentences are connected in meaning, it is sometimes better to link them to make one longer sentence using a clause. The connecting element may be time, a place, a reason, a condition, a concession, a result or a purpose.

If it is time, use 'after', 'before', 'since', 'when' or 'while'
e.g. Before he could set up the business, he had to apply for a loan.

If it is a place, use 'where',
e.g. The goods are made in China, where production costs are lower.

If it is a reason, use 'as', 'because' or 'since',
e.g. As the company has a cash flow problem, we cannot approve the loan.

If it is a condition, use 'if' or 'unless',
e.g. Unless the economy improves, sales will go on falling.

If it is a concession, use 'although' or 'though',
e.g. They decided to invest in new machinery though sales were poor.

If it is a result, use 'so … that' or 'such a … that',
e.g. The new product was such a success that profits rose by 25%.

If it is a purpose, use 'so that'
e.g. They bought land so that they could build new premises.

## 11 Starting out

21 Twenty-nine-year-old entrepreneur Julian Davis is talking to Tania Pohl, who works in the corporate business department of a German bank.

**a** Before you listen to their conversation, do these tasks:

1 Find out what the following expressions mean and explain them in English:

a work placement | a gap in the market | cut your overheads | face a setback | have plans in the pipeline

2 Say what you think a person needs to set up a business successfully. List the points.

**b** Listen to the dialogue and decide why Julian Davis has been successful. Compare the reasons with the points on your list.

Note: The Prince's Trust is a charity which helps people aged 18–30 to start up in business.

**c** Listen again and write a memo in German about this company.

## 12 A rights issue of shares

In April 2008, when HBOS (Halifax Bank of Scotland) decided to raise capital by issuing new shares to existing shareholders at a discount, its share price stood at nearly 500p (= £5).

Read this article from July 20th 2008 and describe in German what happened.

### HBOS £4 bn rights issue is massive flop

HBOS will tomorrow reveal that its £4 bn rights issue has been one of the biggest flops in UK corporate history.

Almost all the new shares on offer to existing shareholders will be left with underwriting banks Morgan Stanley and Dresdner Kleinwort. Under the terms of the underwriting arrangements, Morgan and Dresdner must try to place the offer with institutions as long as the market price is the same as the rights issue price of 275p, or higher.

Because the shares had been trading below the rights issue price for several weeks, shareholders did not take up the issue as they could buy HBOS shares for less on the market.

HBOS will still receive its £4 bn as the issue is fully underwritten, which means that it gets the money, no matter how poor the take-up.

Since HBOS announced the rights offer in April, sentiment has turned against banks as the UK and US housing markets have deteriorated amid fears of a recession. Many banks have seen their share prices fall by as much as 45 per cent in the last ten weeks.

(Source: Abridged from *The Observer*)

## 13 A bond issue

Read this report and then do the tasks below.

### Das Land Berlin nimmt 500 Millionen Euro auf

Das Land Berlin begibt eine zweijährige Anleihe im Volumen von 500 Millionen Euro. Die Titel werden zu pari und in Stückelungen zu 1000 Euro ausgegeben. Der Kupon beträgt 5,156 Prozent. Konsortialführer ist Unicredit. Die Agentur Moody's benotet die Anleihe mit „Aa1".

*(Frankfurter Allgemeine Zeitung)*

**a** Find German expressions in the report which mean the following:

at par | federal state | in denominations of | lead manager | to issue | to rate

**b** Explain in English how Berlin will raise the sum of 500 million euros.

## 14 Group work

Divide your class into three groups and do the following task.

One of your bank's largest corporate clients, a publicly-owned company, needs capital to expand. In your groups consider the pros and cons of financing the expansion a) by a bank loan, b) by an issue of bonds and c) by issuing new shares. Then compare your results.

# Going public

## 15 Two IPOs

These two articles describe initial public offerings (IPOs) in China. Read them and do the tasks below.

### Märchenhafter Börsenstart für Alibaba

Die chinesischen Aktien-Handelsplätze sind seit Monaten auf Rekordjagd, aber das Börsendebüt des von Lehrer Jack Ma vor gerade sieben Jahren gegründeten Unternehmens Alibaba übertrifft selbst die kühnsten Träume aus tausend und einer Anleger-Nacht. Am Tag der Erstnotierung konnten Börsianer, die Alibaba für 13,50 Hongkong-Dollar pro Stück gezeichnet hatten, ihren Einsatz fast verdreifachen. Die Aktie kostete zum Handelsende 39,50 Hongkong-Dollar. Der Börsengang spülte dem Unternehmen umgerechnet rund eine Milliarde Euro in die Kasse. Die Nachfrage nach der Aktie war 250-mal größer als das Angebot.

Der Alibaba-Boom ist umso überraschender, als die Dimensionen des Unternehmens bescheiden anmuten. Im ersten Halbjahr erwirtschaftete die Firma einen Umsatz von 958 Millionen Yuan (88,5 Millionen Euro). Der Gewinn belief sich auf 295 Millionen Yuan (27,5 Millionen Euro). Als Internet-Portal bringt Alibaba verschiedene Unternehmen mit potentiellen Kunden zusammen – ein Marktplatz wie E-bay, nur ohne Auktion und für Geschäftsprofis. Anleger finden das offensichtlich so großartig, dass die Aktie jetzt zum 155-fachen der für 2008 erwarteten Gewinne gehandelt wird. Ein zehnmal kleineres Kurs-Gewinn-Verhältnis gilt als normal, aber in China scheint Normalität gegenwärtig das falsche Wort zu sein.

(Abridged from *Frankfurter Allgemeine Zeitung*, $7^{\text{th}}$ November 2007)

### Tepid IPO in China is sign of end to bull run

Shares in China Railway Construction rose Monday by less than expected in their trading debut in the largest IPO of this year, a further sign that the Chinese bull market was ending its extraordinary run. The company, which has built more than half of China's railroads, rose 28 per cent in Shanghai, but it was the worst debut in more than a year. 'Investors have already factored in that spectacular gains won't be a guarantee any more,' said Mona Chung of Daiwa Asset Management in Hong Kong.

The lackluster IPO for China Railway's $5.4 billion stock listing, split between Shanghai and Hong Kong, was expected to hurt new share offerings in China because it signaled a bearish turn in market conditions.

(Abridged from *International Herald Tribune*, $11^{\text{th}}$ March 2008)

**a** Compare the two IPOs.

**b** Describe indicators in the first article which link it to the second.

## 16 Group discussion

Discuss this question: "What makes for a successful IPO?"

# Global Banking

## 1 Warm-up

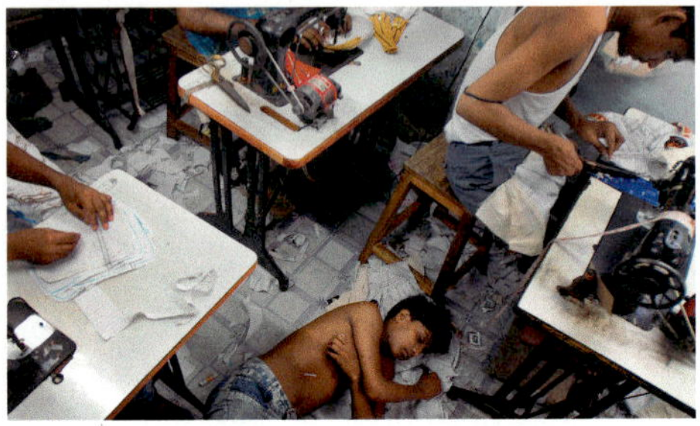

**a** Describe these pictures. Point out how they are connected.

**b** Say what globalization is. Explain why it is a recent phenomenon.

**c** Point out some positive and some negative effects of globalization.

**d** Describe how banks have been affected by globalization.

## 2 World trade

Describe this chart and this graph. Say which facts you find the most interesting. Suggest what the figures might look like in ten years' time.

**Aufschwung des Welthandels**

Warenausfuhr
Anteil am Weltmarkt

| | | |
|---|---|---|
| Deutschland | 1327 | (9.5) |
| China | 1218 | (8.8) |
| Vereinigte Staaten | 1163 | (8.4) |
| Japan | 713 | (5.1) |
| Frankreich | 552 | (4.0) |
| Niederlande | 551 | (4.0) |
| Italien | 492 | (3.5) |
| Großbritannien | 436 | (3.1) |
| Belgien | 432 | (3.1) |
| Kanada | 418 | (3.0) |
| Brasilien | 161 | (1.2) |
| Indien | 145 | (1.0) |

Globales Handelsvolumen
in Milliarden Dollar

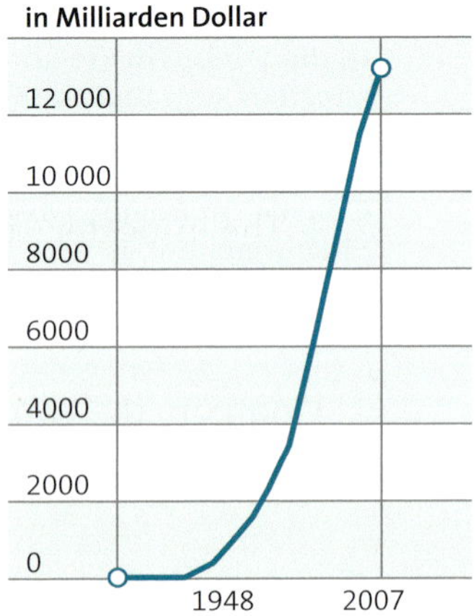


(Source: WTO/F.A.Z.-Grafik Kaiser)

**LANGUAGE How to clarify and summarize information**

| To make sure you have understood someone correctly, you can say: | To summarize what someone has said, you can say: |
|---|---|
| If I understand you correctly, …<br>So what you're saying is, …<br>Could you give an example of that?<br>Could you be more specific? | To sum up, we can say that …<br>So the key points are …<br>If I may/Let me just go through the main points again, … |

## 3 Chairing a discussion

Either alone or with a partner, look at the charts in Exercise 2 again and prepare answers to the questions below. Then discuss them in a group:

For each question, choose one person in the group to chair the discussion and note the main points on an OHP. When it is your turn as chairperson, use expressions from the last box.

1 Germany exports more than the USA. What are the reasons for this?
2 Why is the level of Britain's exports so low? Is this a danger signal?
3 The volume of global trade has risen steeply in recent years. Why is this so?
4 What are Germany's main exports? How can Germany stay competitive?
5 Where does Germany mostly export to? Is globalization changing this?

## 4 Terms of payment

**a** Match each of these five terms of payment with one of the definitions (1–5).

payment on open account | payment in advance | a documentary credit
documents against acceptance | documents against payment

1 The exporter dispatches the goods after receiving payment for them.
2 The exporter dispatches the goods, sends the invoice and waits for payment.
3 The importer's bank guarantees to make payment against presentation of documents.
4 The importer's bank releases the documents when the importer has paid the invoice.
5 The importer's bank releases the documents when the importer has accepted a bill of exchange.

**b** Discuss where the advantage/disadvantage of each of the terms of payment lies

1 for the exporter.
2 for the importer.

## 5 Payment in foreign trade

22

Harry Oldham has a small business which makes industrial glue. He has received an enquiry from Malaysia and consults his adviser Jim Asbury.

**a** Before you listen to their conversation, say what advice you think Harry Oldham is going to need.

**b** Listen to the dialogue and see whether you were right.

JIM: What can I do for you, Mr Oldham?

HARRY: I need a bit of advice on exporting. This company in Kuala Lumpur saw our website, asked for a sample of our products and are now enquiring about placing a large order with us.

JIM: Oh! Congratulations! Is this your first export transaction?

HARRY: Yes, going global at last! And I don't know much about the Far East, so I thought I'd better ask you about arranging the payment.

JIM: Of course. You can hardly allow payment on open account, can you?

HARRY: You mean, ship the goods, send an invoice and then wait for them to transfer the money? Goodness, no! I can't take a risk like that.

JIM: And I doubt the buyer will agree to payment in advance –

HARRY: They pay the bill first and I only send off the shipment when the money's in my account? That'd be nice, but I can't see them agreeing to it!

JIM: That's why it would be safer for you to arrange collection of documents –

HARRY: Hang on a minute. You've lost me there. What documents?

JIM: I'm sorry, the shipping documents – that's the bill of lading, the commercial invoice, the certificate of insurance, the certificate of origin and the packing list.

HARRY: I see. I suppose my freight forwarder will deal with all those?

JIM: Yes. Collection of documents works in two different ways. If you agree on documents against payment, the buyers will have to pay your invoice before they can get the documents from their bank.

HARRY: But what if they want to pay later? We let some of our customers in this country pay 30 days after sight.

JIM: That would be the second way. If you agree on documents against acceptance, the buyers will have to accept a bill of exchange in order to get the documents from their bank.

HARRY: Hmm. I'm not so sure I'd trust a bank that I don't know to get it right.

JIM: I'd recommend asking the buyers to apply for a documentary credit.

HARRY: I've heard of a letter of credit. Are documentary credits the same?

JIM: Yes, they are. With a documentary credit a bank guarantees to make the payment when the documents are presented to them. It's the safest of all the terms of payment.

HARRY: D'you know, exporting might be a lot less risky than I thought! Can you tell me how a documentary credit works?

**c** Now read the dialogue and find the five terms of payment mentioned in it. Which one does Harry Oldham prefer?

**d** Say what these abbreviations stand for: B/E B/L D/A D/C D/P L/C

**GRAMMAR** Gerunds

1 **Exporting** might be a lot less risky than I thought.
2 I'd recommend **asking** the buyers to apply for a documentary credit.
3 I thought I'd ask you about **arranging** the payment.
4 I need a bit of advice on **exporting.**

- The gerund is formed with the *-ing* form of the verb. (1–4)
- Gerunds can be used as the subject of a sentence (1) or as the object after certain verbs (2). Here are some common ones:
advise – avoid – consider – dislike – enjoy – finish – hate* – imagine - involve – like* – love* – (not) mind – recommend – risk – suggest
- Verbs used after prepositions must be in the form of the gerund. (3, 4)
- These expressions are followed by a gerund:
advantage of – advice on (4) – disadvantage of – information about – means of – method of – possibility of – reason for – service of – way of

* The verbs *hate, like* and *love* can also be followed by an infinitive.

## 6 Practice: using gerunds

**a** Replace the words in italics with an expression that uses a gerund.

Example Mr Oldham sees the advantage *he will have if he asks for a L/C.*
Mr Oldham sees the advantage of asking for a L/C.

1 Mr Oldham is worried about the risk *that he may lose money.*
2 He wants to find a way *how he can avoid this.*
3 Jim Asbury gives him advice on *how to secure the payment.*
4 They discuss the reasons *why he should ask for a documentary credit.*
5 Mr Oldham sees the possibility *that he can export his goods safely.*
6 The importers' bank will charge for the service *when they issue a L/C.*

**b** Complete these sentences using gerunds.

1 My bank specialises in …
2 Working in a bank, I particularly enjoy …
3 Of all the departments I have worked in, I most liked …
4 At the moment, my daily work mainly consists of …
5 In future I look forward to …

## 7 Documentary credits

Working with a partner, do the tasks below.

**a** The points 1–10 on this chart show how a documentary credit works. Use them to put the 10 sentences below into the right order.

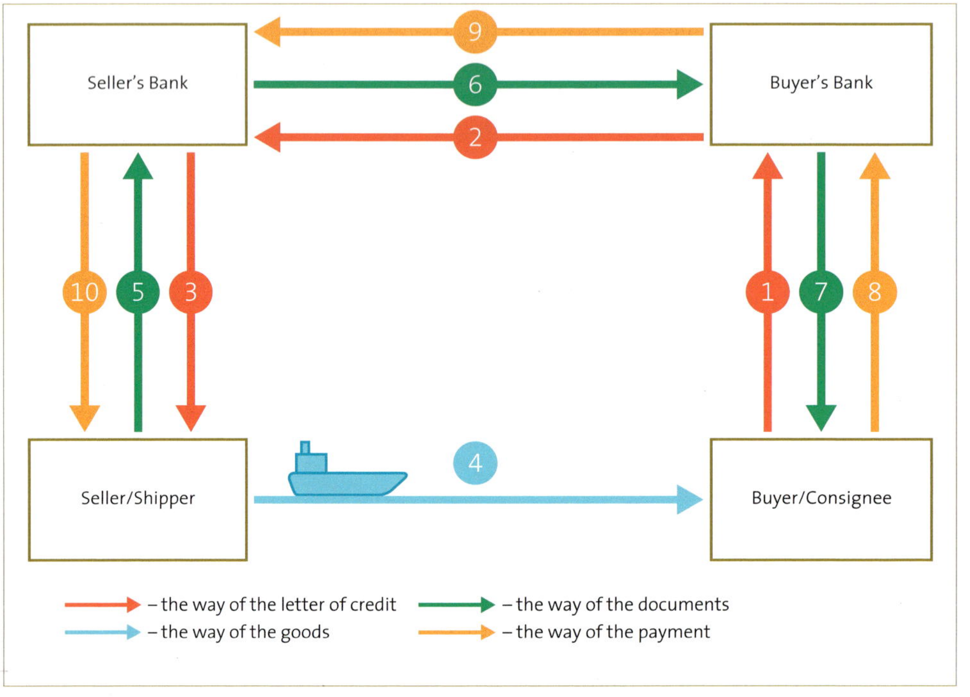


A The seller's bank credits the sum to the seller's account.
B The buyer's bank issues an *irrevocable* D/C and *notifies* the seller's bank.
C The buyer asks his bank to open a documentary credit *in favour of* the seller.
D The buyer's bank transfers the money to the seller's bank.
E The seller gives the shipping documents to his bank.
F The seller *ships* the goods.
G The buyer pays or accepts a B/E and the documents are *released.*
H The seller's bank either *advises* or *confirms* the D/C and informs the seller.
I The buyer's bank *presents* the documents to the buyer for payment or for acceptance of a B/E.
J The seller's bank checks that the documents *conform* with the D/C and *forwards* them to the buyer's bank.

**b** Translate the words that are in italics in the sentences above.

**c** Look at the documentary credit on page 120 and say what documents it requires.

## 8 Using a D/C

23

Listen to the dialogue and then do the tasks below.

Jim Asbury is telling Harry Oldham how a documentary credit works.

**a** Say who has to apply for the documentary credit.

**b** Explain the difference between advising and confirming a documentary credit.

**c** Describe when the importers can receive the shipping documents.

**d** Point out who pays the costs of a documentary credit.

### CULTURE Dealing with Far-Eastern customers

There are many ethnic groups and cultures in the Far East, but here are some basic points.

- Be careful: if you have offended someone, they may say nothing or even keep smiling.
- Avoid direct confrontation. Look for other ways to resolve differences of opinion.
- Read between the lines. Many Asians communicate indirectly or implicitly, e.g. a Japanese person who says "That would be difficult" means "That is impossible".
- Always ask after the client's family in small talk.
- Never say the word "no" in China. Use expressions like "That is not correct" or "I see things differently".
- Avoid the numbers 13, 4 and any number ending in a 4 (these numbers are considered unlucky). In China, the number 8 brings good luck, especially if it is at the end of a long number.

## 9 Work with words

Match the numbers on this diagram with the terms below.

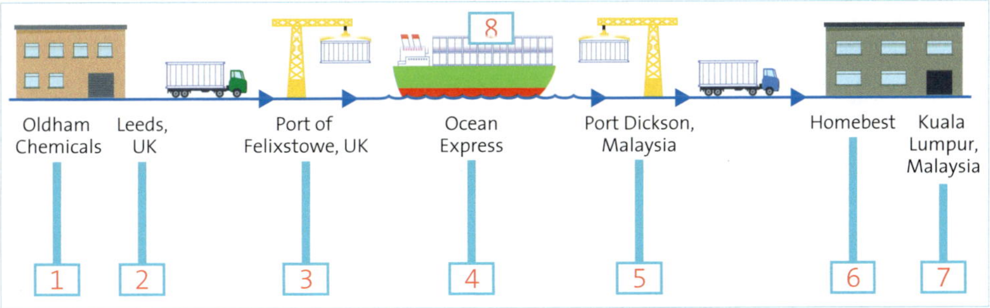


**a** buyer / consignee / importer

**b** place of delivery / place of destination

**c** place of dispatch / place of loading

**d** port of discharge / port of destination

**e** port of loading / port of shipment

**f** seller / shipper / exporter

**g** vessel / ship

**h** consignment / shipment

## 10 Over to you

**a** Choose one of the cases on page 119 and create a role play card in English about it. Make up details about yourself and your business, your trading partner, the transaction and the problem involved.

**b** Find a partner who chose a different case and use your card to play the roles below. Use words from the last exercise and expressions for clarifying and summarizing information. Then swap roles.

If you are the bank adviser:
- Find out who your customer is.
- Make sure you understand the problem.
- Summarize the situation.
- Give advice.
- Answer questions.

If you are the customer:
- Introduce yourself.
- Explain where your problem lies.
- Make sure you understand the advice you are given.
- Ask questions about the risk, the costs etc.
- Summarize the steps you will have to take.

## 11 Bills of lading

**a** Read this text and decide whether the statements below are true or false or contain information that is not in the text. Correct the false ones.

### What is a Bill of Lading?

A bill of lading is a receipt signed at the port of loading by the agent of the shipping company or the captain of the vessel. It confirms that the consignment has been received either on board a ship (a Shipped on Board B/L) or at the quay (a Received for Shipment B/L). A third type of bill, a Combined Transport B/L, can be issued for multi-modal transport. The letter of credit specifies which type of bill is required. If the issuer is satisfied that the shipment appears to be in good condition, the B/L is clean; any visible damage must be noted on the B/L which is then unclean.

Bills of lading are usually issued in full sets – that means there are two or three signed originals which are all identical. The shipper sends them by separate posts to the consignee in case they get lost. As the bill of lading is a title document, the consignee (or his forwarding agent) needs it to take possession of the shipment when it arrives at the port of discharge.

Bills of lading are also negotiable: an importer may sell the shipment while the ship is still at sea, simply by endorsing the B/L and transferring the rights to another person.

1 A bill of lading shows that a consignment has been loaded onto a ship.
2 A bill of lading can cover both sea and land transport.
3 A clean bill of lading means that the goods are not damaged in any way.
4 The holder of a signed original B/L can take possession of the goods.
5 Importers often pledge bills of lading to receive short-term bank loans.
6 Only the original consignee named on the bill can receive the shipment.

**b** Look at the bill of lading on page 121 and say what type of bill it is.

## 12 The Incoterms

Work with a partner.

Read the information about the Incoterms on pages 122–124. Choose one incoterm and say what costs and risks the seller and the buyer each have to bear. See if your partner can name the Incoterm you have described. Keep changing the roles.

## 13 Global stock markets

**a** Read this article and then do the tasks below in German.

### Panic on Global Markets

21st January 2007 was one of the blackest Mondays ever on the world's stock exchanges. Growing fears of a recession in the USA and anxiety about the outlook for the financial sector triggered a sell-off on global equity markets. Turbulences on the Asian markets caused European share prices to tumble in the biggest one-day fall since 9/11.

In Asia, indices declined across the board. In Tokyo, the Nikkei 225 dropped 3.9% to a new 27-month low on Monday and fell a further 4.4% by midday on Tuesday, while Hong Kong slumped 5,5% on Monday and crashed a further 8% on Tuesday. In Mumbai trading was halted on Monday after shares dived 9.8% in the opening minutes and finally closed 7.4% down. Shanghai lost 5.1% and Singapore 6% at the end of the day. The Dubai stock exchange was down by 10% and shares in Sydney slid for the eleventh successive trading session.

In Europe, in one day, about $490 bn was wiped off the market value of the FTSE Eurofirst 300 index. The FTSE 100 index in London lost $148 bn, its biggest slide ever. Germany's Xetra Dax plunged 7.2% and France's CAC-40 sank 6.8%. As investors rushed to the safety of government bonds, the yield on the ten-year Bund fell to 3.9%, while the two-year Schatz yield fell to 3.5%. US markets were closed for the Martin Luther King holiday.

Many analysts believe that there is worse to come and that markets have not bottomed out yet. "September 11 aside, I can't remember a day like this," said Jimmy Yates, a share dealer in London. "We've had four or five really good years but this looks like the end of the bull run."

(Adapted from FT.com)

1 Nennen Sie die Auslöser für den schwarzen Montag.
2 Fassen Sie die Vorgänge des Tages kurz zusammen.
3 Begründen Sie, warum ein Land verschont blieb.
4 Beschreiben Sie die Prognose der Analysten.
5 Geben Sie die Meinung von Aktienhändler Jimmy Yates wieder.

**b** Give your opinion:
Why did a financial problem in one country trigger a global crisis?

## 14 Mediation

Look at this chart and then do the tasks below. The photos show Dirk Müller, a broker on the Frankfurt stock exchange.

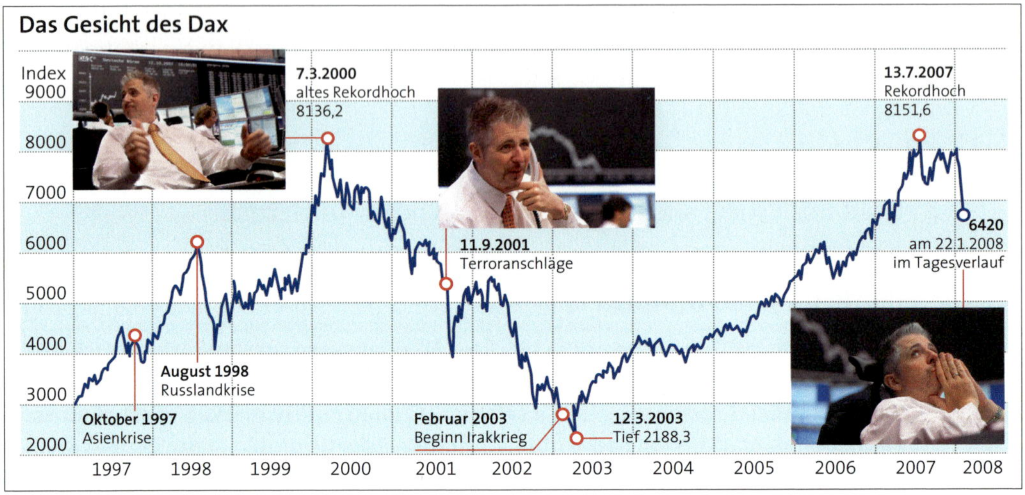


Source: FAZ 23.01.08 (NR 19, S.9)

1 Collect information about the global events that influenced the Dax in the period shown in the chart.
2 Find out how the Dax has performed since January 2008.
3 Present your findings in English to your fellow students.

## 15 Currency fluctuations

Working in a group, do the following tasks.

1 Name as many currencies as you can. Say whether they are strong or weak.
2 Has the euro fallen or risen against the US dollar over the past months? Give reasons why.
3 Explain how the recent development of the euro has affected Germany's import and export trade. Say how banks can help.

**LEARNING** **Wie kann ich mein Englisch weiter verbessern?**

Hier sind ein paar Tipps:

- Wenn Sie Nachrichten auf deutsch gehört haben, schalten Sie um zu BBC World, CNN oder NBC und hören Sie sie sich dann auf Englisch an.
- Sehen Sie Filme im Kino oder auf DVD in der englischen Fassung.
- Lesen Sie ein spannendes Buch oder eine Zeitung auf Englisch.
- Schicken sie englischsprachigen Bekannten öfter eine E-mail oder SMS.
- Suchen Sie nach Möglichkeiten, auch in Ihrer Freizeit Englisch zu sprechen.

# Islamic finance

## 16 Islamic banking

Read this article and summarize the differences between conventional German and Scharia-compliant banking.

### Scharia-compliant banking products

The Kuwait Finance House Automall offers its customers not only cars but also Islamic finance and insurance to go with them. Experts estimate that the worldwide demand for Scharia-compliant banking products is growing at the rate of 15% annually.

Scharia law does not allow banks to charge or pay interest. This prohibition, called *Riba*, is based on the teachings of the Koran, which sees money only as a means of exchange that defines value but does not have any value in itself. Money should therefore not generate more money in the form of fixed interest payments, simply by being lent out or deposited. A ban on gambling and speculation also affects investment business: the provider and the receiver of capital have to share the risk in a business venture.

How can a bank function without its two main sources of income: loans and investment products? Let us return to the car showroom. When the motorist has chosen a car, he orders the bank to buy it for him. The bank then resells it to him at a higher price, which the buyer pays off in instalments. This type of loan, *murabahah,* together with *arbun,* a non-refundable deposit which a buyer has to pay the seller on concluding a contract of sale, forms the basis of financial transactions. Islamic banks also sell *sukuks,* bonds that are Sharia-compliant in that, instead of a coupon, a rent is paid to the holder and the issuer undertakes to repay the nominal value on maturity or in case of default. However, these bonds have recently been criticized by Islamic scholars as being unacceptable because they offer a guaranteed return.

## 17 A presentation

Your bank wants to attract more Muslim customers.

In a small group, consider suitable changes regarding:

1 the branches and branch network
2 the staff and staff training
3 the financial products
4 marketing

Make a group presentation, with your fellow students taking the role of your colleagues in the bank. Ask for their feedback.

# Role cards and cases

**ROLE CARD 1**

You are 18 years old, from California, and have got a job in a hotel in Germany. Your employer says you will need a bank account. You only had a savings account in the States.

**ROLE CARD 2**

You come from South Africa. You have got a current account and are getting married next month. You and your fiancé(e) hope to buy a flat of your own one day and need advice.

**ROLE CARD 5**

**Your role**
You are a 19-year-old Canadian student
- single with no children
- on a 3-year bachelor course in Germany
- receive €750 a month from your parents
- want to save a small sum regularly
- plan to travel to see more of Europe

**Your requirements**
A current account with:
- low costs
- online banking
- an overdraft facility
- a credit card
- a debit card
- ways to pay regular bills (e.g. cell phone, rent)

**ROLE CARD 7**

You are Paul/Pauline Godet from France.

You speak good English but no German.

Your account number is 6577342.

You want to transfer €1250 to Giselle de Plessis in Bordeaux, because she has paid the deposit on a holiday villa for you. Her IBAN is FR14 2004 1010 0505 0001 3M02 606 and the BIC is AGRIFRPP833.

You want to know
- what IBAN and BIC are.
- how much the transfer will cost and who will pay the charge.
- how long the transfer will take.

## INFORMATION Loan terms

**Ratenkredit über € 10.000**

*Beispielrechnung*

| | |
|---|---|
| Darlehenssumme: | 10.000 EUR |
| Laufzeit: | 72 Monate |
| Jährlicher Nominalzins*: | 8,45 % |
| Einmaliges Bearbeitungsentgelt: | 2 % |
| Effektiver Jahreszins: | 9,56 % |
| Monatliche Rate: | 181,09 EUR |
| Einmaliger Kreditversicherungsbeitrag: | 946,11 EUR |

* nominal interest rate

**Annuitätendarlehen* über 15.000 EUR**

*Beispielrechnung*

| | |
|---|---|
| Darlehenssumme: | 15.000 EUR |
| Auszahlung: | 15.000 EUR |
| Monatliche Rate: | 304,17 EUR |
| Anfänglicher effektiver Jahreszins: | 7,67 % (veränderlich) |
| Disagio: | 1 % 150 EUR |
| Anzahl der Raten: | 60 (unverbindlich) |
| Kreditversicherung: | auf Wunsch möglich |

* annuity loan / loan with fixed instalments

## ROLE CARD 9

You have started a traineeship as a cook and want to save €5,000 to buy a motorbike. You do not always have the same sum left in your current account at the end of the month. At the moment you have no savings or investments at all.

## ROLE CARD 10

After selling your car, you have got €15,000 in your current account. You plan to get married in two years' time and will need the money then to pay for the wedding. You already have a savings plan for *vermögenswirksame Leistungen.*

## ROLE CARD 3

You have just come to Germany from Canada. You are thinking of opening an account but you have to work till 5 p.m. on weekdays so you want information about the opening hours and ways of doing your banking at other times.

## ROLE CARD 4

You are from Australia and earn a regular salary in Germany as an IT-specialist. You have a current account and a savings account with this bank but now you are interested in saving for a private pension.

## ROLE CARD 6

**Your role**

You are a 39 year-old engineer from New Zealand

- married with two small children
- want your wife to be able to use the account as well
- two-year contract with a German company
- net monthly salary of €2850

**Your requirements:**

A current account with:

- credit interest
- a credit card
- an overdraft facility
- online and telephone banking
- additional benefits

## ROLE CARD 8

You are Miloslav/Miloslava Czydzc from Serbia.

You speak no German and your English is not very good so you ask the clerk to fill the form in for you.

IMPORTANT: You do not know the following English words – payee, amount, purpose, signature – so you do not understand if the adviser uses them. Ask the adviser to explain any words that you don't understand.

Your account number is 6579953.

You want to transfer €150 to Kris Svenson in Stockholm, Sweden, as a wedding present.

His IBAN is SE35 5000 0000 0549 1994 5673

His BIC is SWEDSESSXXX.

**ROLE CARD 11**

You recently sold all your investments on the stock exchange and now have €62,000 in your current account. You intend to use the money to buy a flat but have decided to wait and see whether property prices fall in the near future. You are self-employed.

**ROLE CARD 12**

As a single parent working part-time, you have a net income of €15,000 a year and have to save to pay for large items like a new washing-machine, car repairs or holiday trips. You can afford to save €60 a month. You have never heard of the *Arbeitnehmer-Sparzulage.*

**CASE 1**

Sie sind Verkaufsleiter/in eines Unternehmens, das eine Anfrage aus Südamerika erhalten hat. Der potentielle Kunde hat um ein Zahlungsziel von 30 Tagen nach Erhalt der Dokumente gebeten. Ihr Unternehmen hat bisher nur im Inland verkauft. Sie bitten Ihre Bank um Rat.

**CASE 2**

Sie sind Mitbesitzer(in) einer Firma, die eine Warenbestellung aus dem Ausland erhalten hat (nennen Sie selbst das Land). Sie haben Zweifel an der Bonität sowohl des Auftraggebers als auch seiner Bank. Sie suchen einen Weg, diesen lukrativen Auftrag anzunehmen, und wenden sich an Ihre Bank.

**CASE 3**

Sie haben ein kleines Unternehmen gegründet und möchten Waren aus Asien importieren. Der Verkäufer hat Ihnen ein gutes Angebot unterbreitet, verlangt jedoch ein Akkreditiv, da Ihre Firma neu und unbekannt ist. Sie haben ein Akkreditiv noch nie benutzt und bitten Ihre Bank um Informationen.

# Documentary Credit

**Deutsche Bank**
Musterstadt Branch
P.O. BOX 222777
D-12345 Musterstadt

**DOCUMENTARY-CREDIT ISSUANCE**
**PAGE 1 OF 2**

| Ihre Nr./Your No. | | |
|---|---|---|
| Unsere Nr./Our No. | 7770550128IA | |

| | Währung/Currency | Betrag/Amount |
|---|---|---|
| +05%/-05% | EUR | 45.130,00 |

TELEX : 888833
SWIFT : DEUTDEDE987
PHONE : 0123/456-789 MEIER

PER SWIFT ERLEDIGT
14. FEB 2003

PUSAN BANK
P.O. BOX 5555

SEOUL
KOREA, SUED

BY ORDER OF

FREIZEIT & WELLNESS GMBH
STADTGARTEN 15
D-12345 MUSTERSTADT

WE ISSUE OUR IRREVOCABLE DOCUMENTARY CREDIT IN FAVOUR OF
SUN FUN & WIRELESS LTD.
7TH FLOOR, DONGWOO BLDG.
123 YEOKSAM-DONG, KANGNAM-KU
SEOUL, KOREA 987654
FOR AN AMOUNT OF EUR 45.130,00
AMOUNT IN WORDS
****** ****** ****** ****** ****** FOUR** FIVE** ONE*** THREE* ZERO**
DECIMAL PLACES, IF ANY, AS STATED ABOVE.
UP TO AN AMOUNT OF 05 PERCENT MORE OR 05 PERCENT LESS
AVAILABLE WITH US
BY DEFERRED PAYMENT AT 30 DAYS AFTER BL-DATE.
THE FOLLOWING DOCUMENTS ARE TO BE PRESENTED:

1) SIGNED COMMERCIAL INVOICE 1 ORIGINAL AND 3 COPIES
2) PACKING LIST IN 3-FOLD CONFIRMING THAT ALL PACKING INSTRUCTIONS AS PER APPLICANT'S LETTER DATED 11. FEB 2003 HAVE BEEN COMPLIED WITH
3) FULL SET (3-3) OF CLEAN ON BOARD SHIPPING COMPANY MARINE BILLS OF LADING ISSUED TO ORDER, BLANK ENDORSED, MARKED: FREIGHT PREPAID TO HAMBURG AND NOTIFY APPLICANT WITH FULL ADDRESS.
4) INSPECTION CERTIFICATES ACC. EN13456-4.2B FOR EACH ITEM SHOWING THE FIGURES OF THE ACTUAL ROPE-DIAM, THE ACTUAL BREAKING LOAD AND THE CHEMICAL ANALYSIS OF THE ROPING WIRES

CERTIFICATE OF ORIGIN
EVIDENCING SHIPMENT OF THE FOLLOWING GOODS:
XYZ AS PER ORDER SPECIFICATION NO. 24681359
QUALITY AISI 124 / ...... = 18.000 M +/- 5 PCT,
QUALITY AISI 236 / ...... = 114.000 M +/- 5 PCT.
DDP 20359 HAMBURG

Dokumenten-Akkreditive unterliegen den Einheitlichen Richtlinien und Gebräuchen für Dokumenten
Documentary credits are subject to Uniform Customs and Practice for Documentary Cred
Inkassi unterliegen den Einheitlichen Richtlinien für Inkassi, Revision 199
Collections are subject to Uniform Rules for Collections, 1995 Revision,

**Deutsche Bank**
Musterstadt Branch
P.O. BOX 222777
D-12345 Musterstadt

**DOCUMENTARY-CREDIT ISSUANCE**
**PAGE 2 OF 2**

| Ihre Nr./Your No. | | |
|---|---|---|
| Unsere Nr./Our No. | 7770550128IA | |

| | Währung/Currency | Betrag/Amount |
|---|---|---|
| +05%/-05% | EUR | 45.130,00 |

TELEX : 888833
SWIFT : DEUTDEDE987
PHONE : 0123/456-789 MEIER

PER SWIFT ERLEDIGT
14. FEB 2003

PUSAN BANK
P.O. BOX 5555

SEOUL
KOREA, SUED

FROM ANY SOUTH KOREAN PORT
TO ANY NORTH SEA PORT SHOWING PLACE OF DELIVERY DDP 20359 HAMBURG
ON 30. APR 2003 AT THE LATEST.
THE CREDIT IS VALID UNTIL 21. MAY 2003.
PRESENTATION OF DOCUMENTS WITHIN 21 DAYS AFTER THE DATE OF SHIPMENT, BUT WITHIN THE VALIDITY OF THE CREDIT.
PARTIAL SHIPMENTS ARE NOT ALLOWED.
TRANSHIPMENT IS ALLOWED.
ADDITIONAL CONDITIONS:
A FEE OF EUR 175,00 OR EQUIVALENT WILL BE DEDUCTED FOM THE PROCEEDS FOR EACH FULL SET OF DOCUMENTS EVEN IF PRESENTED UNDER ONE REMITTANCE LETTER WHEN IT IS NECESSARY TO CONTACT THE APPLICANT VOR APPROVAL OF DISCREPANT DOCUMENTS.
FURTHERMORE WE WILL DEDUCT OUR SWIFT/TELEX CHARGES FOR EACH ADVICE OF PAYMENT.
AN ADDITIONAL FEE OF EUR 50,00 OR EQUIVALENT PER MONTH WILL BE DEDACTED FOR UNPAID DOCUMENTS IN OUR CUSTODY.
PLEASE SEND DOCUMENTS TO THE FOLLOWING ADDRESS: DEUTSCHE BANK AG, MUSTERSTADT BRANCH, FINANZPLATZ 24, 12345 MUSTERSTADT, GERMANY.
PLEASE ADVISE THIS CREDIT TO THE BENEFICIARY WITHOUT ADDING YOUR CONFIRMATION.
PLEASE ADVISE THROUGH
PUSAN BRANCH, KANG NAM BRANCH
1923-33 SEOCHO-KU, SEOCHO-DONG
SEOUL, KOREA
ACC. 012-34-56789-9
ALL CHARGES OTHER THAN OURS ARE FOR ACCOUNT OF THE BENEFICIARY.

PLEASE FORWARD THE DOCUMENTS TO US BY REGISTERED AIRMAIL. PROVIDED THE TERMS AND CONDITONS OF THIS CREDIT HAVE BEEN FULLY COMPLIED WITH AND WE HAVE RECEIVED THE DOCUMENTS; WE SHALL EFFECT PAYMENT AT MATURITY IN ACCORDANCE WITH YOUR INSTRUCTIONS.

DEUTSCHE BANK AG
MUSTERSTADT BRANCH

Dokumenten-Akkreditive unterliegen den Einheitlichen Richtlinien und Gebräuchen für Dokumenten-Akkreditive, Revision 1993, ICC Publikation Nr. 500. /
Documentary credits are subject to Uniform Customs and Practice for Documentary Credits, 1993 Revision, ICC Publication No. 500.
Inkassi unterliegen den Einheitlichen Richtlinien für Inkassi, Revision 1995, ICC Publikation Nr. 522. /
Collections are subject to Uniform Rules for Collections, 1995 Revision, ICC Publication No. 522.

# Bill of Lading

Bill of Lading for Combined Transport shipment or Port to Port shipment

Shipper
P&O NEDLLOYD LTD
BERTH 204/205/206
WESTERN DOCKS,
SOUTHAMPTON

B/L No.: PONLBHX23009678

Reference: LGM0099535

Consignee or Order (for U.S. Trade only: Not Negotiable unless consigned 'To Order')
YUSIF BIN YUSIF FAKHRO
P.O.BOX 214
MANAMA
BAHRAIN

Notify Party/Address (It is agreed that no responsibility shall attach to the carrier or his Agents for failure to notify (see clause 20 on reverse))
YUSIF BIN YUSIF FAKHRO
P.O.BOX 214
MANAMA
BAHRAIN

Place of Receipt (Applicable only when this document is used as a Combined Transport Bill of Lading)
SOUTHAMPTON

Vessel and Voy. No.
OOCL FREEDOM OFM0234

Place of Delivery (Applicable only when this document is used as a Combined Transport Bill of Lading)
PORT OF MINA SULMAN
STATE OF BAHRAIN

| Port of Loading | Port of Discharge |
|---|---|
| SOUTHAMPTON | BAHRAIN |

Undermentioned particulars as declared by Shipper, but not acknowledged by the Carrier (see clause 11)

| Marks and Nos; Container Nos; | Number and kind of Packages; Description of Goods | Gross Weight (kg) | Measurement (cbm) |
|---|---|---|---|
| POCU0432963<br>SEAL: 000204 | 1x20'GP CONTAINER SAID TO CONTAIN | | |
| TEST DATA<br>TEST DATA<br>TEST DATA | 20 C/S FCL/FCL<br>TEST DATA FOR REMOTE BILL PRINTING<br>FREIGHT COLLECT<br><br>SHIPPERS LOAD, STOW & COUNT<br><br>SHIPPED ON BOARD PER OCEAN VESSEL OOCL FREEDOM<br>AT SOUTHAMPTON<br>ON XXXXXXXXXXXXXXX<br>FOR P&O NEDLLOYD LIMITED | 6240.0000 | |

TOTAL: PART OF 1x20' CONTAINER(S) ONLY

---

FREIGHT AND CHARGES:

| | | |
|---|---|---|
| ORIGIN INLAND HAULAGE CHARGE | P | HAI |
| ORIGIN TERMINAL HANDLING/LCL SERVICE CHARGE | P | HAI |
| OCEAN FREIGHT | C | BAH |
| DESTINATION TERMINAL HANDLING/LCL SERVICE CHARGE | C | BAH |
| DESTINATION INLAND HAULAGE CHARGE | C | BAH |

| * Total No. of Containers/Packages received by the carrier | Movement | Freight Payable at |
|---|---|---|
| 1 PART | FCL/FCL | KANOO, BAHRAIN |

Received by the Carrier from the Shipper in apparent good order and condition (unless otherwise noted herein) the total number or quantity of Containers or other packages or units indicated in the box above entitled "*Total No. of Containers/Packages received by the Carrier" for Carriage subject to all the terms and conditions hereof (INCLUDING THE TERMS AND CONDITIONS ON THE REVERSE HEREOF AND THE TERMS AND CONDITIONS OF THE CARRIER'S APPLICABLE TARIFF) from the Place of Receipt or the Port of Loading, whichever is applicable, to the Port of Discharge or the Place of Delivery, whichever is applicable. If the acknowledged tally is of Containers, this indicates that the Container has been packed and sealed by the Merchant at his premises without the Carrier being represented and able to check or verify either the tally of Goods or the stowage, which are consequently unknown to him (See Clause 8). The Merchant accepts that, except by special arrangement or pursuant to Clause 9 hereof, Containers are not weighed by the Carrier at any time. If the Carrier so requires, before he arranges delivery of the Goods one original Bill of Lading, duly endorsed, must be surrendered by the Merchant to the Carrier at the Port of Discharge or at some other location acceptable to the Carrier. In accepting this Bill of Lading the Merchant expressly accepts and agrees to all its terms and conditions whether printed, stamped or written, or otherwise incorporated, not withstanding the non-signing of this Bill of Lading by the Merchant. Without prejudice to the generality of this reference, attention is drawn, inter-alia, to Clause 12 (Shipper's/Merchant's Responsibility), 19 (Dangerous Goods) and 24 (Law & Jurisdiction).

| Number of Original Bills of Lading | Place and Date of Issue | |
|---|---|---|
| 2/TWO | PONL BIRMINGHAM | 23/09/00 |

IN WITNESS of the contract herein contained the number of originals stated opposite has been issued, one of which being accomplished, the other(s) to be void.

EXCESS VALUATION: REFER TO CLAUSE 7(3) ON REVERSE SIDE (U.S. TRADE ONLY).....

*** ORIGINAL ***

This Bill of Lading has been printed remotely via the Internet, at the customer's premises.

# Incoterms® 2010

In international trade the eleven Incoterms® 2010 Rules (international commercial terms) are used in contracts of sale to define the rights and obligations of the buyer and seller as regards risk, transport, insurance, packing, customs duty and documentation. They are terms of delivery.

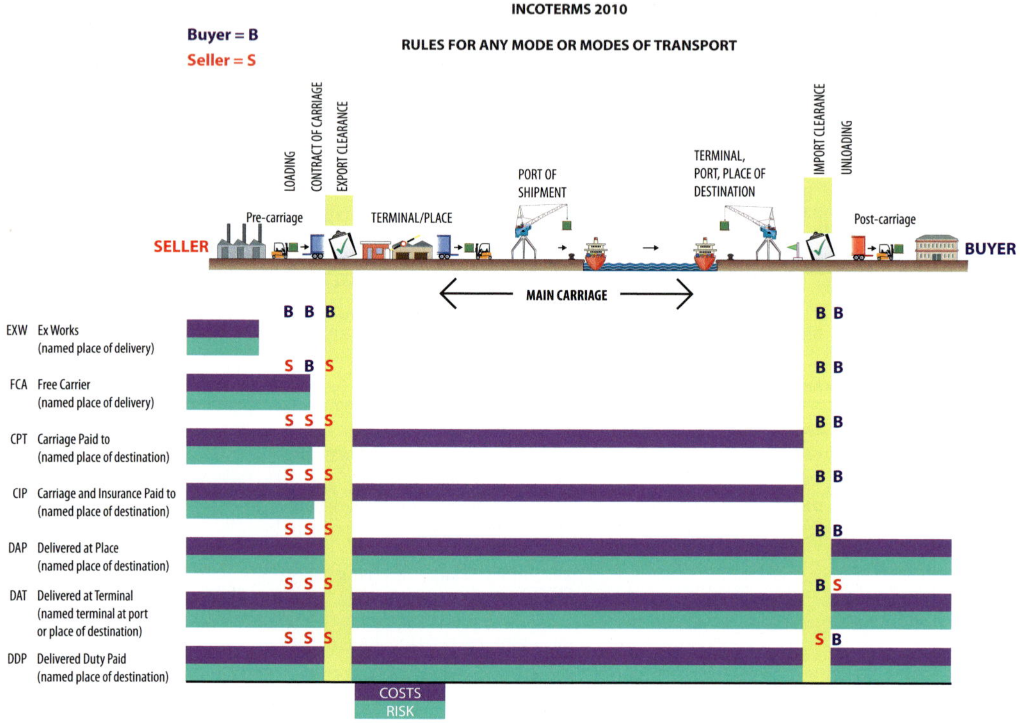


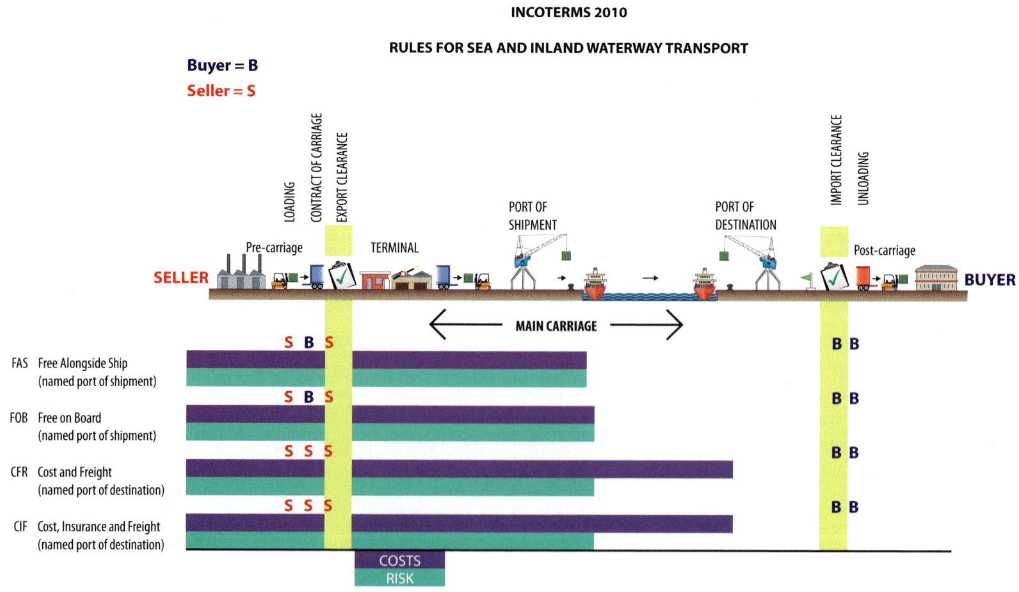

## Rules for any mode or modes of transport

**EXW – EX WORKS (… named place of delivery)**
The seller makes the goods available at his premises in the customary packing. The seller assists the buyer in obtaining any documentation needed at the buyer's expense. The buyer is responsible for loading the goods, transporting them to their destination, customs clearance and insurance.

**FCA – FREE CARRIER (… named place of delivery) Multimodal transport**
The seller is not responsible for the main carriage of the goods. The seller delivers the goods at his own expense and risk, in the customary packing, cleared for export to the carrier nominated by the buyer. The seller provides the commercial invoice and, if requested, a certificate of origin at the buyer's expense. If the goods are collected at the seller's premises, the seller loads the goods. The seller bears the risks until the goods are in the custody of the first carrier. After that the buyer bears all the costs and risks of transporting the goods to their destination.

**CPT – CARRIAGE PAID TO (… named place of destination) Multimodal transport**
The seller pays for the main carriage of the goods. The seller delivers the goods, in the customary packing, cleared for export to the carrier which he nominates. The seller bears the risk until the goods have been delivered into the custody of the first carrier. The seller pays the transport costs for the goods, excluding transport insurance, up to the named destination. The buyer is responsible for insuring the goods for the main carriage and pays all import duties and taxes.

**CIP – COST AND INSURANCE PAID TO (… named place of destination) Multimodal transport**
The seller pays for the main carriage of the goods. The seller delivers the goods in the customary packing, cleared for export to the carrier which he nominates. The seller bears the risk until the goods have been delivered into the custody of the first carrier. The seller pays the transport costs for the goods, including transport insurance, up to the named destination. The buyer pays all import duties and taxes.

**DAP – DELIVERED AT PLACE (… named place of destination) Multimodal transport**
The seller is responsible for the carriage of the goods in the customary packing, cleared for export to the named terminal at the destination by the carrier which he nominates. He bears the risk until the goods have been delivered to the named terminal. The buyer is responsible for unloading the goods at the place of destination and pays all import duties and taxes.

**DAT – DELIVERED AT TERMINAL (… named terminal at port or place of destination) Multimodal transport**
The seller is responsible for the carriage of the goods in the customary packing, cleared for export to the named terminal at the destination by the carrier which he nominates. He bears the risk until the goods have been delivered to the named terminal. The seller is responsible for unloading the goods at the place of destination. The buyer pays all import duties and taxes.

**DDP – DELIVERED DUTY PAID (… named place of destination) Multimodal transport**
The seller is responsible for the carriage of the goods in the customary packing, cleared for export to the named terminal at the destination by the carrier which he nominates. He bears the risk until the goods have been delivered to the named destination. The seller pays all import duties and taxes. The buyer is responsible for unloading the goods at the place of destination.

## Rules for sea and inland waterway transport

**FAS – FREE ALONGSIDE SHIP (… named port of shipment)**
The seller is not responsible for the main carriage of the goods. The seller delivers the goods at his own expense and risk, in the customary packing, cleared for export, alongside the vessel selected by the buyer at the named port of shipment. Thereafter, the buyer bears all the costs and risks of transporting the goods to their destination.

**FOB – FREE ON BOARD (… named port of shipment)**
The seller is not responsible for the main carriage of the goods. The seller delivers the goods at his own expense and risk, in the customary packing, cleared for export, on board the vessel selected by the buyer unless otherwise agreed, at the named port of shipment. Thereafter, the buyer bears all the costs and risks of transporting the goods to their destination.

**CFR – COST AND FREIGHT (… named port of destination)**
The seller pays for the main carriage of the goods. The seller delivers the goods at his own expense and risk, in the customary packing, cleared for export, on board the vessel selected by the buyer, at the named port of shipment. The seller pays the transport costs for the goods, excluding transport insurance, up to the named port of destination. The buyer is responsible for insuring the goods for the main carriage and pays all import duties and taxes.

**CIF – COST INSURANCE FREIGHT (… named port of destination)**
The seller pays for the main carriage of the goods. The seller delivers the goods at his own expense and risk, in the customary packing, cleared for export, on board the vessel selected by the buyer, at the named port of shipment. The seller pays the transport costs for the goods, including transport insurance, up to the named port of destination. The buyer pays all import duties and taxes.

# Account application form

**FIRST APPLICANT**

## Personal Details

Mr/Mrs/Miss/Ms/Other ☐ Surname

First name Other initials

Proof of identity (e.g. Passport no.)

Relationship status: Single ☐ Married ☐ Divorced ☐ Widowed ☐ Separated ☐ Living with partner ☐

Date of birth

Gender: Female ☐ Male ☐ No. of dependent children: ☐

House no. and street name

City/Town County

Postcode Date moved to this address Mth. Yr.

Work/Daytime Tel. No. (incl. area code) Evening Tel. No. (incl. area code)

Mobile Tel. No. Email Address

Please provide previous address if less than 3 years spent at present address.

House no. and street name

City/Town County

Postcode Date moved to this address Mth. Yr.

## Details of employment

Are you:

In full-time employment ☐ Employed part-time ☐

Self-employed ☐ Studying full-time ☐ Retired ☐

Homemaker ☐ Unemployed ☐

If you are in employment/self-employed please enter:

Employer's name

Business address (in full) Postcode

Type of business

Date started present employment Mth. Yr. Occupation

Total annual income (before tax and deductions) £

Net Monthly Income £ Net Monthly Expenditure £

If you are in employment/self-employed

Income paid:
Directly to bank ☐ By cheque ☐ In cash ☐ Other ☐

Income payments made on (e.g. monthly, every Monday, 15th, etc.):

Type of pension:
Company pension ☐ Private pension ☐ None ☐

## Financial details

Name of present bank or building society branch and address (in full)

Date account opened Mth. Yr.

Sort code Account No.

Will this relationship continue? Yes ☐ No ☐

Are you already a holder of:

Our Credit Cards Yes ☐ No ☐

Other Credit Cards Yes ☐ No ☐

Other Cheque Cards Yes ☐ No ☐

## Details of residency

Residency status: Homeowner ☐ Tenant ☐

Living with parents ☐ Living with partner and/or friends ☐

If you are a homeowner, please provide:

Estimated value of residence £ Mortgage outstanding £

Name of lender

## Requirements

Would you like to be considered for an overdraft? Yes ☐ No ☐

How much? £

I/We would like my/our statements on monthly.

If you would like to apply for a personal loan, please tick the box. ☐

## Declaration

I/We request you to open a bank account in my/our name(s). I/We agree that my/our account is subject to the personal banking terms and conditions, a copy of which I have received. I/We confirm that the information given is true to the best of my/our knowledge.

## Signature of first applicant

**Date:**

## Signature of second applicant

**Date:**

# KMK exam practice



## 1 Rezeption: Hörverstehen*

Webcode MMU0101

Ein britischer Radiosender informiert junge Leute wöchentlich über verschiedene Berufe. Sie interessieren sich für ein Praktikum in einer britischen Bank und hören sich die Informationen über den *banker / bank teller* an.

**Machen Sie sich Notizen zu folgenden Punkten.**

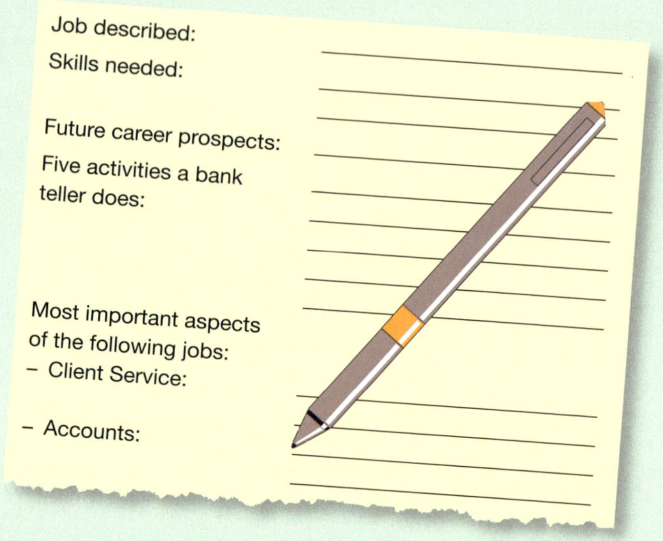


## 2 Interaktion

**Erstellen Sie in Partnerarbeit einen Dialog mithilfe der folgenden Rollenkarten.**

Julia/Jake Stone macht ein dreiwöchiges Praktikum in Ihrem Kreditinstitut. Ein/e Auszubildende/r stellt die Firma vor und informiert über Tätigkeiten, die gemacht werden müssen.

**Student A**

**Sie sind Julia/Jake Stone.**
Sie stellen sich vor und erzählen:
- woher Sie kommen
- welchen Schulabschluss Sie haben
- warum Sie das Praktikum absolvieren.

Sie bieten an, sich mit dem Vornamen anzusprechen.

**Kreditinstitut**
Sie möchten wissen:
- wie groß das Kreditinstitut ist
- wie viele Mitarbeiter es gibt
- wie die Öffnungszeiten sind.

Fragen Sie nach dem Arbeitsplatz.

**Service**
Sie fragen nach Tätigkeiten, die ein/e Auszubildende/r zu machen hat.

**Student B**

**Sie sind der/die Auszubildende/r des Kreditinstituts.**
Sie stellen sich vor und berichten über:
- Ihren Schulabschluss
- Ihre Berufsschule
- Ihre Ausbildung.

**Kreditinstitut**
Sie informieren darüber, dass es neben der Hauptstelle noch fünf Zweigstellen in Ihrer Stadt gibt.
Sie teilen Julia/Jake Stone Arbeits- und Öffnungszeiten mit.
Sie zeigen ihr/ihm den Kundenraum.

**Service**
Sie nennen einige Ihrer Tätigkeiten.

* Geben Sie den Webcode im Webcode-Suchfeld auf www.cornelsen.de/matters ein, um den Hörtext anzuhören.

## Rezeption: Leseverstehen

Ihre Bank plant Veränderungen bezüglich der Konten, die für Kinder oder Jugendliche eingerichtet werden können. Ihr Chef bittet Sie, im Internet zu recherchieren, was andere Kreditinstitute anbieten. Sie finden zwei Angebote einer englischen Bank.

**1** http://www.bank-uk.uk/starter-account/details

BANK UK gives your kids the right stepping stone towards a future of smart spending.

Our STARTER ACCOUNT, a current or savings account, offers specialized features and benefits making it the perfect present for young people.

Anyone under 18 years of age can apply for our STARTER ACCOUNT.

Our account features are:

- first cheque book free
- free printouts of bank statements
- interesting welcome kit when opening account

We offer:

- a special ID card for your child. Along with the basic banking necessities, with the STARTER ACCOUNT, the child will get a specialized photographic membership card. This card gives access to great events and interesting offers thanks to our special partners. Your child will be offered discounts and vouchers in different areas of entertainment, as well as in toy and book stores.
- free insurance cover for parents provided by our special partners.

**2** http://www.bank-uk.uk/student-account/details

Our STUDENT ACCOUNT offers everything you need to help you make the most of your time at college or university. It helps you manage your money.

Should you need to go into your overdraft, we offer you a £20 overdraft limit. No overdraft fees apply if you overdraw your account by less than this amount or exceed your Planned Overdraft limit by this amount.
Overdrafts that exceed this sum are available subject to application and approval and are repayable on demand. You will get a grace period if you go over your limit. This means that you have until 2.00 p.m. (GMT) to lodge enough money to avoid any overdraft fees that may be incurred that day.
You have the choice of transferring money from another personal account you have with us via mobile or internet banking, or you can pay the fee in cash in one of our branches.
On opening the account you will be provided with a welcome pack offering you discounts in different areas of entertainment, or in toy and book stores.

**Beantworten Sie diese Verständnisfragen in kurzen Stichworten auf Deutsch.**

**1** Welches der beiden Angebote richtet sich an die Kontoinhaber?

**2** Wieviel kostet es, einen Kontoauszug beim *Starter Account* auszudrucken?

**3** Warum ist das *Starter Account* ein perfektes Geschenk von Eltern an ihre Kinder?

**4** Wodurch unterscheiden sich die beiden Angebote hinsichtlich:

**a** Alter? **b** Inhalt und Fokus? (je Angebot mind. 2 Antworten)

**5** Was passiert beim *Student Account*, wenn man das Konto überzieht?

**6** Was für unterschiedliche Sonderangebote bieten die beiden Konten?

## Interaktion

Ein älterer englischsprachiger Tourist / Eine ältere englischsprachige Touristin besucht Freunde in Deutschland. Er/Sie hat bisher nie mit der Geldkarte selbst Geld abheben müssen und steht verzweifelt vor einem Geldautomaten. Ein/e Mitarbeiter/in Ihres Kreditinstituts erläutert dem/der Tourist/in die Funktionsweise des Geldautomaten und gibt auch Hinweise zur Sicherheit.

**Führen Sie das Gespräch.**

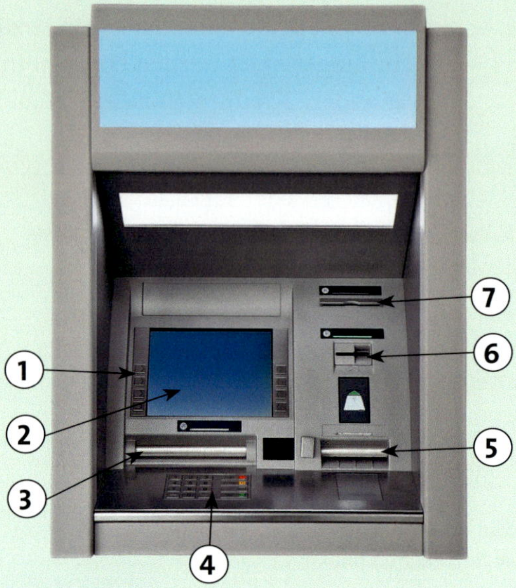


**Student A**

**Mitarbeiter/in der Bank**

Begrüßen Sie den/die Tourist/in.

Beschreiben Sie die einzelnen Teile und Funktionen des Geldautomaten (siehe Foto oben).

Erläutern Sie, dass der/die Tourist/in auf seine/ihre Sicherheit achten soll und die PIN niemandem sagen oder zeigen darf.

Teilen Sie auch mit, dass man die PIN aus Sicherheitsgründen nicht aufschreiben sollte – und wenn doch, dass man den Zettel nicht im Portemonnaie aufbewahren sollte.

Teilen Sie ebenfalls mit, dass man bei Eingabe der PIN und Entnahme des Geldes direkt vor dem Automaten stehen sollte.

Machen Sie den/die Tourist/in darauf aufmerksam, dass man nicht vergessen darf, die Karte, das Geld und die Quittung einzustecken.

**Student B**

**Tourist/in**

Ihr Problem ist, dass sie nicht wissen, was Sie machen sollen, um Geld zu erhalten.

Fragen Sie immer wieder nach, was Sie genau machen müssen.

Teilen Sie dem/der Bankmitarbeiter/in mit, dass Sie extra eine Nummer aufgeschrieben haben, um sie nicht zu vergessen – und ziehen ein Stückchen beschriebenes Papier mit Ihrer PIN aus dem Portemonnaie.

Fragen Sie, warum diese ganzen Sicherheitsmaßnahmen so wichtig sind.

Bedanken Sie sich.

## 1 Produktion

Nach dem Besuch mit einer Delegation deutscher Lehrer in England erhält der Organisator der Fahrt, Herr Schröder, durch den Kollegen David Deas eine Rechnung der englischen Schule über Mittagessen in deren Kantine. Lehrer Peter Schröder möchte das Geld überweisen, aber es fehlen noch einige Daten.

**Peter Schröders Englischkenntnisse reichen nicht aus, um selbst einen Brief zu verfassen. Daher bittet er Sie, eine E-Mail an die Schule zu schreiben, um die fehlenden Daten zu erhalten. Er zeigt Ihnen folgende Rechnung.**

**Invoice**

Business College Cramlington
High Street 5
Cramlington
NE22 3BN
Email: BCC@bcc.uk

| | | | |
|---|---|---|---|
| Name: | Mr Peter Schröder | Invoice no.: | 232 |
| Address: | Business College Hamburg, Hochstraße 10 | Date: | 1 October 20.. |
| City: | Hamburg, D – 22283 | | |

| Quantity | Description | Unit Price | Total |
|---|---|---|---|
| 22 | lunch | 8.50 | 187.00 |

**Verfassen Sie eine E-Mail an das englische College.**

## 2 Interaktion

Mark/Michaela Miller aus Newcastle, der/die für ein Jahr als Fremdsprachenassistent/in in einem kleinen Ort in der Nähe Bremens arbeiten wird, möchte ein Bankkonto eröffnen. Er/Sie erhält regelmäßig 950 Euro vom Pädagogischen Austauschdienst.

**Führen Sie das Gespräch.**

**Student A**

**Bankmitarbeiter/in**
Zur Eröffnung eines Bankkontos benötigt der Kunde / die Kundin Informationen
- zur Person, zum Wohnort und Einkommen.

Sie beantworten Fragen zum
- Online Banking
- Voraussetzungen zur Ausstellung einer Bank- und Kreditkarte
- Unterschied zwischen Dauerauftrag und Einzugsverfahren.

Fragen Sie Herr/Frau Miller, ob er/sie weitere Fragen hat.

**Student B**

**Mark/Michaela Miller aus Newcastle**
Sie möchten:
- günstiges Angebot für ein Kontokorrentkonto
- Möglichkeit zum Online Banking
- Bankkarte, evtl. auch Kreditkarte
- Information zu Überweisung oder Bankeinzugsverfahren, da Sie die Miete für ein 1-Zimmer-Apartment zahlen müssen und auch die Kosten für Ihr Handy haben.

Überlegen Sie sich ggf. weitere Fragen und bedanken Sie sich.

## Mediation

**In einem Newsletter Ihres Kreditinstituts finden Sie folgenden Text. Übertragen Sie den Artikel für Ihre Praktikantin aus Nordirland ins Englische.**

# Sparen in Deutschland

Sparen heißt, Geld für die Zukunft zurückzulegen. Man spart für Notfälle, für die Alterssicherung oder für größere Anschaffungen. Wie viel des verfügbaren Einkommens gespart wird, gibt die Sparquote an. Sie bezeichnet den prozentualen Anteil der Ersparnisse privater Haushalte am verfügbaren Einkommen.

Generell ist eine ansteigende Sparquote in allen EU-Ländern zu verzeichnen. Die Deutschen sparen in der Regel ca. 10 Prozent ihres Einkommens an, und dies vor allem in regelmäßigen Abständen. Damit sind sie ungefähr doppelt so sparsam wie US-Amerikaner. Chinesen dagegen sind mit einer Sparquote von nahezu der Hälfte ihres Einkommens Weltmeister im Sparen. Das ungleiche Sparverhalten von Bürgern verschiedener Staaten ist hauptsächlich auf ein unterschiedliches wirtschaftliches Wachstum zurückzuführen: Demgemäß sparen die Bürger exportorientierter Länder wie China und Deutschland mehr als die konsumorientierter Wirtschaftsgesellschaften wie die USA. Aber auch unterschiedliche Rahmenbedingungen von Banken, wie z.B. günstige Privatkredite, beeinflussen das Sparverhalten wesentlich. So ist es in den USA sehr gängig, für den privaten Konsum einen Kredit aufzunehmen.
Inzwischen ist allerdings auch in Deutschland zu beobachten, dass immer mehr Leute Schulden machen. Ein Auto wird fast nur noch finanziert; und auch bei Anschaffungen wie Waschmaschinen, Kühlschränken, Fernsehgeräten oder Computern wird bei vielen Händlern bereits in den Prospekten die monatliche Rate mitausgewiesen. Verschulden wird immer mehr zur Selbstverständlichkeit! Die Wirtschaft lebte und lebt von der Kauflaune ihrer Bürger.

## Produktion

Sie arbeiten zurzeit in der Abteilung Ihrer Bank, die Newsletter zu unterschiedlichen statistischen Daten erstellt.

**Sie werden gebeten, folgende Kurve für die englischsprachige Ausgabe zu beschreiben.**

**Pound sterling (GBP)**

Latest (5 December 2012); EUR 1 = GBP 0.81190 -0.00040 (0.0%)

Date range: 1m | 3m | 6m | 1y | 2y | 5y | 10y | All    See EUR vs. GPB

Change from 5 December 2011 to 5 December 2012 -0.04735 (-5.5%)

Minimum (20 July 2012): 0.77835 / Maximum (5 December 2011): 0.85925 / Average: 0.81309

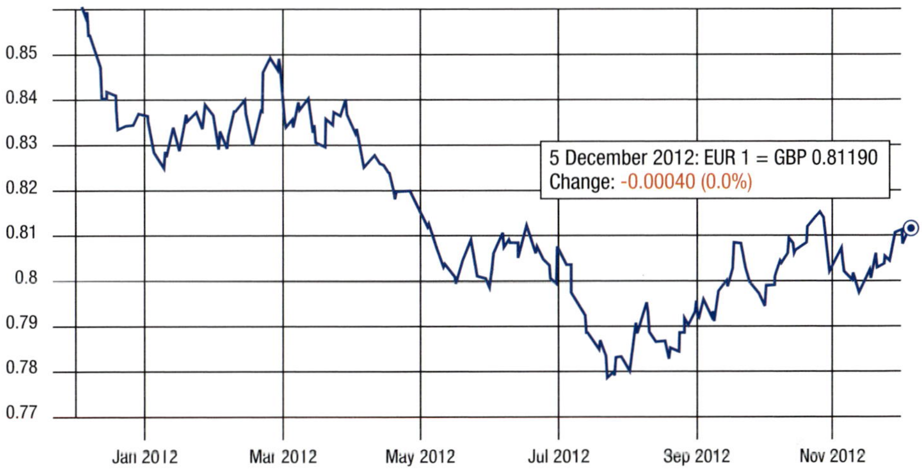


(Source: European Central Bank)

## 1 Rezeption: Hörverstehen

Webcode MMU0701

Als Auszubildende/r der XY Bank absolvieren Sie ein Praktikum bei einer schottischen Bank. Sie helfen zurzeit am Schalter aus und dürfen auch Kundengesprächen beiwohnen. Eines Morgens betritt Rebecca Derek die Bank und bittet den Abteilungsleiter Stewart Ferguson um ein Beratungsgespräch.

**Hören Sie dem Gespräch aufmerksam zu und machen Sie folgende Aufgaben. Sie hören den Text zwei Mal.**

**a Entscheiden Sie, ob die folgenden Aussagen richtig oder falsch sind.**

1. Rebecca hat Geld geerbt.
2. Sie möchte ein Reisebüro für Geschäftskunden anbieten.
3. Rebeccas Eltern hatten auch ein Reisebüro.
4. Der Businessplan muss Antworten auf alle Fragen der Bank beinhalten.

**b Fertigen Sie mithilfe der folgenden Fragen eine Gesprächsnotiz in kurzen Stichworten auf Deutsch an.**

1. Welches Anliegen hat Rebecca?
2. Warum bittet sie um das Beratungsgespräch?
3. Welche Erfahrungen kann Rebecca vorweisen?
4. Was muss Rebecca tun, um die Bank davon zu überzeugen, ihr ein Darlehen zu gewähren?
5. Welche wesentlichen Voraussetzungen für ein Darlehen nennt Stewart?

## 2 Produktion

Um ein Darlehen zu erhalten, muss Rebecca Derek der Bank einen detaillierten *business plan* präsentieren. Sie findet im Internet eine Beschreibung, was der *business plan* enthalten sollte.

**Wählen Sie aus den drei Sektionen A, B oder C insgesamt drei Aspekte aus, die Sie Rebecca erläutern.**

http://www.planningyourbusiness.co.uk

**Section A – Planning**
- Explain why you chose your business idea.
- Explain your proposed legal form, aims and objectives.

**Section B – Managing business activities**
- Run through your marketing strategies.
- Describe which human resources are needed for your business.
- List and explain all physical resources needed.
- Present the financial resources required to start and run the business.

**Section C – Financial management in business**
- List and explain the function of a few financial documents you must present to the bank, e.g. projected profit and loss account, etc.

## 1 Mediation

Während eines Praktikums in Großbritannien stellen Sie fest, dass sich das Angebot britischer und deutscher Bausparkassen unterscheiden. Das berichten Sie einem Kollegen, der Sie bittet, diesen Unterschied in einem Kurzbericht für den wöchentlichen Newsletter der Bank zu erläutern.

**Fassen Sie die Unterschiede in einem kurzen Text auf Englisch zusammen.**

**Worin unterscheiden sich Bausparkassen in Großbritannien und Deutschland?**

In Deutschland betreiben Bausparkassen als spezielle Kreditinstitute hauptsächlich die Wohnungsbaufinanzierung. Das Bausparkassengesetz schreibt vor, dass Bausparkassen eigenständige Gebilde sein müssen. Daher können Banken das Bauspargeschäft nicht direkt, sondern nur über Tochtergesellschaften durchführen.

Die Förderung des Bausparens besteht im Wesentlichen aus:
1. der Gewährung von Wohnungsbauprämien für Sparleistungen auf Bausparkonten
2. der Zahlung von Arbeitnehmersparzulagen für die vermögenswirksamen Leistungen.

Seit 2008 gibt es das Eigenheimrentengesetz, das eine zusätzliche Förderung des Bausparens beschließt.
Bauherren und Wohnungskäufer können zwischen einem klassischen Bankdarlehen mit direkter Tilgung oder einem Kombikredit einer Bausparkasse mit festen Zinsen während der gesamten Laufzeit wählen. Laut einem Finanztest schnitten die Kombidarlehen der Bausparkassen günstiger ab als die Angebote der Banken mit ähnlich langer Zinsbindung.

In Großbritannien entstanden die Bausparkassen im 18. Jahrhundert aus den sogenannten *cooperative savings groups*. Sie bieten Bank- und Finanzdienstleistungen an und konkurrieren in diesem Bereich stark mit den Banken, vor allem, wenn es um Sparkonten und Hypothekendarlehen geht.

## 2 Produktion

Ihr englischsprachiger Kunde David Stone möchte gern sein Eigenheim modernisieren und benötigt dafür 10.000 Euro. Er sendet Ihnen per Mail folgendes Angebot einer Bausparkasse, das er im Internet gefunden hat.

**Ihr Kunde bittet Sie um eine Erklärung auf Englisch. Beantworten Sie seine Mail schriftlich. Erläutern Sie auch die Begriffe „Sollzinsbildung“ und „effektiver Jahreszins“.**

http://www.bspkasse.de/renovieren/angebot

**Angebot**
Benötigen Sie Geld, um Ihre Immobilie zu modernisieren? Dann nutzen Sie unser Angebot!

**Beispiel***
Sie benötigen 10.000 Euro
Sollzinsbindung: 5 Jahre

Dann zahlen Sie bei einer Gesamtlaufzeit von ca. 14 Jahren 83 Euro im Monat bei einem effektiven Jahreszins von 2,87 %.

* Weitere Informationen finden Sie in unserer Broschüre *Bausparen und mehr*

## Rezeption: Leseverstehen

Sie sind im Rahmen Ihrer Ausbildung in der Abteilung für Geschäftskredite. Ein Kollege findet auf der Internetseite einer englischen Bank folgende Informationen und bittet Sie, ihn über den Inhalt zu informieren.

http://www.xxbank.co.uk/businessbanking/businessloans_finance

**XX Bank**

| Personal Banking | **Business Banking** | Private Banking |
|---|---|---|
| Internet Banking | Business Accounts | **Business Loans & Finance** |

**Are you an XX Bank customer?**

**Do you need a business loan over £25,000?**
Do you have big business plans for the future, do you want to refurbish or develop new property, has your old machinery or equipment seen better days and you need up to £500,000 to cover the costs? Just give us a call and we'll see what we can do for you. As part of the new Funding for Lending Scheme (supported by the Bank of England), we have reduced the interest rate on all new approved business loan applications by 1%!

**Our special offer:**
***Fixed Rate Business Loan*** for up to 15 years!
A fixed-rate loan has a fixed interest rate for the whole repayment period – from one to fifteen years. This means you know exactly how much you have to repay each month. Fixed interest rates are less dependent on market conditions, allowing you to meet your financial obligations more easily.

**Key features and benefits of our *Fixed Rate Business Loan*:**
- interest rate already reduced by 1% (Funding for Lending Scheme)
- business loans available from £25,001 – £500,000
- 1–15 year repayment terms available
- fixed repayment rate for whole term of repayment
- capital repayment holiday of up to 18 months available
- lump sum repayment possible (a prepayment fee and fixed breakage costs will be charged)

**Interested in applying?**
If you are already an XX Bank customer, simply call us or apply online for a *Fixed Rate Business Loan*.

**Please confirm that ...**
- you are a sole trader, partner or director
- you are aged 18 or over
- you need the loan for business use <u>only</u>.

All loans are subject to a satisfactory credit assessment.

**Notieren Sie wichtige Hinweise stichpunktartig in deutscher Sprache.**

1 Welche Kunden berücksichtigt die XX Bank in dem Angebot besonders?

2 Welche Angebote unterbreitet die XX Bank ihren Kunden? Informieren Sie Ihren Kollegen stichwortartig zu folgenden Punkten:

– Kredithöhe
– Wofür kann der Kredit verwendet werden?
– Zeitraum
– Wofür wird 1% Zinsersparnis erteilt?
– Welche Hauptmerkmale zeichnet dieses Darlehen noch aus?
– Wie und unter welchen Voraussetzungen kann ein XX Bank-Kunde einen Kreditantrag stellen?
– Voraussetzung für die Gewährung des Kredits

## Mediation

Ein Kunde möchte ins Auslandsgeschäft einsteigen und zeigt Ihnen den Auszug aus den Bedingungen eines britischen Spediteurs. Da seine Englischkenntnisse noch nicht so gut sind, bittet er Sie, ihm weiterzuhelfen.

**Lesen Sie folgenden Text und übertragen Sie für Ihren Kunden die wesentlichen Punkte auf Deutsch.**

With years of experience in helping customers to complete major projects, **Newcastle Logistics** is the number one choice for all of your logistic needs.

**How do we do it?**
We do it by building a project team, led by a project manager, around each specific project's requirements. Transport, warehousing and administration teams also become involved, if and when needed, to ensure success. The project manager co-ordinates Newcastle Logistics' involvement and keeps the customer up-to-date with events.

The planning stage is very important. Therefore customers are invited to contact Newcastle Logistics as early as possible to take full advantage of all services offered.

We are constantly working to improve our services for our customers and have therefore prepared the following booking form to help organize consignments from receipt right through to delivery. The following fields must be completed:

| | |
|---|---|
| **Consignor** | ... |
| **Consignee** | ... |
| **Quantity, gross weight and volume**<br>(Number of cartons, packages, pallets, bundles, etc.; gross weight of the whole consignment including packaging and pallets; measurement of the goods in cubic metres) | ... |
| **Incoterms**<br>• EXW<br>• FOB<br>• DAP | ... |
| **Charges payable by**<br>(State full name and address of party responsible for payment of our shipping charges. If this is the shipper or consignee please state 'Shipper' or 'Consignee') | ... |
| **Customs declaration**<br>(Mandatory! You should answer all of the questions with 'Yes' or 'No'.) | ... |

Once you have completed the requested information, send your booking form to our customer services team by email (NLservices@NL.uk) or by fax to 0123 456 7778.

**Schriftliche Prüfung**

| | |
|---|---|
| **Zeit:** | **90 Minuten** |
| **Hilfsmittel:** | **allgemeines zweisprachiges Wörterbuch** |
| **Maximale Punktzahl:** | **100 Punkte** |

**Im Rahmen der schriftlichen Prüfung werden die Aufgabenanteile für die drei Kompetenzbereiche wie folgt gewichtet:**

- **Rezeption – Hörverstehen 20 %**
- **Rezeption – Leseverstehen 20 %**
- **Produktion 30 %**
- **Mediation 30 %**

Im Folgenden werden vier Aufgaben vorgelegt, die Sie bearbeiten sollen. Die erste und die zweite Aufgabe beziehen sich auf Ihre Fähigkeit, englische Texte (gesprochene und geschriebene) zu verstehen = **Rezeption**. Bei der dritten Aufgabe sollen Sie ein Schriftstück erstellen = **Produktion** eines englischen Textes. Bei der vierten Aufgabe wird von Ihnen erwartet, dass Sie Texte von der deutschen oder englischen in die jeweils andere Sprache übertragen = **Mediation**.

Die Prüfung beginnt mit der Hörverstehensaufgabe.
Alle weiteren Aufgaben können in beliebiger Reihenfolge bearbeitet werden.

## Rezeption I (Hörverstehen)

Erreichbare Punkte: (hier) 20

Webcode MMKMK01

**Situation:** Sie nehmen an einer Fortbildungsveranstaltung zum Thema Beratung ausländischer Kunden teil. Dort werden Ihnen drei Dialoge in englischer Sprache vorgespielt. Demnächst werden Sie in Ihrer Filiale bei solchen Beratungsgesprächen assistieren und müssen daher in der Lage sein, wichtige Angaben festzuhalten. Dafür wurde ein Formular entwickelt (siehe unten).

**Aufgabe:** Notieren Sie sich die Angaben bzgl. der Wünsche oder Probleme der Kunden (Frau Morris, Herr Friday und Herr Coley) in deutscher Sprache.

**Kundengespräch**

Name des Kunden / der Kundin ____________________

Kundenwunsch/Problem ____________________
____________________

Beratung durch den Bankangestellten ____________________
____________________
____________________
____________________

## Rezeption II (Leseverstehen)

Erreichbare Punkte: (hier) 20

**Situation:** Sie nehmen an einer internationalen Fachtagung teil. Es geht um das Thema „Kontoführungsgebühren und deren Inklusivleistungen". Sie und ein Kollege wurden aufgefordert, eine Präsentation über die Situation in Großbritannien zu halten. Dazu ziehen Sie den untenstehenden Text von *BBC News – Business* heran. Ihr Kollege erstellte bereits Angaben bzgl. der wichtigen Aspekte, die im Text aufgeführt werden. Leider wurde er krank, sodass Sie die Tabelle mit Details allein vervollständigen müssen (siehe S. 138).

**Aufgabe:** Finden Sie die betreffenden Angaben für Ihre Präsentationsfolien mit Hilfe des Textes heraus und schreiben Sie diese in englischer Sprache stichwortartig auf.

### Packaged accounts: How paid-for current accounts work

*by David Black, Banking specialist, Defaqto*

**Packaged current accounts receive somewhat mixed publicity, so it is worth spending some time examining what is actually on offer before deciding whether or not to open one.**

There is a choice of 69 packaged current accounts available in the UK, and many of the High Street banks offer a range of accounts from entry level through to premium accounts.

The monthly fees charged for them vary from £6.50 up to as much as £40, although the typical account charges about £15 per month.

In exchange for this monthly fee they offer various benefits. The typical high-value incentives are travel insurance, motor breakdown assistance and mobile phone insurance. [...]

**Suitability**

The Financial Services Authority (FSA) is currently in a consultation period looking at the insurance-based incentives offered by packaged current accounts. [...]

There will also be an annual statement setting out the benefits, with a recommendation that the customer reviews their suitability. This is a really salient issue and highlights the fact that differing circumstances dictate different needs.

But is it worth having a packaged account or should you just use a free in-credit current account?

It has long been the case that the informed consumer should look at the incentives on offer and decide whether they need the incentive.

If so, is it suitable for them, do they already have a similar product in place or could they buy it more cheaply – independently – elsewhere?

**Examples of cover**

To give you a flavour of the sort of things to consider, have a look at travel insurance where there is a wide variation in the cover details on offer. Some just cover European travel whereas others provide worldwide cover. [...]

(Source: abridged from BBC News – Business, http://www.bbc.co.uk/news/business-16596949)

| | |
|---|---|
| **1** Subject | … |
| **2** Number of variations in the UK | … |
| **3** Variations | • possible forms: …<br>• fees: … |
| **4** Typical incentives for packaged accounts | • …<br>• … |
| **5** Action taken by the FSA | • …<br>• … |
| **6** Examples of cover | • …<br>• …<br>• … |
| **7** Recommendations | • …<br>• …<br>• … |

## Produktion

Erreichbare Punkte: (hier) 30

**Situation:** Sie sind seit einigen Wochen im Rahmen Ihrer Ausbildung in Ihrer Bank in der Anlageberatung eingesetzt. Nachdem der Umsatz von Fondsanlagen in der letzten Zeit stark rückläufig verlief, beauftragt Sie Ihre Vorgesetzte damit, für sie eine E-Mail in **englischer Sprache** an alle ausländischen Kunden zu entwerfen.

**Aufgabe:** Ihre Vorgesetzte schrieb: „Entwerfen Sie bitte umgehend eine E-Mail an unsere englischsprachigen Kunden. Bieten Sie den Kunden die Anlage in den Mischfonds *NG-Invest* an. Weisen Sie dabei auf unten aufgeführte Vorzüge des *NG-Invest-Fonds* hin:

- Zurzeit versprechen sehr günstige Einstiegskurse hohe zukünftige Gewinne
- Risikostreuung durch Anlage in verschiedenste Werte und dadurch geringe Fluktuation (Zusammensetzung des Fonds: 30 % europäische Aktien, 15 % US-Aktien, 25 % deutsche Unternehmensanleihen, 20 % deutsche Staatsanleihen, 10 % liquide Mittel)
- Professionelles Management
- Monatliche Anlage: bereits ab € 25
- Jederzeitige Rückgabemöglichkeit: hohe Liquidität
- Geringe Gebühren: Ausgabeaufschlag 2,5 %; Verwaltungsvergütung derzeit 1 % p. a.

Wählen Sie einen geeigneten Betreff sowie einen ansprechenden Einführungssatz und beenden Sie die E-Mail angemessen.

## Mediation

Erreichbare Punkte: (hier) 30

**Situation:** Sie nahmen an einer internationalen Tagung teil. Es ging um die veränderten Zahlungsgewohnheiten der Konsumenten. Die Konferenzsprache war Englisch, und deshalb wurde auch das Informationsmaterial in englischer Sprache verteilt. Nun sind Sie wieder am Arbeitsplatz in Ihrer Bank und sollen Ihren Kolleginnen und Kollegen von der Tagung berichten.

**Aufgabe:** Übertragen Sie bitte die Aussagen des folgenden Textes inhaltlich genau für Ihre Kollegen in die deutsche Sprache, jedoch ohne Auflistung von Zahlen. Dies kann stichwortartig erfolgen.

### THE UK CARDS ASSOCIATION

**A Decade of Cards**
**2000–2010 ... and beyond**

**The decade in numbers: An overview**

- The 2000s see plastic come of age as credit and debit cards dominate the way we pay; by 2010, cash loses its crown as top method of consumer payment for the first time in history as debit card spending continues to grow.
- Consumers find debit cards more appropriate for daily use, but still value credit cards for large purchases [...].
- Use of cards instead of cash and cheques enables the growth of a new industry – internet retailing. In 2000, two per cent of card spending is online. This is 13% in 2010 and will keep growing.
- Average spend on credit and charge cards rises in the second half of the decade, reaching £2,151 per card in 2010 as multiple card holding falls and dormant accounts are closed. [...]
- Over six and a half billion transactions are made on debit cards in 2010 to a value of £299 billion, compared to two billion credit card purchases, totalling £111 billion.
- Credit cards are still favoured for use overseas. 63% of overseas card spending by value is on a credit card in 2010, although this is down from 86% in 2000. Debit cards are increasingly widely accepted and account for 37% of overseas card spending by value in 2010, but much more in terms of the number of transactions.
- Cash acquisition overseas moves from credit cards to debit cards, shrinking from 28% of cash taken out on a card to 10% by 2010. Travellers acquire £7 billion on all cards in 2010, up from £2 billion in 2000.
- In the UK, £3.8 billion is taken out on credit cards in 2010, down from £9.2 billion in 2005. Debit card cash withdrawals hit £172 billion in 2010, more than doubling since 2000.
- Borrowing on credit cards peaks at £69 billion in April 2006, falling to £58 billion in 2010. [...]
- Card crime falls sharply as industry moves to keep ahead of criminals. Fraud losses fall 40% in 2010 compared to their 2008 peak and are lower than at any time since 2000.

(Source: abridged from http://www.theukcardsassociation.org.uk/wm_documents/decade_of_cards_final.pdf)

### Mündliche Prüfung

Die Prüfung ist eine Gruppenprüfung, bei der Sie Gespräche persönlichen und fachlichen Inhalts in der Fremdsprache führen sollen. Es wird von Ihnen erwartet, dass Sie der vorgegebenen Situation entsprechend sprachlich agieren und reagieren. Es kommt dabei vor allem darauf an, dass Sie sich spontan äußern, dass Sie versuchen, sich verständlich zu machen und dass Sie gut zuhören.

Die Prüfung besteht aus zwei Teilen (ggf. noch einer dritten Zusatzaufgabe) und dauert insgesamt ca. 20 Minuten. Zur Vorbereitung haben Sie 20 Minuten Zeit.

Im ersten Teil der mündlichen Prüfung werden Sie gebeten, sich zu persönlichen oder beruflichen Themen zu äußern.

Im zweiten Teil sollen Sie zusammen mit einem anderen Kandidaten ein Rollenspiel durchführen. Dazu erhalten Sie vom Prüfer Rollenkarten, auf denen eine Situation beschrieben ist, die Sie vorspielen sollen. Eventuell nehmen Sie in einem dritten Teil zu einer vorgegebenen Situation Stellung.

**Hilfsmittel:** allgemeines zweisprachiges Wörterbuch.

## Mündliche Prüfung Teil II

**Situation:** Sie werden demnächst im Rahmen eines europäischen Austauschprogramms vier Wochen mit mehreren deutschen Kolleginnen und Kollegen ein Praktikum in einer englischen Filiale absolvieren. Genau wie Ihre Bank plant auch die Bank in England, eine kleine Filiale in einem dünn besiedelten Vorort zu eröffnen. Alle Mitarbeiter werden aufgefordert, Gestaltungsvorschläge beizutragen.

**Aufgabe:** Diskutieren Sie zu Vorbereitungs- und Trainingszwecken gemeinsam mit Ihrer Kollegin / Ihrem Kollegen, die an diesem Austauschprogramm teilnehmen werden, in englischer Sprache verschiedene Möglichkeiten der Einrichtung der kleinen Filiale. Hier ist die Liste der Dinge, die platziert werden sollen:

| Schalterbereich | SB-Zone |
|---|---|
| • Schalterbereich für 2 Personen<br>• 2 Schreibtische<br>• 1 Beratungsraum<br>• Kasse<br>• Tresorraum<br>• Kopiergerät | • Geldausgabeautomat<br>• Kontoauszugsdrucker<br>• Informationsbereich „Investment“ (festverzinsliche Wertpapiere, Aktienkurse)<br>• Informationsbereich „Kredit“ (Kreditzinsen, Immobilienangebote) |

**Hier ist der Grundriss:**

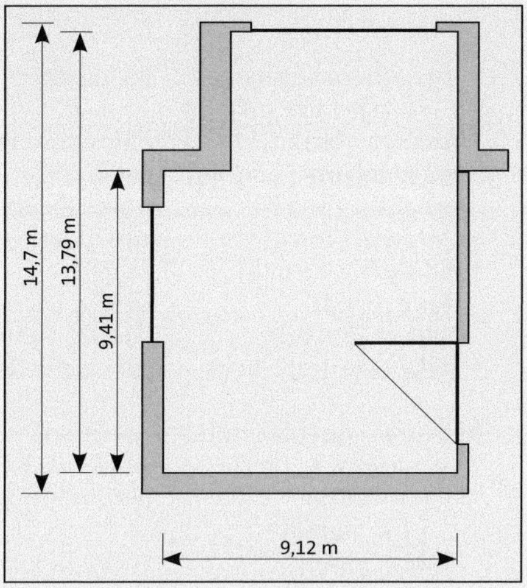


**Weitere mögliche Aufgaben (auch geeignet für Phase III)**

- Diskutieren Sie, wie wichtig **Spielecken** für Kinder in einer Bank sein können.
- Diskutieren Sie, ob Vorschriften für weitgehend vereinheitlichte Dienstkleidung zur Verbesserung der **„Corporate Identity“** beitragen können – wie z. B. die gleichen Krawatten für alle Mitarbeiter, die gleichen Farben für Hemden, Blusen usw.
- Diskutieren Sie, wie wichtig **Werbegeschenke** der Bank oder preiswerte Gegenstände des täglichen Gebrauchs (Becher usw.) **mit dem Banken-Logo** sind.
- Planen Sie gemeinsam einen **„Tag der offenen Tür“**, der an einem Sonnabend stattfinden soll. Sie haben dafür einen Etat von € 1000 zur Verfügung. Einigen Sie sich auf einen thematischen Schwerpunkt.
- Betrachten Sie die **Internetseite** einer Bank und prüfen Sie diese mit Ihrem Partner / Ihrer Partnerin auf Kundenfreundlichkeit, farbliche Gestaltung, Übersichtlichkeit usw. (Alternativ: Gegenüberstellung zweier Internetseiten von englischen und/oder deutschen Banken).

# Unit word list

Dieses Wörterverzeichnis enthält alle Wörter in der Reihenfolge ihres Erscheinens, die nicht in der Liste des Grundwortschatzes enthalten sind, d. h. die nicht vorausgesetzt werden.
t = das Wort befindet sich in den Transcripts (Hörverständnisübungen).

In der Liste werden folgende Abkürzungen verwendet:
pl. only = nur Plural
sing. only = nur Singular
coll. = umgangssprachlich
AE = Amerikanisches Englisch
BE = Britisches Englisch

## UNIT 1

6 **savings bank** ['seɪvɪŋz bæŋk] – Sparkasse
**attract** [ə'trækt] – anwerben, gewinnen
**trainee** [treɪ'ni:] – Auszubildende/r, Praktikant/in
**task** [tɑ:sk] – Aufgabe
**source** [sɔ:s] – Quelle
**pressure** ['preʃə] – Druck
**polite** [pə'laɪt] – höflich
**popular** ['pɒpjələ] – beliebt
**serious** ['sɪəriəs] – ernsthaft
**trustworthy** ['trʌstwɜ:ði] – vertrauenswürdig
**advertisement** [əd'vɜ:tɪsmənt] – Anzeige
**express** [ɪk'spres] – ausdrücken
**apply for** [ə'plaɪ fə] – sich bewerben um, beantragen
**traineeship** [treɪ'ni:ʃɪp] – Ausbildung(sverhältnis), Praktikum

7 **on the job** [ɒn ðə ˌdʒɒb] – im Beruf, bei der Arbeit
**apprentice** [ə'prentɪs] – Lehrling, Auszubildende/r im Handwerk
**manual trade** ['mænjuəl treɪd] – Handwerk
**clerk** [klɑ:k] – kaufmännische/r Angestellte/r
**old-fashioned** [ˌəʊld 'fæʃənd] – veraltet
**staff (pl. only)** [stɑ:f] – Personal, Mitarbeiter(stab)
**cashier** [kæ'ʃɪə] – Kassierer/in
**adviser** [əd'vaɪzə] – Berater/in
**personal banking manager** [ˌpɜ:sənl 'bæŋkɪŋ mænɪdʒə] – Kundenberater/in
**branch manager** ['brɑ:ntʃ mænɪdʒə] – Filialleiter/in
**branch** [brɑ:ntʃ] – Filiale, Zweigstelle
**be going on** [ˌgəʊ 'ɒn] – passieren
**wealthy** ['welθi] – wohlhabend, reich
**foreign** ['fɒrən] – ausländisch
**counter** ['kaʊntə] – Schalter
**loan** [ləʊn] – Kredit, Darlehen
**salary** ['sæləri] – Gehalt, Lohn
**take care** [teɪk 'keə] – pass auf dich auf!

8 **expression** [ɪk'spreʃn] – Ausdruck
**similarity** [ˌsɪmə'lærəti] – Ähnlichkeit
**show round** [ˌʃəʊ 'raʊnd] – herumführen
**lobby** ['lɒbi] – Foyer, Eingangshalle
**automatic teller machine (ATM)** [ˌɔ:təmætɪk 'telə məʃi:n, eɪ ti: 'em] – Geldautomat
**statement** ['steɪtmənt] – (Konto-)Auszug
**statement printer** ['steɪtmənt prɪntə] – Kontoauszugsdrucker
**self-service terminal** [ˌself 'sɜ:vɪs tɜ:mɪnl] – Selbstbedienungsterminal
**security** [sɪ'kjʊərəti] – Sicherheit
**straight ahead** [ˌstreɪt ə'hed] – geradeaus
**meeter-greeter** [ˌmi:tə 'gri:tə] – Empfang(smitarbeiter/in)
**appointment** [ə'pɔɪntmənt] – Termin, Verabredung
**enquiry** [ɪn'kwaɪəri] – Anfrage
**stand in line (AE)** [stænd ɪn 'laɪn] – anstehen
**queue (BE)** [kju:] – anstehen
**till** [tɪl] – Kasse
**amount** [ə'maʊnt] – Betrag
**withdraw** [wɪð'drɔ:] – abheben
**teller (AE)** ['telə] – Kassierer/in

9 **basement** ['beɪsmənt] – Untergeschoss
**strongroom** ['strɒŋru:m] – Stahlkammer, Tresorraum
**safe** [seɪf] – Tresor
**account** [ə'kaʊnt] – Konto
**advice** [əd'vaɪs] – Beratung
**invest** [ɪn'vest] – anlegen, investieren
**suppose** [sə'pəʊz] – annehmen, vermuten
**open-plan** ['əʊpən plæn] – Großraum(büro)
**floor** [flɔ:] – Stock(werk)
**corporate** ['kɔ:pərət] – Firmen-
**pop into** [ˌpɒp 'ɪntə] – hineingehen

| | | |
|---|---|---|
| | **elevator (AE)** ['elɪveɪtə] | Fahrstuhl |
| | **hang on** [ˌhæŋ 'ɒn] | warte! |
| | **colleague** ['kɒliːg] | Kollege / Kollegin |
| 10 | **limited** ['lɪmɪtɪd] | begrenzt |
| 11 | **give directions** [gɪv də'rekʃnz] | den Weg beschreiben |
| | **ground floor** [ˌgraʊnd 'flɔː] | Erdgeschoss |
| | **payment** ['peɪmənt] | Zahlung |
| 12 | **current account** ['kʌrənt əkaʊnt] | Girokonto, Kontokorrentkonto |
| | **savings account** ['seɪvɪŋz əkaʊnt] | Sparkonto |
| | **debit card** ['debɪt kɑːd] | Bankkarte, ec-Karte |
| | **overdraft** ['əʊvədrɑːft] | Überziehung(skredit) |
| | **building society policy** [ˌbɪldɪŋ səˌsaɪəti 'pɒləsi] | Bausparvertrag |
| | **insurance policy** [ɪn'ʃʊərəns pɒləsi] | Versicherung (spolice) |
| | **foreign currency** [ˌfɒrən 'kʌrənsi] | Fremdwährung, Sorten |
| | **securities (pl. only)** [sɪk'jʊərətiz] | Wertpapiere |
| | **senior** ['siːniə] | vorgesetzt, leitend |
| | **member of staff** [ˌmembər əf 'stɑːf] | Mitarbeiter/in |
| | **surname** ['sɜːneɪm] | Nach-, Familienname |
| | **introduce** [ˌɪntrə'djuːs] | (sich) vorstellen |
| 13t | **enter** ['entə] | eingeben |
| | **thief** [θiːf] | Dieb |
| | **damaged** ['dæmɪdʒd] | geschädigt |
| | **overdraw** [ˌəʊvə'drɔː] | überziehen |
| | **overdraft** ['əʊvədrɑːft] | Dispositionskredit |
| | **work contract** [wɜːk 'kɒntrækt] | Arbeitsvertrag |
| | **finance** ['faɪnæns] | finanzieren |
| | **savings** ['seɪvɪŋz] | Ersparnisse |
| | **mortgage** ['mɔːgɪdʒ] | Hypothek, Hypothekendarlehen |
| | **diary** ['daɪəri] | Kalender |
| | **benefit** ['benɪfɪt] | Vorteil, zusätzliche Leistung |
| | **government** ['gʌvənmənt] | Regierung |
| | **permanent contract** [ˌpɜːmənənt 'kɒntrækt] | unbefristeter Vertrag |
| | **wedding** ['wedɪŋ] | Hochzeit |
| | **withdrawal form** [wɪð'drɔːəl fɔːm] | Auszahlungsformular |
| 13 | **advise** [əd'vaɪz] | beraten |
| | **available** [ə'veɪləbl] | anwesend, zu sprechen |
| | **convenient** [kən'viːniənt] | passend |
| 14 | **transfer** [træns'fɜː] | überweisen |
| | **retail banking** ['riːteɪl bæŋkɪŋ] | Privatkundengeschäft |
| | **froth** [frɒθ] | (auf)schäumen |
| | **portfolio** [pɔːt'fəʊliəʊ] | Portefeuille, Depot |
| | **whip sth up for sb (coll.)** [ˌwɪp 'ʌp fə] | jdm (etw) zusammenstellen |
| | **premises** ['premɪsɪz] | Geschäft(sräume) |
| | **building society** ['bɪldɪŋ səsaɪəti] | Bausparkasse |
| | **cooperate with** [kəʊ'ɒpəreɪt wɪð] | zusammenarbeiten mit |
| | **on sale** [ɒn 'seɪl] | zum Verkauf |
| | **package holiday** ['pækɪdʒ hɒlədeɪ] | Pauschalreise |
| | **split** [splɪt] | (auf)teilen |
| | **pros and cons** [ˌprəʊz ənd 'kɒnz] | Für und Wider, Vor- und Nachteile |
| | **suggestion** [sə'dʒestʃən] | Vorschlag |
| | **representative** [ˌreprɪ'zentətɪv] | Vertreter/in |
| | **present** [prɪ'zent] | vorlegen, -stellen |
| | **conclusion** [kən'kluːʒn] | (Schluss-)Folgerung |

## EXTRA MATERIALS

| | | |
|---|---|---|
| 15 | **examine** [ɪg'zæmɪn] | untersuchen |
| | **separate** ['seprət] | getrennt, separat |
| | **fellow** ['feləʊ] | Mit- |
| | **chart** [tʃɑːt] | Karte, (Wand-)Bild |
| | **consequence** ['kɒnsɪkwəns] | Folge, Konsequenz |
| | **overcome** [ˌəʊvə'kʌm] | überwinden |
| | **phishing** ['fɪʃɪŋ] | Bankbetrug durch Datenklau |
| | **decide** [dɪ'saɪd] | (sich) entscheiden |
| | **increase** [ɪn'kriːs] | steigen |
| | **awareness** [ə'weənəs] | Bewusstsein |
| | **encourage** [ɪn'kʌrɪdʒ] | auffordern |
| | **precaution** [prɪ'kɔːʃn] | Vorsichtsmaßnahme |

## UNIT 2

| | | |
|---|---|---|
| 16 | **survey** ['sɜːveɪ] | (Meinungs-)Umfrage |
| | **carry out** [ˌkæri 'aʊt] | aus-, durchführen |
| | **conclude** [kən'kluːd] | schließen, folgern |
| | **annoy** [ə'nɔɪ] | ärgern, belästigen |
| | **charge** [tʃɑːdʒ] | Kosten, Gebühr |
| | **opening hours** ['əʊpənɪŋ aʊəz] | Geschäfts-, Öffnungszeiten |
| | **nasty** ['nɑːsti] | scheußlich, böse |

| | | |
|---|---|---|
| | **get a good press** [get ə gʊd 'pres] | eine gute Presse haben |
| | **satisfaction** [ˌsætɪs'fækʃn] | Zufriedenheit |
| 17 | **keen** [kiːn] | (sehr) interessiert, eifrig |
| | **satisfied** ['sætɪsfaɪd] | zufrieden |
| | **regarding** [rɪ'gɑːdɪŋ] | hinsichtlich |
| | **fee** [fiː] | Gebühr |
| | **connect to** [kə'nekt tə] | verbinden mit |
| | **review** [rɪ'vjuː] | überprüfen |
| | **abbreviation** [əˌbriːvi'eɪʃn] | Abkürzung |
| | **corporation (US)** [ˌkɔːpə'reɪʃn] | (Aktien-)Gesellschaft, Konzern |
| | **trustee** [trʌ'stiː] | Treuhänder |
| | **get in touch** [get ɪn 'tʌtʃ] | (sich) in Verbindung setzen |
| | **engaged** [ɪn'geɪdʒd] | besetzt |
| | **message** ['mesɪdʒ] | Nachricht |
| | **look forward to** [ˌlʊk 'fɔːwəd tə] | sich freuen auf |
| 17t | **fund** [fʌnd] | Fond |
| | **urgent** ['ɜːdʒənt] | dringend |
| | **pronounce** [prə'naʊns] | aussprechen |
| 18 | **swap** [swɒp] | tauschen |
| | **digit** ['dɪdʒɪt] | einstellige Zahl, Ziffer |
| | **dash** [dæʃ] | Bindestrich, Minus-Zeichen |
| | **slash** [slæʃ] | Schrägstrich |
| | **dot** [dɒt] | Punkt |
| | **lower case** [ˌləʊə 'keɪs] | Kleinbuchstaben |
| | **underscore** [ˌʌndə'skɔː] | unterstreichen |
| | **I didn't catch that** [aɪ dɪdnt 'kætʃ ðət] | das habe ich nicht verstanden |
| | **uncertain** [ʌn'sɜːtn] | unsicher |
| | **sign** [saɪn] | unterschreiben |
| 19 | **formality** [fɔː'mæləti] | Formalität |
| | **shortly** ['ʃɔːtli] | in Kürze, bald |
| | **proof of identity** [pruːf əv aɪ'dentəti] | Identitätsnachweis |
| | **certificate** [sə'tɪfɪkət] | Urkunde, Bescheinigung |
| | **residents' registration office** [ˌrezɪdənts ˌredʒɪ'streɪʃn ɒfɪs] | Einwohnermeldeamt |
| | **application** [ˌæplɪ'keɪʃn] | Antrag |
| | **fill in** [ˌfɪl 'ɪn] | ausfüllen, eintragen |
| | **details** ['diːteɪlz] | Daten |
| | **declaration** [ˌdeklə'reɪʃn] | Erklärung |
| | **reference** ['refrəns] | Auskunft, Referenz |
| | **agency** ['eɪdʒənsi] | Agentur, Büro |
| | **procedure** [prə'siːdʒə] | Verfahren, Maßnahme |
| | **regulation** [ˌregju'leɪʃn] | Bestimmung, Vorschrift |
| | **specimen signature** [ˌspesɪmən 'sɪgnətʃə] | Unterschriftsprobe |
| | **comparison** [kəm'pærɪsn] | Vergleich |
| | **signature** ['sɪgnətʃə] | Unterschrift |
| | **genuine** ['dʒenjuɪn] | echt |
| | **protection** [prə'tekʃn] | Schutz |
| | **grant** [grɑːnt] | gewähren, erteilen |
| | **third party mandate** [ˌθɜːd pɑːti 'mændeɪt] | Vollmacht |
| | **withdrawal** [wɪð'drɔːəl] | Abhebung |
| | **account holder** [ə'kaʊnt həʊldə] | Kontoinhaber/in |
| | **sole** [səʊl] | einzig, alleinig |
| | **joint account** [ˌdʒɔɪnt ə'kaʊnt] | gemeinsames Konto |
| 20 | **prove** [pruːv] | nachweisen |
| | **protect** [prə'tekt] | schützen |
| 21 | **given name** ['gɪvn neɪm] | Vorname |
| | **nationality** [ˌnæʃə'næləti] | Nationalität, Staatsangehörigkeit |
| | **date of birth** [ˌdeɪt əv 'bɜːθ] | Geburtsdatum |
| | **sex** [seks] | Geschlecht |
| | **place of birth** [ˌpleɪs əv 'bɜːθ] | Geburtsort |
| | **date of issue** [ˌdeɪt əv 'ɪʃuː] | Ausstellungsdatum |
| | **place of issue** [ˌpleɪs əv 'ɪʃuː] | Ausstellungsort |
| | **date of expiry** [ˌdeɪt əv ɪk'spaɪəri] | Ablaufdatum |
| | **compare** [kəm'peə] | vergleichen |
| | **identity card** [aɪ'dentəti kɑːd] | Ausweis |
| | **extract** ['ekstrækt] | Auszug |
| | **applicant** ['æplɪkənt] | Antragsteller/in |
| 22 | **gap** [gæp] | Lücke |
| | **declare** [dɪ'kleə] | erklären |
| | **file** [faɪl] | Akte, Datei |
| | **fund** [fʌnd] | Fonds |
| | **acceptance** [ək'septəns] | Annahme |
| | **general business conditions** [ˌdʒenrəl 'bɪznəs kəndɪʃnz] | allgemeine Geschäftsbedingungen |
| | **solely** ['səʊlli] | (einzig und) allein |
| | **purpose** ['pɜːpəs] | Zweck |
| | **congratulate** [kən'grætʃuleɪt] | beglückwünschen |

| | | |
|---|---|---|
| | **folder** ['fəʊldə] | Ordner |
| | **brochure** ['brəʊʃə] | Broschüre, Prospekt |
| | **required** [rɪ'kwaɪəd] | erforderlich |
| | **Money Laundering Act** [ˌmʌni 'lɔːndərɪŋ ækt] | Geldwäschegesetz |
| 24 | **celebrity** [sə'lebrəti] | Prominente/r, Berühmtheit |
| | **endorsement** [ɪn'dɔːsmənt] | Unterzeichnung, hier: Werbung |
| | **engagement** [ɪn'geɪdʒmənt] | Verpflichtung, Engagement |
| | **leading** ['liːdɪŋ] | führend |
| | **claim** [kleɪm] | behaupten, erklären |
| | **honestly** ['ɒnɪstli] | ehrlich |
| | **interest rate** ['ɪntrəst reɪt] | Zinssatz |
| | **brand** [brænd] | Marke |
| | **ambassador** [æm'bæsədə] | Botschafter/in |
| | **state** [steɪt] | bekannt geben, feststellen |
| | **coupled with** ['kʌpld wɪð] | verbunden mit |
| | **popularity** [ˌpɒpju'lærəti] | Beliebtheit |
| | **abroad** [ə'brɔːd] | im Ausland |
| | **endorse** [ɪn'dɔːs] | unterzeichen, hier: werben (für) |
| | **act** [ækt] | spielen |
| | **audience** ['ɔːdiəns] | Publikum |
| | **be glad** [bi 'glæd] | sich freuen |
| | **represent** [ˌreprɪ'zent] | vertreten, repräsentieren |
| | **admit** [əd'mɪt] | zugeben, gestehen |
| | **terminology** [ˌtɜːmɪ'nɒlədʒi] | Terminologie |
| | **give it your best shot** [gɪv ɪt jɔː ˌbest 'ʃɒt] | sein Bestes geben |
| | **soap opera** ['səʊp ɒprə] | Fernsehserie, Seifenoper |
| | **star in** ['stɑːr ɪn] | eine Hauptrolle spielen in |
| | **donation** [dəʊ'neɪʃn] | Spende |
| | **charity** ['tʃærəti] | Wohltätigkeit, wohltätiger Zweck |
| | **fund** [fʌnd] | finanzieren |
| | **ward** [wɔːd] | (Kranken-)Station |
| | **contribute** [kən'trɪbjuːt] | beitragen |
| | **generous** ['dʒenərəs] | großzügig |
| | **Prime Minister** [ˌpraɪm 'mɪnɪstə] | Premierminister/in |
| | **relief** [rɪ'liːf] | Hilfe |
| | **suitable** ['suːtəbl] | geeignet, passend |

## EXTRA MATERIALS

| | | |
|---|---|---|
| 25 | **premier customer** [ˌpremiə 'kʌstəmə] | Private-Banking Kunde/in |
| | **advertising** ['ædvətaɪzɪŋ] | Werbe- |
| | **treat** [triːt] | behandeln |
| | **affluent** ['æfluənt] | wohlhabend |
| | **development** [dɪ'veləpmənt] | Entwicklung |
| | **range** [reɪndʒ] | Reihe |
| | **explore** [ɪk'splɔː] | erkunden |
| | **increasingly** [ɪn'kriːsɪŋli] | zunehmend |
| | **wealth management** ['welθ mænɪdʒmənt] | Vermögensverwaltung |
| | **opportunity** [ˌɒpə'tjuːnəti] | Möglichkeit |
| | **access** ['ækses] | Zugang |
| | **support** [sə'pɔːt] | Unterstützung, Hilfe |
| | **worldwide** ['wɜːldwaɪd] | weltweit |
| | **recognise** ['rekəgnaɪz] | anerkennen |
| | **location** [ləʊ'keɪʃn] | (Stand-)Ort |
| | **extend** [ɪk'stend] | erweitern, zukommen lassen |
| | **award winning** [ə'wɔːd wɪnɪŋ] | preisgekrönt |
| | **offshore** [ˌɒf'ʃɔː] | Übersee- |
| | **provide** [prə'vaɪd] | liefern, (an)bieten |
| | **guidance** ['gaɪdəns] | Beratung |
| | **implication** [ˌɪmplɪ'keɪʃn] | Auswirkung |
| | **enclosed** [ɪn'kləʊzd] | beigefügt |
| | **reacquaint** [ˌriːə'kweɪnt] | sich (wieder) vertraut machen mit |
| | **launch** [lɔːntʃ] | Einführung, Start |
| | **certain** ['sɜːtn] | bestimmt |
| | **eligibility** [ˌelədʒə'bɪləti] | Berechtigung, Eignung |
| | **criteria** [kraɪ'tɪəriə] | Kriterien |
| | **annual** ['ænjuəl] | jährlich |
| | **ensure** [ɪn'ʃʊə] | sicherstellen, gewährleisten |
| | **overleaf** [ˌəʊvə'liːf] | umseitig |
| | **list** [lɪst] | verzeichnen |
| | **be of service** [bi əv 'sɜːvɪs] | dienlich sein |
| | **Yours sincerely** [jɔːz sɪn'sɪəli] | Mit freundlichen Grüßen |

## UNIT 3

| | | |
|---|---|---|
| 26 | **trust** [trʌst] | vertrauen |
| | **high street bank** ['haɪ striːt bæŋk] | Großbank |
| | **avoid** [ə'vɔɪd] | vermeiden |
| 27 | **personalized** ['pɜːsənəlaɪzd] | personalisiert |

| | |
|---|---|
| **paying-in book** [ˌpeɪɪŋ 'ɪn bʊk] | Einzahlungsbeleg-block |
| **deposit** [dɪ'pɒzɪt] | Einzahlung |
| **balance** ['bæləns] | Kontostand, Saldo |
| **account statement** [ə'kaʊnt steɪtmənt] | Kontoauszug |
| **mini statement** ['mɪni steɪtmənt] | Mini-Auszug |
| **transaction** [træn'zækʃn] | Zahlungseingang, -ausgang |
| **set up** [ˌset 'ʌp] | einrichten |
| **view** [vjuː] | durchsehen |
| **top up (v.)** [ˌtɒp 'ʌp] | (mit Guthaben) aufladen |
| **top up (n.)** ['tɒp ʌp] | (Karten-)Aufladung |
| **standing order** [ˌstændɪŋ 'ɔːdə] | Dauerauftrag |
| **direct debit** [dəˌrekt 'debɪt] | Einzug(sverfahren), Lastschrift |
| **extra charge** ['ekstrə tʃɑːdʒ] | Zusatzgebühren |
| **include** [ɪn'kluːd] | einschließen, enthalten |
| **straightforward** [ˌstreɪt'fɔːwəd] | einfach, schlicht |
| **feature** ['fiːtʃə] | Merkmal, Eigenschaft |
| **cheque book** ['tʃek bʊk] | Scheckheft |
| **credit interest** [ˌkredɪt 'ɪntrəst] | Guthabenzinsen |
| **Cashpoint (BE)** ['kæʃpɔɪnt] | Geldautomat |
| **suit** [suːt] | entsprechen, passen zu |
| **need** [niːd] | Bedürfnis |
| **interest (sing. only)** ['ɪntrəst] | Zinsen |
| **agreed** [ə'griːd] | vereinbart |
| **similar** ['sɪmələ] | ähnlich |

28

| | |
|---|---|
| **additional** [ə'dɪʃənl] | zusätzlich |
| **match** [mætʃ] | passen zu |
| **insurance** [ɪn'ʃʊərəns] | Versicherung |
| **(insurance) cover** [ɪnˌʃʊərəns 'kʌvə] | Deckung |
| **backup** ['bækʌp] | abspeichern, sichern |
| **restore** [rɪ'stɔː] | wieder holen, wieder herstellen |
| **rating** ['reɪtɪŋ] | Bewertung |
| **discounted** [dɪs'kaʊntɪd] | ermäßigt |
| **emergency** [ɪ'mɜːdʒənsi] | Notfall, Not- |
| **extended** [ɪk'stendɪd] | erweitert |
| **warranty** ['wɒrənti] | Garantie |
| **identity theft** [aɪ'dentəti θeft] | Identitätsdiebstahl |
| **tailored** ['teɪləd] | maßgeschneidert |
| **instant access** [ˌɪnstənt 'æksəs] | Sofortzugang |
| **preferential** [ˌprefə'renʃl] | Vorzugs- |
| **text alert** ['tekst əlɜːt] | SMS-Benachrichtigung |
| **potential** [pə'tenʃl] | potenziell |
| **annual saving** [ˌænjuəl 'seɪvɪŋ] | jährliche Ersparnis |

29

| | |
|---|---|
| **current** ['kʌrənt] | derzeitig |
| **previous** ['priːviəs] | vorherig |
| **overdraft facility** [ˌəʊvədrɑːft fə'sɪləti] | Dispositionskredit |
| **bank sort code** [ˌbæŋk 'sɔːt kəʊd] | Bankleitzahl |
| **international bank account number (IBAN)** [ˌɪntənæʃnəl 'bæŋk əkaʊnt nʌmbə] | internationale Bankkontonummer |
| **SWIFT** [swɪft] | Code für internationale Überweisungen (Society for Worldwide Financial Telecommunication) |
| **entry** ['entri] | Buchung, Eintrag |
| **debit** ['debɪt] | abbuchen, belasten |
| **debit (entry)** ['debɪt entri] | Abbuchung, Belastung |
| **credit** ['kredɪt] | gutschreiben |
| **credit (entry)** ['kredɪt entri] | Gutschrift |
| **in the red** [ɪn ðə 'red] | in den roten Zahlen |
| **in the black** [ɪn ðə 'blæk] | in den schwarzen Zahlen |

30

| | |
|---|---|
| **exchange** [ɪks'tʃeɪndʒ] | Austausch |
| **American Studies** [əˌmerɪkən 'stʌdiz] | Amerikanistik |
| **gonna** ['gɒnə] | = going to |
| **checking account (US)** ['tʃekɪŋ əkaʊnt] | Gehaltskonto, Girokonto |
| **free of charge** [friː əv 'tʃɑːdʒ] | gebührenfrei |
| **cheque (BE), check (AE)** [tʃek] | **Scheck** |
| **utility bill** [juː'tɪləti bɪl] | Rechnung für Strom-, Wasserversorger etc. |
| **credit transfer** [ˌkredɪt 'trænsfɜː] | Überweisung |
| **line of credit (AE)** [laɪn əv 'kredɪt] | Dispositionskredit, Kreditlinie |
| **charge** [tʃɑːdʒ] | berechnen |

| | | |
|---|---|---|
| 31 | **exceed** [ɪk'siːd] | überschreiten, -steigern |
| | **miss** [mɪs] | versäumen |
| 32 | **native speaker** [ˌneɪtɪv 'spiːkə] | Muttersprachler/in |
| | **rarely** ['reəli] | selten |
| | **impolite** [ˌɪmpə'laɪt] | unhöflich |
| | **definitely** ['defɪnətli] | genau |
| | **widely** ['waɪdli] | weit (verbreitet) |
| | **regret** [rɪ'gret] | Bedauern |
| | **crash** [kræʃ] | abstürzen |
| | **guideline** ['gaɪdlaɪn] | Hinweis |
| | **deputy** ['depjəti] | stellvertretend |
| | **efficient** [ɪ'fɪʃnt] | leistungsfähig |
| 33 | **occasional** [ə'keɪʒənl] | gelegentlich |
| | **pension** ['penʃn] | Rente, Pension |
| 34 | **gang** [gæŋ] | Bande |
| | **strike** [straɪk] | zuschlagen |
| | **a couple of** [ə 'kʌpl əv] | ein paar |
| | **refuse** [rɪ'fjuːz] | ablehnen |
| | **cleared** [klɪəd] | leer (geräumt) |
| | **victim** ['vɪktɪm] | Opfer |
| | **furious** ['fjʊəriəs] | wütend |
| | **afford** [ə'fɔːd] | (es) sich leisten (können) |
| | **gardening** ['gɑːdnɪŋ] | Gartenarbeit |
| | **investigate** [ɪn'vestɪgeɪt] | untersuchen, nachprüfen |
| | **solve** [sɒlv] | lösen |
| | **mystery** ['mɪstri] | Geheimnis, Rätsel |
| | **beat** [biːt] | Streife, Runde |
| | **catch sb's eye** [kætʃ 'aɪ] | jds Aufmerksamkeit erregen |
| | **slot** [slɒt] | Schlitz |
| | **insert** [ɪn'sɜːt] | einschieben, einführen |
| | **strip** [strɪp] | Streifen |
| | **stuck** [stʌk] | geklebt |
| | **panel** ['pænl] | Platte |
| | **target** ['tɑːgɪt] | ins Visier nehmen |
| | **issue** ['ɪʃuː] | herausgeben |
| | **crime** [kraɪm] | Verbrechen |
| | **harm** [hɑːm] | Schaden |
| | **damage** ['dæmɪdʒ] | beschädigen |
| | **illegal** [ɪ'liːgl] | gesetzwidrig, illegal |
| | **equipment** [ɪ'kwɪpmənt] | Geräte |
| | **spokesperson** ['spəʊkspɜːsn] | Sprecher/in |
| | **reimburse** [ˌriːɪm'bɜːs] | entschädigen |
| | **rob** [rɒb] | ausrauben |
| | **remove** [rɪ'muːv] | entfernen |
| | **area** ['eəriə] | Gegend |
| 35 | **safety** ['seɪfti] | Sicherheit |
| | **prompt** [prɒmpt] | Stichwort, Vorgabe |
| | **communicate** [kə'mjuːnɪkeɪt] | übermitteln |
| | **misuse** [ˌmɪs'juːz] | Missbrauch |
| | **device** [dɪ'vaɪs] | Vorrichtung, Gerät |
| | **keypad** ['kiːpæd] | Tastenfeld, Tastatur |
| | **cancel** ['kænsl] | löschen, (hier: sperren) |
| 36 | **target group** ['tɑːgɪt gruːp] | Zielgruppe |
| | **identify** [aɪ'dentɪfaɪ] | festlegen, -stellen |
| | **visual aid** ['vɪʒuəl eɪd] | Anschauungsmaterial |
| | **overview** ['əʊvəvjuː] | Überblick, -sicht |
| | **structure** ['strʌktʃə] | Aufbau, Struktur |
| | **insight** ['ɪnsaɪt] | Einblick |
| | **section** ['sekʃn] | Teil, Abschnitt |
| | **move on to** [muːv 'ɒn tə] | übergehen zu |
| | **comment on** ['kɒment ɒn] | kommentieren |
| | **stage** [steɪdʒ] | Phase, Abschnitt |
| | **summarize** ['sʌməraɪz] | zusammenfassen |
| | **EXTRA MATERIALS** | |
| 37 | **interior** [ɪn'tɪəriə] | Innenausstattung |
| | **employee** [ɪm'plɔɪiː] | Angestellte/r |
| | **topic** ['tɒpɪk] | Thema |
| | **experience** [ɪk'spɪəriəns] | Erfahrung |
| 37t | **account manager** [ə'kaʊnt mænɪdʒə] | Kundenbetreuer/in |
| | **follow-up appointment** [ˌfɒləʊ ʌp ə'pɔɪntmənt] | Folgetermin |
| | **properly** ['prɒpəli] | korrekt, richtig |
| | **digit** ['dɪdʒɪt] | Ziffer |
| | **qualify** ['kwɒlɪfaɪ] | sich qualifizieren |
| | **that won't cut any ice** [wəʊnt ˌkʌt eni 'aɪs] | das macht nichts her |
| | **learn on the job** [lɜːn ɒn ðə 'dʒɒb] | bei der Arbeit / am Arbeitsplatz lernen |
| | **personal quality** [ˌpɜːsənl 'kwɒləti] | persönliche Eigenschaft |
| | **deal with people** [ˌdiːl wɪð 'piːpl] | mit Menschen umgehen |
| | **sales geared** ['seɪlz gɪəd] | auf den Verkauf ausgerichtet |
| | **gear (coll.)** [gɪə] | Zeug, Sachen, Kleidung |
| | **pin-striped suit** [ˌpɪn straɪpt 'suːt] | Nadelstreifenanzug |
| | **waistcoat** ['weɪskəʊt] | Weste |
| | **ring the changes** [rɪŋ ðə 'tʃeɪndʒɪz] | variieren, für Abwechslung sorgen |

| | | |
|---|---|---|
| | **affluence** ['æfluəns] | Wohlstand |
| | **casual** ['kæʒuəl] | locker, salopp |
| | **competitive** [kəm'petətɪv] | konkurrenzbetont, umkämpft |
| | **pilot scheme** ['paɪlət ski:m] | Pilotprojekt |
| | **generate** ['dʒenəreɪt] | erbringen |
| | **drop** [drɒp] | fallen lassen |

## UNIT 4

| | | |
|---|---|---|
| 38 | **contents** ['kɒntents] | Inhalt |
| | **item** ['aɪtəm] | Artikel, Gegenstand |
| | **means of payment** [ˌmi:nz əv 'peɪmənt] | Zahlungsmittel, -modalität |
| 39 | **via** ['vaɪə] | über |
| | **payee** [ˌpeɪ'i:] | Zahlungsempfänger/in |
| | **purpose** ['pɜ:pəs] | Verwendungszweck |
| | **authorize** ['ɔ:θəraɪz] | ermächtigen |
| | **confirm** [kən'fɜ:m] | bestätigen |
| | **button** ['bʌtn] | Taste, Knopf |
| 40t | **hard drive** [ˌhɑ:d 'draɪv] | Festplatte |
| | **alter** ['ɔ:ltə] | ändern |
| | **quarter** ['kwɔ:tə] | Quartal |
| 41 | **due** [dju:] | fällig |
| | **due date** [ˌdju: 'deɪt] | Fälligkeitsdatum |
| | **claim** [kleɪm] | einziehen |
| | **authorization** [ˌɔ:θəraɪ'zeɪʃn] | Ermächtigung |
| | **membership fee** ['membəʃɪp fi:] | Mitgliedsbeitrag |
| | **revoke** [rɪ'vəʊk] | widerrufen |
| 42 | **vary** ['veəri] | verändern, sich verändern |
| | **instalment** [ɪn'stɔ:lmənt] | Rate |
| | **hire purchase** [ˌhaɪə 'pɜ:tʃəs] | Ratenkauf |
| | **subscription** [səb'skrɪpʃn] | Abonnement |
| | **repayment** [rɪ'peɪmənt] | Rückzahlung, Tilgung |
| | **season ticket** ['si:zn tɪkɪt] | Jahres-, Zeitkarte, Abonnement |
| | **partial** ['pɑ:ʃl] | Teil- |
| | **goods** [gʊdz] | Ware(n) |
| | **insurance premium** [ɪnˌʃʊərəns 'pri:miəm] | Versicherungsbeitrag |
| | **delivery** [dɪ'lɪvəri] | Zustellung |
| | **chip and PIN** [tʃɪp ən 'pɪn] | Chip und Geheimzahl |
| | **affect** [ə'fekt] | betreffen |
| | **fraud** [frɔ:d] | Betrug |
| | **loss** [lɒs] | Verlust |
| | **gold** [gəʊld] | Gold |
| | **contain** [kən'teɪn] | enthalten |
| | **encrypted** [ɪn'krɪptɪd] | verschlüsselt |
| | **increase** [ɪn'kri:s] | erhöhen |
| | **secure** [sɪ'kjuə] | sicher |
| | **forge** [fɔ:dʒ] | fälschen |
| | **log** [lɒg] | aufzeichnen |
| | **consecutive** [kən'sekjətɪv] | aufeinander folgend |
| | **failed** [feɪld] | gescheitert |
| | **attempt** [ə'tempt] | Versuch |
| 43 | **agent** ['eɪdʒənt] | handelnde Person |
| | **leaflet** ['li:flət] | Broschüre, Prospekt |
| | **enclosed** [ɪn'kləʊzd] | beiliegend |
| | **in addition** [ɪn ə'dɪʃn] | außerdem, darüber hinaus |
| | **display** [dɪ'spleɪ] | (an)zeigen |
| | **salesperson** ['seɪlzpɜ:sn] | Verkäufer/in |
| 44 | **Australian** [ɒ'streɪliən] | australisch |
| | **beginning** [bɪ'gɪnɪŋ] | Anfang, Beginn |
| | **head (coll.)** [hed] | fahren |
| | **down under** [daʊn 'ʌndə] | nach Australien |
| | **traveller's cheque** ['trævələz tʃek] | Reisescheck |
| | **why on earth** [waɪ ɒn 'ɜ:θ] | warum um Himmels willen |
| | **in theory** [ɪn 'θɪəri] | theoretisch |
| | **denomination** [dɪˌnɒmɪ'neɪʃn] | Nennwert |
| | **denominations (pl.)** [dɪˌnɒmɪ'neɪʃnz] | Stückelung |
| | **theft** [θeft] | Diebstahl |
| | **notify** ['nəʊtɪfaɪ] | benachrichtigen |
| | **stop payment on** [stɒp 'peɪmənt ɒn] | sperren |
| | **bear** [beə] | tragen |
| | **misuse** [ˌmɪs'ju:z] | missbrauchen |
| | **replacement** [rɪ'pleɪsmənt] | Ersatz |
| | **baggage** ['bægɪdʒ] | Gepäck |
| | **cover** ['kʌvə] | Deckung |
| 45 | **expiry date** [ɪk'spaɪəri deɪt] | Ablaufdatum |
| | **issuer** ['ɪʃu:ə] | Aussteller |
| | **undertake** [ˌʌndə'teɪk] | unternehmen |
| | **campaign** [kæm'peɪn] | Kampagne |
| | **persuade** [pə'sweɪd] | überreden |
| | **unsolicited mail** [ˌʌnsə'lɪsɪtɪd meɪl] | nicht erbetene Post, Wurfsendung |
| | **be in debt** [bi ɪn 'det] | verschuldet sein, Schulden haben |
| | **repay** [rɪ'peɪ] | tilgen, zurückzahlen |
| | **remaining** [rɪ'meɪnɪŋ] | restlich, verbleibend |

| | | |
|---|---|---|
| | **variable** ['veəriəbl] | variable |
| | **get (deeply) into debt** [get ˌdi:pli ɪntə 'det] | sich (tief) verschulden |
| | **in contrast** [ɪn 'kɒntrɑ:st] | im Gegensatz |
| | **cover** ['kʌvə] | decken |
| 47 | **combi-card** ['kɒmbi kɑ:d] | Kombi-Karte |
| | **variety** [və'raɪəti] | Vielfalt, Auswahl |
| | **major** ['meɪdʒə] | Haupt-, wichtig |
| | **purchase** ['pɜ:tʃəs] | Kauf |
| | **vending machine** ['vendɪŋ məʃi:n] | Verkaufsautomat |
| | **collaboration** [kəˌlæbə'reɪʃn] | Zusammenarbeit |
| | **retailer** ['ri:teɪlə] | Einzelhändler/in |
| | **handle** ['hændl] | umgehen mit |
| | **newsagent** ['nju:zeɪdʒənt] | Zeitungshändler/in |
| | **scheme** [ski:m] | Programm, Projekt |
| | **install** [ɪn'stɔ:l] | einrichten |
| | **decipher** [dɪ'saɪfə] | entziffern, lesen |
| | **deduct** [dɪ'dʌkt] | abziehen, abbuchen |
| | **emphasize** ['emfəsaɪz] | betonen, hervorheben |
| | **consumer** [kən'sju:mə] | Verbraucher/in |
| | **usability** [ˌju:zə'bɪləti] | Brauchbarkeit |
| | **convenience** [kən'vi:niəns] | Annehmlichkeit |
| 48 | **clue** [klu:] | Hinweis |
| | **fraudulent** ['frɔ:djələnt] | betrügerisch |
| | **human being** [ˌhju:mən 'bi:ɪŋ] | Mensch, menschliches Wesen |
| | **pattern** ['pætn] | Muster |
| | **behave** [bɪ'heɪv] | sich verhalten, sich benehmen |
| | **in the field of** [ɪn ðə 'fi:ld əv] | auf dem Gebiet von |
| | **detection** [dɪ'tekʃn] | Entdeckung |
| | **evaluate** [ɪ'væljueɪt] | bewerten, evaluieren |
| | **purchase** ['pɜ:tʃəs] | kaufen |
| | **bar code** ['bɑ: kəʊd] | Strichcode |
| | **score** [skɔ:] | Punktzahl, Punktestand |
| | **query** ['kwɪəri] | beanstanden, bezweifeln |
| | **pump attendant** [ˌpʌmp ə'tendənt] | Tankstellenwärter/in |
| | **adapt** [ə'dæpt] | adaptieren |
| 49 | **redeem** [rɪ'di:m] | einlösen |
| | **blackout date** ['blækaʊt deɪt] | Terminbeschränkung |
| | **expiration** [ˌekspə'reɪʃn] | Ablaufdatum |
| | **collectables** [kə'lektəbl] | Sammlergegenstände |
| | **one-of-a-kind** [wʌn əv ə kaɪnd] | einmalig |
| | **associate** [ə'soʊʃieɪt] | Servicemitarbeiter/in |

## UNIT 5

| | | |
|---|---|---|
| 50 | **piggy bank** ['pɪgi bæŋk] | Sparschwein |
| | **decimal** ['desɪml] | Dezimalzahl, -stelle |
| | **inhabitant** [ɪn'hæbɪtənt] | Einwohner/in |
| | **billion (AE)** ['bɪljən] | Milliarde |
| | **one thousand million (BE)** [wʌn ˌθaʊznd 'mɪljən] | Milliarde |
| | **trillion (AE)** ['trɪljən] | Billion |
| | **billion (BE)** ['bɪljən] | Billion |
| 51 | **wealth** [welθ] | Vermögen |
| | **distribution** [ˌdɪstrɪ'bju:ʃn] | Verteilung |
| | **net** [net] | Netto- |
| | **assets** ['æsets] | Vermögen(swerte) |
| | **ethnic** ['eθnɪk] | ethnisch |
| | **background** ['bækgraʊnd] | Herkunft, Hintergrund |
| | **percentage** [pə'sentɪdʒ] | Prozentsatz |
| | **distribute** [dɪ'strɪbju:t] | verteilen |
| | **unequal** [ʌn'i:kwəl] | ungleich |
| | **increase** [ɪn'kri:s] | zunehmen |
| | **decrease** ['di:kri:s] | abnehmen |
| | **react** [ri'ækt] | reagieren |
| | **agreement** [ə'gri:mənt] | Zustimmung |
| | **disagreement** [ˌdɪsə'gri:mənt] | Widerspruch |
| 52 | **disagree** [ˌdɪsə'gri:] | nicht zustimmen |
| | **my pleasure** [maɪ 'pleʒə] | gern geschehen |
| | **share** [ʃeə] | Aktie |
| | **stock exchange** ['stɒk ɪkstʃeɪndʒ] | (Wertpapier-)Börse |
| | **willing** ['wɪlɪŋ] | gewillt (sein) |
| | **economic** [ˌi:kə'nɒmɪk] | wirtschaftlich, Wirtschafts- |
| | **recession** [rɪ'seʃn] | Rezession, Wirtschaftsflaute |
| | **unemployment** [ˌʌnɪm'plɔɪmənt] | Arbeitslosigkeit |
| | **think twice about** [θɪŋk 'twaɪs əbaʊt] | es sich gut überlegen |
| | **hard-earned** [ˌhɑ:d 'ɜ:nd] | schwer verdient |
| | **competition** [ˌkɒmpə'tɪʃn] | Konkurrenz, Wettbewerb |
| | **saver** ['seɪvə] | Sparer/in |
| | **on offer** [ɒn 'ɒfə] | im Angebot |

| | | |
|---|---|---|
| 53 | **penalty fee** ['penlti] fi: | Strafgebühr |
| | **deposit** [dɪ'pɒzɪt] | einzahlen |
| | **lump sum** [ˌlʌmp 'sʌm] | einmalige Summe |
| | **affect** [ə'fekt] | sich auswirken auf |
| | **rise** [raɪz] | steigen |
| | **syllable** ['sɪləbl] | Silbe |
| 54 | **competitive** [kəm'petətɪv] | umkämpft, konkurrenzfähig |
| | **ECB (European Central Bank)** [ˌjʊərəʊˌpi:ən 'sentrəl bæŋk] | Europäische Zentralbank |
| | **raise** [reɪz] | erhöhen |
| | **base rate** ['beɪs reɪt] | Leitzins(satz) |
| | **profitable** ['prɒfɪtəbl] | gewinnbringend |
| | **mattress** ['mætrəs] | Matratze |
| | **notice account** ['nəʊtɪs əkaʊnt] | Festgeldkonto, Termingeldkonto |
| | **give notice** [ˌgɪv 'nəʊtɪs] | kündigen |
| | **observe a period of notice** [əbˌzɜ:v ə ˌpɪəriəd əv 'nəʊtɪs] | eine Kündigungsfrist einhalten |
| | **term** [tɜ:m] | Laufzeit |
| | **instant** ['ɪnstənt] | sofortig |
| 55 | **deposit bond (BE)** [dɪ'pɒzɪt bɒnd] | Festgeldkonto, Termingeldkonto |
| | **bond** [bɒnd] | festverzinsliches Wertpapier, Anleihe |
| | **upwards** ['ʌpwədz] | aufwärts |
| | **value** ['vælju:] | Wert |
| | **money market account** ['mʌni mɑ:kɪt əkaʊnt] | Geldmarktkonto |
| | **on demand** [ɒn dɪ'mɑ:nd] | auf Abruf |
| 56 | **state** [steɪt] | staatlich |
| | **tax** [tæks] | Steuer |
| | **encourage** [ɪn'kʌrɪdʒ] | ermutigen, ermuntern |
| | **term** [tɜ:m] | Ausdruck |
| | **subsidy** ['sʌbsədi] | Subvention |
| | **employer** [ɪm'plɔɪə] | Arbeitgeber/in |
| | **employee** [ɪm'plɔɪi:] | Arbeitnehmer/in |
| | **asset-building** ['æset bɪldɪŋ] | vermögenswirksam |
| | **appropriate** [ə'prəʊpriət] | angemessen, zutreffend |
| 58 | **mortgage bank** ['mɔ:gɪdʒ bæŋk] | Hypothekenbank |
| | **trigger** ['trɪgə] | auslösen |
| | **fear** [fɪə] | Befürchtung |
| | **default** [dɪ'fɔ:lt] | zahlungsunfähig werden |
| | **be short of** [bi 'ʃɔ:t əv] | zu wenig haben |
| | **funds (pl. only)** [fʌndz] | Kapital |
| | **borrowing** ['bɒrəʊɪŋ] | Kreditaufnahme |
| | **compensation scheme** [ˌkɒmpən'seɪʃn ski:m] | Einlagensicherungsfonds |
| | **solvent** ['sɒlvənt] | solvent |
| | **spin into** ['spɪn ɪntə] | hier: einzahlen |
| | **headline** ['hedlaɪn] | Schlagzeile, Überschrift |
| | **scary** ['skeəri] | beängstigend |
| | **reassurance** [ˌri:ə'ʃʊərəns] | Zusicherung |
| | **overreact** [ˌəʊvəri'ækt] | überreagieren |
| | **close down** [ˌkləʊz 'daʊn] | schließen |
| | **freeze** [fri:z] | einfrieren |
| | **complain** [kəm'pleɪn] | sich beklagen |
| | **meanwhile** ['mi:nwaɪl] | inzwischen |
| | **Chief Executive Officer (CEO)** [ˌtʃi:f ɪg'zekjətɪv ɒfɪsə] | Vorstandsvorsitzende/r |
| | **patient** ['peɪʃnt] | geduldig |
| | **go bust** [gəʊ 'bʌst] | kaputtgehen |
| | **comfortable** ['kʌmftəbl] | wohl |
| 59 | **equity capital** ['ekwəti kæpɪtl] | (haftendes) Eigenkapital |
| | **compensation** [ˌkɒmpən'seɪʃn] | Entschädigung |
| 60 | **economical** [ˌi:kə'nɒmɪkl] | sparsam |

## EXTRA MATERIALS

| | | |
|---|---|---|
| 61 | **gross** [grəʊs] | Brutto- |
| | **European Savings Directive (ESD)** [ˌjʊərə'pi:ən seɪvɪŋz də'rektɪv, ˌi: es 'di:] | Europäische Zinsbesteuerungsrichtlinie |
| | **tax-efficient** [ˌtæks ɪ'fɪʃnt] | steuermindernd |
| | **individual** [ˌɪndɪ'vɪdʒuəl] | (Einzel-)Person |
| | **aim to** ['eɪm tə] | zielen auf |
| | **counter** ['kaʊntə] | entgegenwirken |
| | **cross-border** ['krɒs bɔ:də] | grenzüberschreitend |
| | **tax evasion** ['tæks ɪveɪʒn] | Steuerhinterziehung, Steuerflucht |
| | **essentially** [ɪ'senʃəli] | im Wesentlichen |
| | **proceeds (pl. only)** ['prəʊsi:dz] | Erlös, Erlöse |
| | **deposit** [dɪ'pɒzɪt] | Einlage |
| | **redemption** [rɪ'dempʃn] | Auszahlung, Rückzahlung |
| | **dividend** ['dɪvɪdend] | Dividende |
| | **outside the scope of** [autˌsaɪd ðə 'skəʊp əv] | außerhalb des Bereichs |

| | | |
|---|---|---|
| | **ultimate** ['ʌltɪmət] | End- |
| | **objective** [əb'dʒektɪv] | Ziel |
| | **elect** [ɪ'lekt] | wählen |
| | **apply** [ə'plaɪ] | anwenden |
| | **withholding tax** [wɪð'həʊldɪŋ tæks] | Quellensteuer |
| | **whereby** [weə'baɪ] | wodurch |
| | **request** [rɪ'kwest] | bitten, beantragen |
| | **levy** ['levi] | erheben |
| | **tax authority** [ˌtæks ɔː'θɒrəti] | Finanzamt |
| | **residence** ['rezɪdəns] | Wohnsitz |
| | **certificate of exemption** [səˌtɪfɪkət əv ɪg'zempʃn] | Nichtveranlagungsbescheinigung |
| | **supply** [sə'plaɪ] | liefern |
| | **relate to** [rɪ'leɪt tə] | sich beziehen auf |
| | **tax return** [ˌtæks rɪ'tɜːn] | Steuererklärung |
| | **withhold** [wɪð'həʊld] | abziehen |
| | **retain** [rɪ'teɪn] | einbehalten |

## UNIT 6

| | | |
|---|---|---|
| 62 | **pensioner** ['penʃənə] | Rentner/in, Pensionär/in |
| | **company pension** ['kʌmpəni penʃn] | betriebliche Altersversorgung |
| | **contribution** [ˌkɒntrɪ'bjuːʃn] | Beitrag |
| | **provide for the future** [prəˌvaɪd fə ðə 'fjuːtʃə] | vorsorgen |
| | **make provision for** [meɪk prə'vɪʒn fə] | Vorsorge treffen für |
| | **state pension (fund)** ['steɪt penʃn fʌnd] | staatliche Rente(nkasse) |
| | **determine** [dɪ'tɜːmɪn] | bestimmen |
| | **retirement** [rɪ'taɪəmənt] | Ruhestand |
| | **opportunity** [ˌɒpə'tjuːnəti] | Chance, Gelegenheit |
| 63 | **upturn** ['ʌptɜːn] | Anstieg |
| | **leap** [liːp] | springen |
| | **soar** [sɔː] | steil ansteigen, hochschnellen |
| | **downturn** ['daʊntɜːn] | Rückgang |
| | **decline** [dɪ'klaɪn] | sinken |
| | **plunge** [plʌndʒ] | (ab)stürzen |
| | **slight** [slaɪt] | leicht |
| | **gradual** ['grædʒuəl] | allmählich |
| | **steady** ['stedi] | stetig |
| | **abrupt** [ə'brʌpt] | abrupt, plötzlich |
| | **frequent** ['friːkwənt] | häufig |
| | **volatile** ['vɒlətaɪl] | schwankend, unbeständig |
| | **fluctuate** ['flʌktʃueɪt] | schwanken |
| | **rally** ['ræli] | sich erholen |
| | **rebound** [rɪ'baʊnd] | wieder steigen |
| | **recover** [rɪ'kʌvə] | sich erholen |
| | **constant** ['kɒnstənt] | konstant, stetig |
| | **stable** ['steɪbl] | stabil |
| | **drastic** ['dræstɪk] | drastisch |
| | **perform** [pə'fɔːm] | abschneiden, sich entwickeln |
| | **turbulence** ['tɜːbjələns] | Turbulenz, Aufruhr |
| | **decline** [dɪ'klaɪn] | Rückgang |
| | **rally** ['ræli] | Erholung |
| | **rebound** ['riːbaʊnd] | Wiederanstieg |
| 64 | **incorporate** [ɪn'kɔːpəreɪt] | einbauen, einsetzen |
| | **gain** [geɪn] | Gewinn |
| | **maker** ['meɪkə] | Hersteller/in |
| | **shipment** ['ʃɪpmənt] | Lieferung |
| | **increase** ['ɪŋkriːs] | Steigerung |
| | **beat** [biːt] | übertreffen |
| | **expectation** [ˌekspek'teɪʃn] | Erwartung |
| | **forecast** ['fɔːkɑːst] | vorhersagen |
| | **drop** [drɒp] | fallen |
| | **slump** [slʌmp] | Sturz |
| | **slowdown** ['sləʊdaʊn] | Rückgang |
| | **electronics (pl. only)** [ˌɪlek'trɒnɪks] | Elektronik, elektronische Geräte |
| | **along with** [ə'lɒŋ wɪð] | zusammen mit |
| | **research** [rɪ'sɜːtʃ] | Forschung |
| | **recommend** [ˌrekə'mend] | empfehlen |
| | **well-advised** [ˌwel əd'vaɪz] | gut beraten |
| | **advisable** [əd'vaɪzəbl] | ratsam |
| 65 | **issue** ['ɪʃuː] | Ausgabe |
| | **government bond** ['gʌvənmənt bɒnd] | Staatsanleihe |
| | **issue** ['ɪʃuː] | ausgeben |
| | **yield** [jiːld] | Rendite |
| | **coupon** ['kuːpɒn] | Zinssatz (eines festverzinslichen Wertpapiers) |
| | **corporate bond** ['kɔːpərət bɒnd] | Unternehmensanleihe, Obligation |
| | **rating** ['reɪtɪŋ] | Bewertung, Rating |
| | **bid price** ['bɪd praɪs] | Kauf-, Geldkurs |
| | **US$ denominated** [dɪ'nɒmɪneɪtɪd] | in US-Dollar |
| 66 | **I don't know what got into me** [aɪ dəʊnt ˌnəʊ wɒt ˌgɒt 'ɪntu mi] | ich weiß nicht, was in mich gefahren ist |
| | **you can say that again** [ju kən ˌseɪ ðət ə'gen] | das kann man wohl sagen |
| | **d'you** [dju] | = do you |
| | **cross sb's mind** [krɒs 'maɪnd] | in den Sinn kommen |
| | **long-term** [ˌlɒŋ'tɜːm] | langfristig |

| | | |
|---|---|---|
| | **turn thirty** [tɜːn 'θɜːti] | die Dreißig überschreiten |
| | **wonder** ['wʌndə] | sich fragen |
| | **not necessarily** [nɒt ˌnesə'serəli] | nicht unbedingt |
| | **yield** [jiːld] | erwirtschaften, erzielen |
| | **real estate (sing. only)** ['rɪəl ɪsteɪt] | Immobilien |
| | **consider** [kən'sɪdə] | erwägen, sich überlegen |
| | **pool** [puːl] | sammeln, zusammenlegen |
| | **unit** ['juːnɪt] | Investmentanteil, -zertifikat |
| 67 | **on your behalf** [ɒn ˌjɔː bɪ'hɑːf]] | in Ihrem Namen |
| | **initial charge** [ɪˌnɪʃl 'tʃɑːdʒ] | Ausgabeaufschlag |
| | **reinvest** [ˌriːɪn'vest] | wieder investieren |
| | **bother about** ['bɒðər əbaʊt] | sich kümmern um |
| | **fluctuation** [ˌflʌktʃʊ'eɪʃn] | Schwankung, Ausschlag |
| | **aim** [eɪm] | Ziel |
| | **spread** [spred] | verteilen |
| | **obtain** [əb'teɪn] | erhalten |
| | **huge** [hjuːdʒ] | riesig |
| | **diversified** [daɪ'vɜːsɪfaɪd] | diversifiziert, breit gestreut |
| | **return** [rɪ'tɜːn] | zurückgeben |
| | **medium-term** ['miːdiəm tɜːm] | mittelfristig |
| | **be keen on** [bi 'kiːn ɒn] | auf etwas scharf sein |
| | **emerging markets** [ɪˌmɜːdʒɪŋ 'mɑːkɪts] | Schwellenländer |
| | **fund of funds** [fʌnd əv 'fʌndz] | Dachfonds |
| | **selection** [sɪ'lekʃn] | Auswahl |
| | **growth** [grəʊθ] | Wachstum |
| 68 | **exception** [ɪk'sepʃn] | Ausnahme |
| | **steep** [stiːp] | steil |
| | **eco-friendly** ['iːkə frendli] | umweltfreundlich |
| | **immediate** [ɪ'miːdiət] | sofort, umgehend |
| | **demand** [dɪ'mɑːnd] | Nachfrage |
| 69 | **investor** [ɪn'vestə] | Investor/in, Anleger/in |
| | **treatment** ['triːtmənt] | Behandlung, Umgang |
| | **link** [lɪŋk] | Verbindung |
| 70 | **assess** [ə'ses] | beurteilen, schätzen |
| | **risk tolerance** [ˌrɪsk 'tɒlərəns] | Risikobereitschaft |
| | **consultation** [ˌkɒnsl'teɪʃn] | Beratungsgespräch |
| | **risk-tolerant** [ˌrɪsk 'tɒlərənt] | risikobereit |
| | **scale** [skeɪl] | Skala, Maß(stab) |
| | **conservative** [kən'sɜːvətɪv] | konservativ |
| | **cautious** ['kɔːʃəs] | vorsichtig |
| | **balanced** ['bælənst] | ausgeglichen, ausgewogen |
| | **venturesome** ['ventʃəsəm] | wagemutig |
| | **speculative** ['spekjuleɪtɪv] | spekulativ |
| | **select** [sɪ'lekt] | auswählen |
| | **retire** [rɪ'taɪə] | in Rente/Pension gehen |
| | **mature** [mə'tʃʊə] | fällig werden |
| | **intend** [ɪn'tend] | beabsichtigen, vorhaben |
| | **consult** [kən'sʌlt] | um Rat fragen |
| | **inexperienced** [ˌɪnɪk'spɪəriənst] | unerfahren |
| | **tolerate** ['tɒləreɪt] | tolerieren |
| | **degree** [dɪ'griː] | Grad |
| | **prospect** ['prɒspekt] | Aussicht |
| | **equities (equity shares)** ['ekwətiz] | Aktien |
| 70t | **heart attack** ['hɑːt ətæk] | Herzinfarkt |
| | **go on** [ˌgəʊ 'ɒn] | weitergehen |
| | **manage on one's own** [ˌmænɪdʒ ɒn wʌnz 'əʊn] | alleine zurechtkommen |
| | **sole heir** [səʊl 'eə] | Alleinerbe/-erbin |
| | **estate** [ɪ'steɪt] | (Grund-)Besitz |
| | **be provided for** [bɪ prə'vaɪdɪd fə] | versorgt sein |
| | **widow** ['wɪdəʊ] | Witwe |
| | **civil service** [ˌsɪvl 'sɜːvɪs] | öffentlicher Dienst |
| | **running costs** [ˌrʌnɪŋ 'kɒsts] | laufende Kosten |
| | **foul** [faʊl] | scheußlich |
| | **ballpark figure** [ˌbɔːlpɑːk 'fɪgə] | grobe Schätzung |
| 71 | **tax on investment earnings** [tæks ɒn ɪn'vestmənt ɜːnɪŋz] | Zinsabschlagsteuer |
| | **earnings** ['ɜːnɪŋz] | Einkünfte |
| | **savers' tax-free allowance** [ˌseɪvəz ˌtæks friː ə'laʊəns] | Sparerfreibetrag |
| | **tax-free allowance** [ˌtæks friː ə'laʊəns] | Steuerfreibetrag |
| | **mediate** ['miːdieɪt] | vermitteln |

| | | |
|---|---|---|
| 72 | **divide** [dɪ'vaɪd] | (unter)teilen |
| | **EXTRA MATERIALS** | |
| 73 | **ethical** ['eθɪkl] | moralisch vertretbar, ethisch |
| | **ethically-minded** ['eθɪkli maɪndɪd] | ethisch ausgerichtet |
| | **be worth it** [bi 'wɜːθ ɪt] | sich lohnen |
| | **in the face of** [ɪn ðə 'feɪs əv] | angesichts |
| | **tremendous** [trɪ'mendəs] | gewaltig |
| | **threaten** ['θretn] | bedrohen |
| | **environment** [ɪn'vaɪrənmənt] | Umwelt |
| | **tend to** ['tend tə] | tendieren zu, dazu neigen |
| | **impact** ['ɪmpækt] | (Aus-)Wirkung |
| | **widespread** ['waɪdspred] | weit verbreitet |
| | **issue** ['ɪʃuː] | Frage, Thema |
| | **responsible** [rɪ'spɒnsəbl] | verantwortlich |
| | **ecological** [ˌiːkə'lɒdʒɪkl] | ökologisch |
| | **oriented** ['ɔːriəntɪd] | ausgerichtet, orientiert |
| | **be concerned with** [bi kən'sɜːnd wɪð] | sich befassen mit |
| | **environmental** [ɪnˌvaɪrən'mentl] | Umwelt- |
| | **welfare** ['welfeə] | Wohlergehen |
| | **environmental footprint** [ɪnˌvaɪrənˌmentl 'fʊtprɪnt] | Öko-Bilanz |
| | **latter** ['lætə] | letzte(r,s) |
| | **exclude** [ɪk'skluːd] | ausschließen |
| | **pollute** [pə'luːt] | verschmutzen |
| | **manufacturer** [ˌmænju'fæktʃərə] | Hersteller/in |
| | **priority** [praɪ'ɒrəti] | Priorität |
| | **screen out** [ˌskriːn 'aʊt] | ausschließen |
| | **arms** [ɑːmz] | Waffen, Rüstungs- |
| | **exploit** [ɪk'splɔɪt] | ausbeuten |
| | **developing country** [dɪˌveləpɪŋ 'kʌntri] | Entwicklungsland |
| | **animal testing** ['ænɪml testɪŋ] | Tierversuche |
| | **pharmaceutical** [ˌfɑːmə'suːtɪkl] | pharmazeutisch |
| | **enterprise** ['entəpraɪz] | Unternehmen |
| | **cotton** ['kɒtn] | Baumwolle |
| | **grain** [greɪn] | Getreide |
| | **bio-fuel** ['baɪəu fjuːəl] | Bio-Kraftstoff |
| | **starving** ['stɑːvɪŋ] | (ver)hungernd |
| | **strict** [strɪkt] | streng |
| | **ethics** ['eθɪks] | Ethik |

| | | |
|---|---|---|
| | **sacrifice** ['sækrɪfaɪs] | opfern |
| | **morality** [mə'ræləti] | Moral |
| | **repeatedly** [rɪ'piːtɪdli] | wiederholt |
| | **concern** [kən'sɜːn] | Anliegen |
| | **legislation** [ˌledʒɪs'leɪʃn] | Gesetzgebung |
| | **benefit** ['benɪfɪt] | zugute kommen |
| | **predict** [prɪ'dɪkt] | vorhersagen |
| | **concept** ['kɒnsept] | Konzept |
| | **sustainable** [sə'steɪnəbl] | nachhaltig |
| | **UNIT 7** | |
| 74 | **do without** [ˌduː wɪ'ðaʊt] | verzichten auf, auskommen ohne |
| | **bureau** ['bjʊərəʊ] | Agentur |
| | **accurate** ['ækjərət] | genau, korrekt |
| 75 | **home improvements** [ˌhəʊm ɪm'pruːvmənts] | Renovierungsarbeiten |
| | **consolidate** [kɒn'sɒlɪdeɪt] | konsolidieren, zusammenlegen |
| | **approve** [ə'pruːv] | genehmigen |
| | **set** [set] | fest |
| | **competitive** [kəm'petətɪv] | konkurrenzfähig |
| | **Annual Percentage Rate (APR)** [ˌænjuəl pə'sentɪdʒ reɪt, ˌeɪ ɑː 'piː] | effektiver Jahreszinssatz |
| | **arrangement fee** [ə'reɪndʒmənt fiː] | Bearbeitungsgebühr |
| | **borrower** ['bɒrəʊə] | Kreditnehmer/in |
| | **security (no plur.)** [sɪ'kjʊərəti] | Kreditsicherheiten |
| | **peace of mind** [piːs əv 'maɪnd] | Sorgenfreiheit |
| | **unemployed** [ˌʌnɪm'plɔɪd] | arbeitslos |
| | **through no fault of your own** [θruː nəʊ ˌfɔːlt əv jɔːr 'əʊn] | unverschuldet |
| | **pass away** [ˌpɑːs ə'weɪ] | versterben |
| 76 | **average** ['ævərɪdʒ] | durchschnittlich |
| | **expenditure (sing. only)** [ɪk'spendɪtʃə] | Ausgabe(n) |
| 77 | **clause** [klɔːz] | Satzteil |
| 78 | **vacation (AE)** [və'keɪʃn] | Urlaub |
| | **for instance** [fə'rɪnstəns] | zum Beispiel |
| | **lower** ['ləʊə] | herabsetzen |
| | **significant** [sɪg'nɪfɪkənt] | bedeutend |
| | **reflect** [rɪ'flekt] | spiegeln |
| | **subject to** ['sʌbdʒekt tə] | vorausgesetzt |
| | **approval** [ə'pruːvl] | Genehmigung |

79 **handling charge** ['hændlɪŋ tʃɑ:dʒ] Bearbeitungsgebühr

80 **credit history** ['kredɪt hɪstri] bisheriges Kredit-/Zahlungsverhalten
**take a break from** [teɪk ə 'breɪk frəm] unterbrechen
**freelance** ['fri:lɑ:ns] freiberuflich
**lender** ['lendə] Kreditgeber/in
**influence** ['ɪnfluəns] beeinflussen

81 **amount to** [ə'maʊnt tə] betragen
**total** ['təʊtl] sich belaufen auf
**roughly** ['rʌfli] ungefähr
**average** ['ævərɪdʒ] durchschnittlich betragen
**on average** [ɒn 'ævərɪdʒ] im Durchschnitt
**apply the criteria** [əˌplaɪ ðə kraɪ'tɪəriə] die Kriterien anwenden
**creditworthiness** ['kredɪtwɜ:ðinəs] Kreditwürdigkeit
**prospective** [prə'spektɪv] voraussichtlich

81t **from … onwards** [frəm 'ɒnwədz] von … an
**net salary** ['net sæləri] Nettogehalt
**(regular) commitment** [ˌregjələ kə'mɪtmənt] regelmäßige Verpflichtung
**(joint) disposable income** [dʒɔɪnt dɪˌspəʊzəbl 'ɪnkʌm] verfügbares Einkommen
**bargain** ['bɑ:gɪn] Schnäppchen, Gelegenheit
**dinghy** ['dɪŋɪ] Jolle
**cash in** [ˌkæʃ 'ɪn] hier: verkaufen
**figure** ['fɪgə] Zahl
**living expenses (pl. only)** [ˌlɪvɪŋ ɪk'spensɪz] Lebenskosten
**paid off** [ˌpeɪd 'ɒf] abbezahlt
**maintenance** ['meɪntənəns] Unterhalt
**pack sth in (coll.)** [ˌpæk 'ɪn] hinschmeißen
**start out on one's own** [ˌstɑ:t aʊt ɒn wʌnz əʊn] sich selbstständig machen

82 **profile** ['prəʊfaɪl] Profil, Beschreibung
**creditworthy** ['kredɪtwɜ:ði] kreditwürdig
**estimate** ['estɪmeɪt] (ein)schätzen
**dispose of** [dɪ'spəʊz əv] verfügen über

83 **assignment** [ə'saɪnmənt] Abtretung
**assignment by bill of sale** [ə'saɪnmənt baɪ ˌbɪl əv 'seɪl] Sicherungsübereignung
**land-charge** ['lændtʃɑ:dʒ] Grundschuld
**guaranty** ['gærənti:] Bürgschaft
**pledge** [pledʒ] Pfand
**lien** ['li:ən] Pfandrecht
**be liable** [bi 'laɪəbl] haften
**vehicle** ['vi:əkl] Fahrzeug
**machinery** [mə'ʃi:nəri] Maschinen(park)
**valuable** ['væljuəbl] wertvoll, Wert-
**jewellery** ['dʒu:əlri] Schmuck
**title document** [ˌtaɪtl 'dɒkjumənt] Traditionspapier
**warehouse** ['weəhaʊs] Lager(haus)
**secure** [sɪ'kjuə] sichern
**property** ['prɒpəti] Immobilie, Grundeigentum
**extension** [ɪk'stenʃn] Erweiterung, Anbau
**register** ['redʒɪstə] eintragen lassen
**valued at** ['vælju:d ət] bewertet mit
**worth** [wɜ:θ] im Wert von
**pledge** [pledʒ] pfänden
**renovation** [ˌrenə'veɪʃn] Renovierung
**assign** [ə'saɪn] abtreten
**life assurance** ['laɪf əʃʊərəns] Lebensversicherung
**antique** [æn'ti:k] Antiquität

84 **unwise** [ˌʌn'waɪz] unklug
**caption** ['kæpʃn] Bildunterschrift
**beware of** [bɪ'weər əv] Vorsicht vor
**co-sign** [ˌkəʊ 'saɪn] mitunterzeichnen
**budget** ['bʌdʒɪt] haushalten, wirtschaften

## EXTRA MATERIALS

85 **redundant** [rɪ'dʌndənt] arbeitslos
**owe** [əʊ] schulden
**single parent** [ˌsɪŋgl 'peərənt] Alleinerziehende/r
**in arrears** [ɪn ə'rɪəz] im Rückstand
**set up** [ˌset 'ʌp] gründen
**go bankrupt** [gəʊ 'bæŋkrʌpt] in Konkurs gehen
**divorce** [dɪ'vɔ:s] Scheidung
**supplier** [sə'plaɪə] Lieferant
**accrued** [ə'kru:d] aufgelaufen

## UNIT 8

86 **home ownership** [həʊm 'əʊnəʃɪp] Wohneigentum
**realty (US)** ['ri:əlti] Immobilie
**ladder** ['lædə] Leiter
**move (home)** [mu:v 'həʊm] umziehen

| | | |
|---|---|---|
| | **bedroomed** ['bedru:md] | mit Schlafzimmern |
| 87 | **rent** [rent] | mieten |
| | **savings and loan association (US)** [ˌseɪvɪŋz ən ˌləʊn əˌsəʊsi'eɪʃn] | Bausparkasse |
| | **release** [rɪ'li:s] | Freigabe |
| | **valuation point** [vælju'eɪʃn pɔɪnt] | Bewertungspunkt |
| 88t | **grant** [grɑ:nt] | gewähren, bewilligen |
| 89 | **occupant** ['ɒkjəpənt] | Bewohner/in |
| | **heading** ['hedɪŋ] | Überschrift |
| | **compete** [kəm'pi:t] | konkurrieren |
| 90 | **solicitor's fee** [sə'lɪsɪtəz fi:] | Anwaltskosten, Notargebühr |
| | **commission** [kə'mɪʃn] | Provision, Gebühr |
| | **deposit** [dɪ'pɒzɪt] | Eigengeld |
| | **sense** [sens] | Sinn |
| | **term deposit account** [ˌtɜ:m dɪ'pɒzɪt əkaʊnt] | Festgeldkonto |
| 91 | **eligible** ['elɪdʒəbl] | anspruchsberechtigt |
| | **commitment** [kə'mɪtmənt] | Verpflichtung, Verbindlichkeit |
| | **liability insurance** [ˌlaɪə'bɪləti ɪnʃʊərəns] | Haftpflicht-versicherung |
| | **uncountable** [ˌʌn'kaʊntəbl] | unzählbar |
| 92 | **interruption** [ˌɪntə'rʌpʃn] | Unterbrechung |
| 93 | **property loan** ['prɒpəti ləʊn] | Baudarlehen |
| | **endowment insurance** [ɪn'daʊmənt ɪnʃʊərəns] | Kapitalversicherung |
| | **repayment loan** [rɪ'peɪmənt ləʊn] | Annuitätsdarlehen |
| | **interest-only loan** ['ɪntrəst əʊnli ləʊn] | endfälliges Darlehen |
| | **take possession of** [teɪk pə'zeʃn əv] | in Besitz nehmen |
| 94 | **shortfall** ['ʃɔ:tfɔ:l] | Deckungslücke |
| | **be on track to** [bi ɒn 'træk tə] | auf dem (richtigen) Weg sein |
| | **colour coded** ['kʌlə kəʊdɪd] | farblich gekenn-zeichnet |
| | **fall short** [ˌfɔ:l 'ʃɔ:t] | nicht reichen |
| | **panic** ['pænɪk] | in Panik geraten |
| | **steer clear of** [stɪə 'klɪər əv] | einen Bogen machen um |
| | **broker** ['brəʊkə] | Makler/in |
| | **route** [ru:t] | Weg |
| | **underperform** [ˌʌndəpə'fɔ:m] | sein Ziel verfehlen |

## EXTRA MATERIALS

| | | |
|---|---|---|
| 95 | **beneficiary** [ˌbenɪ'fɪʃəri] | Begünstigte/r |
| | **insure** [ɪn'ʃʊə] | versichern |
| | **on maturity** [ɒn mə'tʃʊərəti] | bei Fälligkeit |
| | **surrender value** [sə'rendə vælju:] | Rückkaufswert |
| | **accumulate** [ə'kju:mjəleɪt] | (sich) ansammeln |
| | **annuity assurance** [əˌnju:əti ə'ʃʊərəns] | als Rente auszahlbare Kapitalversiche-rung |

## UNIT 9

| | | |
|---|---|---|
| 96 | **face** [feɪs] | konfrontiert werden mit |
| | **Middle-Eastern** [ˌmɪdl 'i:stən] | aus dem Nahen Osten |
| | **be patient** [bi 'peɪʃnt] | Geduld haben |
| | **hospitality** [ˌhɒspɪ'tæləti] | Gastfreundschaft |
| | **incompetent** [ɪn'kɒmpɪtənt] | inkompetent, unfähig |
| | **embarrassing** [ɪm'bærəsɪŋ] | peinlich |
| | **upside-down** [ˌʌpsaɪd 'daʊn] | verkehrt herum |
| 97 | **customized** ['kʌstəmaɪzd] | auf den Kunden zugeschnitten |
| | **ex-pat (= expatriate)** [ˌeks 'pæt] | im Ausland Lebende/r |
| | **foreign exchange (sing. only)** [ˌfɒrən ɪks'tʃeɪndʒ] | Devisen(geschäfte) |
| | **round-table discussion** [ˌraʊnd teɪbl dɪ'skʌʃn] | Diskussionsrunde |
| | **syndicated loan** ['sɪndɪkeɪtɪd ləʊn] | Konsortialkredit |
| | **turnover** ['tɜ:nəʊvə] | Umsatz |
| | **standardize** ['stændədaɪz] | standardisieren |
| | **documentary credit** [ˌdɒkju'mentri kredɪt] | (Dokumenten) akkreditiv |
| | **treasury services** ['treʒəri sɜ:vɪsɪz] | Finanzdienst-leistungen |
| | **structured** ['strʌktʃəd] | strukturiert |
| | **takeover** ['teɪkəʊvə] | Übernahme |
| | **merger** ['mɜ:dʒə] | Fusion |
| | **market** ['mɑ:kɪt] | vermarkten |
| | **tent** [tent] | Zelt |

| | | |
|---|---|---|
| 98 | **balance (sheet)** ['bæləns ʃi:t] | Bilanz |
| | **privately-owned** ['praɪvətli əʊnd] | im Privatbesitz |
| | **manufacturing company** [ˌmænjʊ'fæktʃərɪŋ kʌmpəni] | Herstellerfirma |
| | **omit** [ə'mɪt] | weglassen |
| | **assets** ['æsets] | Aktiva, Vermögen(swerte) |
| | **non-current assets** [ˌnɒn kʌrənt 'æsets] | Anlagevermögen |
| | **goodwill** [ˌgʊd'wɪl] | immaterielle Vermögenswerte, Goodwill |
| | **fixed assets** [fɪkst 'æsets] | Sachanlagevermögen |
| | **tool** [tu:l] | Werkzeug |
| | **current assets** [ˌkʌrənt 'æsets] | Umlaufvermögen |
| | **inventory** ['ɪnvəntri] | Inventar, Waren- und Lagerbestand |
| | **accounts receivable** [əˌkaʊnts rɪ'si:vəbl] | Forderungen |
| | **cash equivalents** [kæʃ ɪ'kwɪvələnts] | Zahlungsmittel-equivalente |
| | **cash** [kæʃ] | Zahlungsmittel |
| | **liabilities** [ˌlaɪə'bɪlətiz] | Passiva, Verbindlichkeiten |
| | **retained earnings** [rɪˌteɪnd 'ɜ:nɪŋz] | Rücklagen |
| | **short-term** [ˌʃɔ:t 'tɜ:m] | kurzfristig |
| | **accounts payable** [əˌkaʊnts 'peɪəbl] | Verbindlichkeiten (an Lieferanten) |
| | **provisions** [prə'vɪʒnz] | Rückstellungen |
| | **equivalent** [ɪ'kwɪvələnt] | Entsprechung, Gegenstück |
| | **reputation** [ˌrepju'teɪʃn] | Ruf |
| | **creditor** ['kredɪtə] | Gläubiger/in |
| | **raw material** [ˌrɔ: mə'tɪəriəl] | Rohstoff |
| | **in progress** [ɪn 'prəʊgres] | in Arbeit |
| | **write off** [ˌraɪt 'ɒf] | abschreiben |
| 99 | **measure** ['meʒə] | messen |
| | **liquidity** [lɪ'kwɪdəti] | Liquidität |
| | **closure** ['kləʊʒə] | Schließung |
| | **entrepreneur** [ˌɒntrəprə'nɜ:] | Unternehmer/in |
| | **go into liquidation** [ˌgəʊ ɪntə ˌlɪkwɪ'deɪʃn] | Konkurs anmelden, abgewickelt werden |
| | **found** [faʊnd] | gründen |
| | **recruit** [rɪ'kru:t] | (Personal) einstellen, rekrutieren |
| | **overheads** ['əʊvəhedz] | Betriebskosten |
| | **wage(s)** ['weɪdʒɪz] | Lohn |
| | **resist** [rɪ'zɪst] | widerstehen |
| | **temptation** [temp'teɪʃn] | Versuchung |
| | **expand** [ɪk'spænd] | expandieren |
| | **employ** [ɪm'plɔɪ] | beschäftigen |
| | **accountant** [ə'kaʊntənt] | Buchhalter/in |
| | **book-keeping** ['bʊkki:pɪŋ] | Buchhaltung, Buchführung |
| | **bad debts** [ˌbæd 'dets] | faule, uneinbringliche Forderungen |
| | **fail** [feɪl] | versäumen |
| | **commercial** [kə'mɜ:ʃl] | Handels- |
| | **legal** ['li:gl] | juristisch, rechtlich |
| | **public limited company (plc)** [ˌpʌblɪk ˌlɪmɪtɪd 'kʌmpəni] | Aktiengesellschaft (AG) |
| | **limited company (Ltd)** [ˌlɪmɪtɪd 'kʌmpəni] | Kapitalgesellschaft (KG), Gesellschaft mit beschränkter Haftung (GmbH) |
| 100 | **cf.** [kəm'peə] | vgl. |
| | **rail travel** ['reɪl trævl] | Schienenverkehr |
| | **healthcare** ['helθkeə] | Gesundheitswesen |
| | **retail outlet** ['ri:teɪl aʊtlet] | Einzelhandelsgeschäft |
| | **leisure facility** [ˌleʒə fə'sɪləti] | Freizeiteinrichtung |
| 101 | **temporary** ['temprəri] | vorübergehend |
| 102 | **seize** [si:z] | ergreifen |
| | **arise** [ə'raɪz] | aufkommen |
| | **put sb in charge of sth** [ˌpʊt ɪn 'tʃɑ:dʒ əv] | jdm die Verantwortung für etw übertragen |
| | **access** ['ækses] | Zugang haben zu |
| | **favourable** ['feɪvərəbl] | günstig |
| | **in the long run** [ɪn ðə lɒŋ 'rʌn] | auf lange Sicht |
| | **regardless of** [rɪ'gɑ:dləs əv] | unabhängig von |
| | **buy in bulk** [baɪ ɪn 'bʌlk] | in großen Mengen kaufen |
| | **force** [fɔ:s] | zwingen |
| 103 | **concession** [kən'seʃn] | Zugeständnis, Konzession |
| | **work placement** ['wɜ:k pleɪsmənt] | Praktikum |
| | **setback** ['setbæk] | Rückschlag |
| | **set up a business** [ˌset ʌp ə 'bɪznəs] | eine Firma gründen |
| | **trust** [trʌst] | Stiftung |

| | | |
|---|---|---|
| 103t | **legal department** [ˌliːgl dɪ'pɑːtmənt] | Rechtsabteilung |
| | **run a business** [ˌrʌn ə 'bɪznəs] | ein Unternehmen führen |
| | **bankrupt** ['bæŋkrʌpt] | bankrott |
| 104 | **rights issue** ['raɪts ɪʃuː] | Bezugsrechtsemission |
| | **raise capital** [reɪz 'kæpɪtl] | Kapital aufbringen |
| | **new shares** [njuː 'ʃeəz] | junge Aktien |
| | **at a discount** [ət ə 'dɪskaʊnt] | mit Rabatt |
| | **share price** ['ʃeə praɪs] | Aktienkurs |
| | **shareholder** ['ʃeəhəʊldə] | Aktionär/in, Anteilseigner/in |
| | **massive** ['mæsɪv] | riesig |
| | **reveal** [rɪ'viːl] | enthüllen |
| | **underwrite** [ˌʌndə'raɪt] | garantieren |
| | **sentiment** ['sentɪmənt] | Stimmung |
| | **housing market** ['haʊzɪŋ mɑːkɪt] | Immobilienmarkt |
| | **deteriorate** [dɪ'tɪəriəreɪt] | sich verschlechtern |
| | **amid** [ə'mɪd] | inmitten, unter |
| | **at par** [ət 'pɑː] | zum Nennwert, zu pari |
| | **federal state** [ˌfedərəl 'steɪt] | Bundesland |
| | **lead manager** [liːd 'mænɪdʒə] | Konsortialführer |
| | **rate** [reɪt] | benoten, bewerten |
| | **expansion** [ɪk'spænʃn] | Expansion |

## EXTRA MATERIALS

| | | |
|---|---|---|
| 105 | **initial public offering (IPO)** [ɪˌnɪʃl ˌpʌblɪk 'ɒfərɪŋ, ˌaɪ piː 'əʊ] | Börsengang |
| | **tepid** ['tepɪd] | lauwarm |
| | **bull run** ['bʊl rʌn] | Hausseperiode |
| | **debut** ['deɪbjuː] | Start |
| | **trading** ['treɪdɪŋ] | (Börsen-)Handel |
| | **bull market** ['bʊl mɑːkɪt] | Hausse |
| | **railroad** ['reɪlrəʊd] | Eisenbahn |
| | **factor in** ['fæktər ɪn] | einpreisen |
| | **lackluster (AE)** ['læklʌstə] | glanzlos |
| | **stock listing** ['stɒk lɪstɪŋ] | Börsennotierung |
| | **signal** ['sɪgnəl] | signalisieren |
| | **bearish** ['beərɪʃ] | sinkend, zur Baisse tendierend |

## UNIT 10

| | | |
|---|---|---|
| 106 | **globalization** [ˌgləʊbəlaɪ'zeɪʃn] | Globalisierung |
| | **phenomenon** [fə'nɒmɪnən] | Phänomen |
| | **effect** [ɪ'fekt] | (Aus-)Wirkung |
| 107 | **clarify** ['klærəfaɪ] | klären |
| | **specific** [spə'sɪfɪk] | genau, präzise |
| | **chair** [tʃeə] | moderieren |
| | **chairperson** ['tʃeəpɜːsn] | Moderator/in |
| | **volume** ['vɒljuːm] | Volumen, Umfang |
| | **payment on open account** [ˌpeɪmənt ɒn ˌəʊpən ə'kaʊnt] | Zahlung gegen Rechnung (mit offenem Zahlungsziel) |
| | **payment in advance** [ˌpeɪmənt ɪn əd'vɑːns] | Zahlung im Voraus |
| | **dispatch** [dɪ'spætʃ] | versenden, abschicken |
| | **invoice** ['ɪnvɔɪs] | Rechnung |
| | **release** [rɪ'liːs] | freigeben |
| | **bill of exchange** [ˌbɪl əv ɪks'tʃeɪndʒ] | Wechsel |
| 108 | **foreign trade** [ˌfɒrən 'treɪd] | Außenhandel |
| | **industrial glue** [ɪnˌdʌstriəl 'gluː] | Industrieklebstoff(e) |
| | **sample** ['sɑːmpl] | Muster, Probe |
| | **enquire** [ɪn'kwaɪə] | (an)fragen, sich erkundigen |
| | **ship** [ʃɪp] | verschiffen, versenden |
| | **collection of documents** [kəˌekʃn əv 'dɒkjumənts] | Dokumenteninkasso |
| | **shipping** ['ʃɪpɪŋ] | Versand, Fracht |
| | **bill of lading** [ˌbɪl əv 'leɪdɪŋ] | Konnossement |
| | **certificate of origin** [səˌtɪfɪkət əv 'ɒrɪdʒɪn] | Ursprungszeugnis |
| | **packing list** ['pækɪŋ lɪst] | Packliste |
| | **freight forwarder** ['freɪt fɔːwədə] | Spediteur/in |
| | **after sight** [ˌɑːftə 'saɪt] | nach Sicht |
| | **letter of credit** [ˌletər əv 'kredɪt] | Akkreditiv |
| | **terms of payment** [ˌtɜːmz əv 'peɪmənt] | Zahlungsbedingungen |
| 109 | **dislike** [dɪs'laɪk] | nicht mögen |
| | **involve** [ɪn'vɒlv] | einschließen, beinhalten |
| | **in italics** [ɪn ɪ'tælɪks] | kursiv |
| | **consist of** [kən'sɪst əv] | bestehen aus |

110 **shipper** ['ʃɪpə] Absender, Verschiffer
**consignee** [ˌkɒnsaɪ'ni:] (Waren-)Empfänger, Adressat
**irrevocable** [ɪ'revəkəbl] unwiderruflich
**advise** [əd'vaɪz] avisieren
**in favour of** [ɪn 'feɪvər əv] zugunsten von
**be conform with** [bi kən'fɔ:m wɪð] entsprechen
**forward** ['fɔ:wəd] senden

111 **offend** [ə'fend] beleidigen
**resolve** [rɪ'zɒlv] lösen
**read between the lines** [ri:d bɪˌtwi:n ðə 'laɪnz] zwischen den Zeilen lesen
**implicit** [ɪm'plɪsɪt] stillschweigend, unausgesprochen
**chemicals** ['kemɪklz] Chemikalien
**destination** [ˌdestɪ'neɪʃn] Bestimmungsort, Endziel
**dispatch** [dɪ'spætʃ] Versand
**loading** ['ləʊdɪŋ] Verladung
**discharge** ['dɪstʃɑ:dʒ] Entladung, Löschung
**shipment** ['ʃɪpmənt] Verschiffung, (Schiffs-)Ladung
**vessel** ['vesl] Schiff
**consignment** [kən'saɪnmənt] (Waren-)Sendung, Lieferung, Frachtgut

111t **contract of sale** [ˌkɒntrækt əv 'seɪl] Kaufvertrag
**examine** [ɪg'zæmɪn] prüfen
**bear the charges** [beə ðə 'tʃɑ:dʒɪz] die Gebühren tragen

112 **receipt** [rɪ'si:t] Quittung, Beleg
**quay** [ki:] Kai
**multi-modal transport** [ˌmʌlti məʊdl 'trænspɔ:t] Transport mit verschiedenen Verkehrsmitteln
**specify** ['spesɪfaɪ] angeben, festlegen
**visible** ['vɪzəbl] sichtbar
**damage** ['dæmɪdʒ] Schaden, Schäden
**set** [set] Satz
**forwarding agent** ['fɔ:wədɪŋ eɪdʒənt] Spediteur/in
**negotiable** [nɪ'gəʊʃiəbl] übertragbar
**endorse** [ɪn'dɔ:s] indossieren
**transfer** [træns'fɜ:] übertragen
**damaged** ['dæmɪdʒd] beschädigt

113 **anxiety** [æŋ'zaɪəti] Besorgnis
**outlook** ['aʊtlʊk] Aussicht(en)
**sell-off** ['sel ɒf] Ausverkauf
**cause** [kɔ:z] veranlassen
**tumble** ['tʌmbl] purzeln
**across the board** [əˌkrɒs ðə 'bɔ:d] generell
**slump** [slʌmp] abstürzen
**halt** [hɔ:lt] anhalten
**dive** [daɪv] abstürzen
**slide** [slaɪd] abrutschen
**successive** [sək'sesɪv] aufeinander folgend
**session** ['seʃn] (Börsen)sitzung
**wipe** [waɪp] wischen
**slide** [slaɪd] Abrutschen
**plunge** [plʌndʒ] abtauchen
**sink** [sɪŋk] sinken
**Bund (German government bond)** ['gʌvənmənt bɒnd] deutsche Staatsanleihe
**Schatz (German treasury bond)** ['treʒəri bɒnd] deutscher Schatzbrief
**bottom out** [ˌbɒtəm 'aʊt] die Talsohle erreichen
**aside** [ə'saɪd] ausgenommen

115 **Islamic** [ɪz'læmɪk] islamisch
**compliant** [kəm'plaɪənt] konform
**prohibition** [ˌprəʊɪ'bɪʃn] Verbot
**teachings** ['ti:tʃɪŋz] Lehren
**means of exchange** [mi:nz əv ɪks'tʃeɪndʒ] Tauschmittel
**define** [dɪ'faɪn] definieren, festlegen
**generate** ['dʒenəreɪt] erzeugen, erwirtschaften
**ban** [bæn] Verbot
**gambling** ['gæmblɪŋ] Glücksspiel
**speculation** [ˌspekju'leɪʃn] Spekulation
**receiver** [rɪ'si:və] Empfänger/in
**venture** ['ventʃə] Unternehmen, Unterfangen
**non-refundable** [ˌnɒn rɪ'fʌndəbl] nicht rückerstattbar
**conclude** [kən'klu:d] abschließen
**nominal value** [ˌnɒmɪnl 'vælju:] Nennwert
**scholar** ['skɒlə] Gelehrte/r
**Muslim** ['mʊzlɪm] moslemisch

# A–Z word list

Diese Liste enthält alle Wörter in alphabetischer Reihenfolge. Hier sind jedoch die Wörter, die zum Basic Word List (siehe S. 170) gehören, nicht aufgeführt.

Die Zahl nach dem Stichwort bezieht sich auf die Seite, auf der das Wort zum ersten Mal erscheint.

t = das Wort befindet sich in den Transcripts (Hörverständnisübungen).

In der Liste werden folgende Abkürzungen verwendet:
pl. only = nur Plural
sing. only = nur Plural
coll. = umgangssprachlich
AE = Amerikanisches Englisch
BE = Britisches Englisch

## A

**abbreviation** *17* Abkürzung
**abroad** *24* im Ausland
**abrupt** *63* abrupt, plötzlich
**acceptance** *22* Annahme
**access** *102* Zugang haben zu
**access** *25* Zugang
**account** *9* Konto
**account holder** *19* Kontoinhaber/in
**account manager** *37t* Kundenbetreuer/in
**account statement** *27* Kontoauszug
**accountant** *99* Buchhalter/in
**accounts payable** *98* Verbindlichkeiten (an Lieferanten)
**accounts receivable** *98* Forderungen
**accrued** *85* aufgelaufen
**accumulate** *95* (sich) ansammeln
**accurate** *74* genau, korrekt
**across the board** *113* generell
**act** *24* spielen
**adapt** *48* adaptieren
**additional** *28* zusätzlich
**admit** *24* zugeben, gestehen
**advertisement** *6* Anzeige
**advertising** *25* Werbe-
**advice** *9* Beratung
**advisable** *64* ratsam
**advise** *110* avisieren
**advise** *13* beraten
**adviser** *7* Berater/in
**affect** *42* betreffen
**affect** *53* sich auswirken auf
**affluence** *37t* Wohlstand
**affluent** *25* wohlhabend
**afford** *34* (es) sich leisten (können)
**after sight** *108* nach Sicht
**agency** *19* Agentur, Büro
**agent** *43* handelnde Person
**agreed** *27* vereinbart
**agreement** *51* Zustimmung
**aim** *67* Ziel
**aim to** *61* zielen auf
**along with** *64* zusammen mit
**alter** *40t* ändern
**alter** *42* verändern
**ambassador** *24* Botschafter/in
**American Studies** *30* Amerikanistik
**amid** *104* inmitten, unter
**amount** *8* Betrag
**amount to** *81* betragen
**animal testing** *73* Tierversuche
**annoy** *16* ärgern, belästigen
**annual** *25* jährlich
**Annual Percentage Rate (APR)** *75* effektiver Jahreszinssatz
**annual saving** *28* jährliche Ersparnis
**annuity assurance** *95* als Rente auszahlbare Kapitalversicherung
**antique** *83* Antiquität
**anxiety** *113* Besorgnis
**applicant** *21* Antragsteller/in
**application** *19* Antrag
**apply** *61* anwenden
**apply for** *6* sich bewerben um, beantragen
**apply the criteria** *81* die Kriterien anwenden
**appointment** *8* Termin, Verabredung
**apprentice** *7* Lehrling, Auszubildende/r im Handwerk
**appropriate** *56* angemessen, zutreffend
**approval** *78* Genehmigung
**approve** *75* genehmigen
**area** *34* Gegend
**arise** *102* aufkommen
**arms** *73* Waffen, Rüstungs-
**arrangement fee** *75* Bearbeitungsgebühr
**aside** *113* ausgenommen
**assess** *70* beurteilen, schätzen
**asset-building** *56* vermögenswirksam
**assets** *98* Aktiva, Vermögen(swerte)
**assets** *51* Vermögen(swerte)
**assign** *83* abtreten
**assignment** *83* Abtretung
**assignment by bill of sale** *83* Sicherungsübereignung
**at a discount** *104* mit Rabatt
**at par** *104* zum Nennwert, zu pari
**attempt** *42* Versuch
**attract** *6* anwerben, gewinnen
**audience** *24* Publikum
**Australian** *44* australisch
**authorization** *41* Ermächtigung
**authorize** *39* ermächtigen
**automatic teller machine (ATM)** *8* Geldautomat
**available** *13* anwesend, zu sprechen
**average** *76* durchschnittlich
**avoid** *26* vermeiden
**award winning** *25* preisgekrönt
**awareness** *15* Bewusstsein

## B

**background** *51* Herkunft, Hintergrund
**backup** *28* abspeichern, sichern
**bad debts** *99* faule, uneinbringliche Forderungen
**baggage** *44* Gepäck
**balance (sheet)** *98* Bilanz
**balance** *27* Kontostand, Saldo
**balanced** *70* ausgeglichen, ausgewogen
**ballpark figure** *70t* grobe Schätzung
**ban** *115* Verbot
**bank sort code** *29* Bankleitzahl
**bankrupt** *103t* bankrott
**bar code** *48* Strichcode

**bargain** *81t* Schnäppchen, Gelegenheit
**base rate** *54* Leitzins(satz)
**basement** *9* Untergeschoss
**be concerned with** *73* sich befassen mit
**be conform with** *110* entsprechen
**be glad** *24* sich freuen
**be in debt** *45* verschuldet sein, Schulden haben
**be keen on** *67* auf etwas scharf sein
**be liable** *83* haften
**be of service** *25* dienlich sein
**be on track to** *94* auf dem (richtigen) Weg sein
**be patient** *96* Geduld haben
**be provided for** *70t* versorgt sein
**be short of** *58* zu wenig haben
**be worth it** *73* sich lohnen
**bear** *44* tragen
**bear the charges** *111t* die Gebühren tragen
**bearish** *105* sinkend, zur Baisse tendierend
**beat** *34* Streife, Runde
**beat** *64* übertreffen
**bedroomed** *86* mit Schlafzimmern
**beginning** *44* Anfang, Beginn
**be going on** *7* passieren
**behave** *48* sich verhalten, sich benehmen
**beneficiary** *95* Begünstigte/r
**benefit** *13t* Vorteil, zusätzliche Leistung
**benefit** *73* zugute kommen
**beware of** *84* Vorsicht vor
**bid price** *65* Kauf-, Geldkurs
**bill of exchange** *107* Wechsel
**bill of lading** *108* Konnossement
**bio-fuel** *73* Bio-Kraftstoff
**bond** *55* festverzinsliches Wertpapier, Anleihe
**book-keeping** *99* Buchhaltung, Buchführung
**borrower** *75* Kreditnehmer/in
**borrowing** *58* Kreditaufnahme
**bother about** *67* sich kümmern um
**bottom out** *113* die Talsohle erreichen
**branch** *7* Filiale, Zweigstelle
**branch manager** *7* Filialleiter/in
**brand** *24* Marke
**brochure** *22* Broschüre, Prospekt
**broker** *94* Makler/in
**budget** *84* haushalten, wirtschaften
**building society** *14* Bausparkasse
**building society policy** *12* Bausparvertrag
**bull market** *105* Hausse
**bull run** *105* Hausseperiode
**Bund (German government bond)** *113* deutsche Staatsanleihe
**bureau** *74* Agentur
**button** *39* Taste, Knopf
**buy in bulk** *102* in großen Mengen kaufen

## C

**campaign** *45* Kampagne
**cancel** *35* löschen, (hier: sperren)
**caption** *84* Bildunterschrift
**carry out** *16* aus-, durchführen
**cash** *98* Zahlungsmittel
**cash equivalents** *98* Zahlungsmittelequivalente
**cash in** *81t* hier: verkaufen
**cashier** *7* Kassierer/in
**Cashpoint (GB)** *27* Geldautomat
**casual** *37t* locker, salopp
**catch sb's eye** *34* jds Aufmerksamkeit erregen
**cause** *113* veranlassen
**cautious** *70* vorsichtig
**celebrity** *24* Prominente/r, Berühmtheit
**certain** *25* bestimmt
**certificate** *19* Urkunde, Bescheinigung
**certificate of exemption** *61* Nichtveranlagungsbescheinigung
**certificate of origin** *108* Ursprungszeugnis
**cf.** *100* vgl.
**chair** *107* moderieren
**chairperson** *107* Moderator/in
**charge** *16* Kosten, Gebühr
**charge** *30* berechnen
**charity** *24* Wohltätigkeit, wohltätiger Zweck
**chart** *15* Karte, (Wand-)Bild
**checking account (AE)** *30* Gehaltskonto, Girokonto
**chemicals** *111* Chemikalien
**cheque (BE), check (AE)** *30* Scheck
**cheque book** *27* Scheckheft
**Chief Executive Officer (CEO)** *58* Vorstandsvorsitzende/r
**chip and PIN** *42* Chip und Geheimzahl
**civil service** *70t* öffentlicher Dienst
**claim** *24* behaupten, erklären, einziehen
**clarify** *107* klären
**clause** *77* Satzteil
**cleared** *34* leer (geräumt)
**clerk** *7* kaufmännische/r Angestellte/r
**close down** *58* schließen
**closure** *99* Schließung
**clue** *48* Hinweis
**collaboration** *47* Zusammenarbeit
**colleague** *9* Kollege / Kollegin
**collection of documents** *108* Dokumenteninkasso
**colour coded** *94* farblich gekennzeichnet
**combi-card** *47* Kombi-Karte
**comfortable** *58* wohl
**comment on** *36* kommentieren
**commercial** *99* Handels-
**commission** *90* Provision, Gebühr
**(regular) commitment** *81t* regelmäßige Verpflichtung
**communicate** *35* übermitteln
**company pension** *62* betriebliche Altersversorgung
**compare** *21* vergleichen
**comparison** *19* Vergleich
**compensation** *59* Entschädigung
**compensation scheme** *58* Einlagensicherungsfonds
**compete** *89* konkurrieren
**competition** *52* Konkurrenz, Wettbewerb
**competitive** *37t* konkurrenzbetont, umkämpft, konkurrenzfähig

**complain** *58* sich beklagen
**compliant** *115* konform
**concept** *73* Konzept
**concern** *73* Anliegen
**concession** *103* Zugeständnis, Konzession
**conclude** *16* schließen, folgern, abschließen
**conclusion** *14* (Schluss-) Folgerung
**confirm** *39* bestätigen
**congratulate** *22* beglückwünschen
**connect to** *17* verbinden mit
**consecutive** *42* aufeinander folgend
**consequence** *15* Folge, Konsequenz
**conservative** *70* konservativ
**consider** *66* erwägen, sich überlegen
**consignee** *110* (Waren-) Empfänger, Adressat
**consignment** *111* (Waren-) Sendung, Lieferung, Frachtgut
**consist of** *109* bestehen aus
**consolidate** *75* konsolidieren, zusammenlegen
**constant** *63* konstant, stetig
**consult** *70* um Rat fragen
**consultation** *70* Beratungsgespräch
**consumer** *47* Verbraucher/in
**contain** *42* enthalten
**contents** *38* Inhalt
**contract of sale** *111t* Kaufvertrag
**contribute** *24* beitragen
**contribution** *62* Beitrag
**convenience** *47* Annehmlichkeit
**convenient** *13* passend
**cooperate with** *14* zusammenarbeiten mit
**corporate** *9* Firmen-
**corporate bond** *65* Unternehmensanleihe, Obligation
**corporation (US)** *17* (Aktien-)Gesellschaft, Konzern
**co-sign** *84* mitunterzeichnen
**cotton** *73* Baumwolle
**counter** *61* entgegenwirken
**counter** *7* Schalter
**(a) couple of** *34* ein paar
**coupled with** *24* verbunden mit
**coupon** *65* Zinssatz (eines festverzinslichen Wertpapiers)
**cover** *45* decken
**(insurance) cover** *28* Deckung
**crash** *32* abstürzen
**credit** *29* gutschreiben
**credit (entry)** *29* Gutschrift
**credit history** *80* bisheriges Kredit-/Zahlungsverhalten
**credit interest** *27* Guthabenzinsen
**credit transfer** *30* Überweisung
**creditor** *98* Gläubiger/in
**creditworthiness** *81* Kreditwürdigkeit
**creditworthy** *82* kreditwürdig
**crime** *34* Verbrechen
**criteria** *25* Kriterien
**cross sb's mind** *66* in den Sinn kommen
**cross-border** *61* grenzüberschreitend
**current** *29* derzeitig
**current account** *12* Girokonto, Kontokorrentkonto
**current assets** *98* Umlaufvermögen
**customized** *97* auf den Kunden zugeschnitten

## D

**d'you** *66* – do you
**damage** *112* Schaden, Schäden
**damage** *34* beschädigen
**damaged** *112* beschädigt
**damaged** *13t* geschädigt
**dash** *18* Bindestrich, Minus-Zeichen
**date of birth** *21* Geburtsdatum
**date of expiry** *21* Ablaufdatum
**date of issue** *21* Ausstellungsdatum
**deal with people** *37t* mit Menschen umgehen
**debit** *29* abbuchen, belasten
**debit (entry)** *29* Abbuchung, Belastung
**debit card** *12* Bankkarte, ec-Karte
**debut** *105* Start
**decide** *15* (sich) entscheiden
**decimal** *50* Dezimalzahl, -stelle
**decipher** *47* entziffern, lesen
**declaration** *19* Erklärung
**declare** *22* erklären
**decline** *63* Rückgang; sinken
**decrease** *51* abnehmen
**deduct** *47* abziehen, abbuchen
**default** *58* zahlungsunfähig werden
**define** *115* definieren, festlegen
**definitely** *32* genau
**degree** *70* Grad
**delivery** *42* Zustellung
**demand** *68* Nachfrage
**denomination** *44* Nennwert
**denominations (pl.)** *44* Stückelung
**deposit bond (BE)** *55* Festgeldkonto, Termingeldkonto
**deposit** *27* Einzahlung, einzahlen, Einlage, Eigengeld
**deputy** *32* stellvertretend
**destination** *111* Bestimmungsort, Endziel
**details** *19* Daten
**detection** *48* Entdeckung
**deteriorate** *104* sich verschlechtern
**determine** *62* bestimmen
**developing country** *73* Entwicklungsland
**development** *25* Entwicklung
**device** *35* Vorrichtung, Gerät
**diary** *13t* Kalender
**digit** *18* einstellige Zahl, Ziffer
**dinghy** *81t* Jolle
**direct debit** *27* Einzug(sverfahren), Lastschrift
**disagree** *52* nicht zustimmen
**disagreement** *51* Widerspruch
**discharge** *111* Entladung, Löschung
**discounted** *28* ermäßigt
**dislike** *109* nicht mögen
**dispatch** *107* versenden, abschicken, Versand
**display** *43* (an)zeigen
**(joint) disposable income** *81t* verfügbares Einkommen
**dispose of** *82* verfügen über
**distribute** *51* verteilen
**distribution** *51* Verteilung
**dive** *113* abstürzen

**diversified** *67* diversifiziert, breit gestreut
**divide** *72* (unter)teilen
**dividend** *61* Dividende
**divorce** *85* Scheidung
**do without** *74* verzichten auf, auskommen ohne
**documentary credit** *97* (Dokumenten)akkreditiv
**donation** *24* Spende
**dot** *18* Punkt
**down under** *44* nach Australien
**downturn** *63* Rückgang
**drastic** *63* drastisch
**drop** *37t* fallen lassen
**drop** *64* fallen
**due** *41* fällig
**due date** *41* Fälligkeitsdatum

E

**earnings** *71* Einkünfte
**ECB (European Central Bank)** *54* Europäische Zentralbank
**eco-friendly** *68* umweltfreundlich
**ecological** *73* ökologisch
**economic** *52* wirtschaftlich, Wirtschafts-
**economical** *60* sparsam
**effect** *106* (Aus-)Wirkung
**efficient** *32* leistungsfähig
**elect** *61* wählen
**electronics (pl. only)** *64* Elektronik, elektronische Geräte
**elevator** *9* Fahrstuhl
**eligibility** *25* Berechtigung, Eignung
**eligible** *91* anspruchsberechtigt
**embarrassing** *96* peinlich
**emergency** *28* Notfall, Not-
**emerging markets** *67* Schwellenländer
**emphasize** *47* betonen, hervorheben
**employ** *99* beschäftigen
**employee** *37* Angestellte/r; Arbeitnehmer/in
**employer** *56* Arbeitgeber/in
**enclosed** *25* beigefügt
**enclosed** *43* beiliegend
**encourage** *15* auffordern
**encourage** *56* ermutigen, ermuntern
**encrypted** *42* verschlüsselt
**endorse** *112* indossieren
**endorse** *24* unterzeichen, hier: werben (für)
**endorsement** *24* Unterzeichnung, hier: Werbung
**endowment insurance** *93* Kapitalversicherung
**engaged** *17* besetzt
**engagement** *24* Verpflichtung, Engagement
**enquire** *108* (an)fragen, sich erkundigen
**enquiry** *8* Anfrage
**ensure** *25* sicherstellen, gewährleisten
**enter** *13t* eingeben
**enterprise** *73* Unternehmen
**entrepreneur** *99* Unternehmer/in
**entry** *29* Buchung, Eintrag
**environment** *73* Umwelt
**environmental footprint** *73* Ökö-Bilanz
**environmental** *73* Umwelt-
**equipment** *34* Geräte
**equities (equity shares)** *70* Aktien
**equity capital** *59* (haftendes) Eigenkapital
**equivalent** *98* Entsprechung, Gegenstück
**essentially** *61* im Wesentlichen
**estate** *70t* (Grund-)Besitz
**estimate** *82* (ein)schätzen
**ethical** *73* moralisch vertretbar, ethisch
**ethically-minded** *73* ethisch ausgerichtet
**ethics** *73* Ethik
**ethnic** *51* ethnisch
**European Savings Directive (ESD)** *61* Europäische Zinsbesteuerungsrichtlinie
**evaluate** *48* bewerten, evaluieren
**examine** *15* untersuchen, prüfen
**exceed** *31* überschreiten, -steigern
**exception** *68* Ausnahme
**exchange** *30* Austausch
**exclude** *73* ausschließen
**expand** *99* expandieren
**expansion** *104* Expansion
**ex-pat (= expatriate)** *97* im Ausland Lebende(r)
**expectation** *64* Erwartung
**expenditure (sing. only)** *76* Ausgabe(n)
**experience** *37* Erfahrung
**expiry date** *45* Ablaufdatum
**exploit** *73* ausbeuten
**explore** *25* erkunden
**express** *6* ausdrücken
**expression** *8* Ausdruck
**extend** *25* erweitern, zukommen lassen
**extended** *28* erweitert
**extension** *83* Erweiterung, Anbau
**extra charge** *27* Zusatzgebühren
**extract** *21* Auszug

F

**face** *96* konfrontiert werden mit
**factor in** *105* einpreisen
**fail** *99* versäumen
**failed** *42* gescheitert
**fall short** *94* nicht reichen
**favourable** *102* günstig
**fear** *58* Befürchtung
**feature** *27* Merkmal, Eigenschaft
**federal state** *104* Bundesland
**fee** *17* Gebühr
**fellow** *15* Mit-
**figure** *81t* Zahl
**file** *22* Akte, Datei
**fill in** *19* ausfüllen, eintragen
**finance** *13t* finanzieren
**fixed assets** *98* Sachanlagevermögen
**floor** *9* Stock(werk)
**fluctuate** *63* schwanken
**fluctuation** *67* Schwankung, Ausschlag
**folder** *22* Ordner
**follow-up appointment** *37t* Folgetermin
**for instance** *78* zum Beispiel
**force** *102* zwingen
**forecast** *64* vorhersagen
**foreign** *7* ausländisch
**foreign currency** *12* Fremdwährung, Sorten
**foreign exchange (sing. only)** *97* Devisen(geschäfte)
**foreign trade** *108* Außenhandel
**forge** *42* fälschen
**formality** *19* Formalität
**forward** *110* senden

**forwarding agent** *112* Spediteur/in
**foul** *70t* scheußlich
**found** *99* gründen
**fraud** *42* Betrug
**fraudulent** *48* betrügerisch
**free of charge** *30* gebührenfrei
**freelance** *80* freiberuflich
**freeze** *58* einfrieren
**freight forwarder** *108* Spediteur/in
**frequent** *63* häufig
**from … onwards** *81t* von … an
**froth** *14* (auf)schäumen
**fund** *17t* Fond(s); finanzieren
**fund of funds** *67* Dachfonds
**funds (pl. only)** *58* Kapital
**furious** *34* wütend

G

**gain** *64* Gewinn
**gambling** *115* Glücksspiel
**gang** *34* Bande
**gap** *22* Lücke
**gardening** *34* Gartenarbeit
**gear (coll.)** *37t* Zeug, Sachen, Kleidung
**general business conditions** *22* allgemeine Geschäftsbedingungen
**generate** *115* erzeugen, erwirtschaften
**generate** *37t* erbringen
**generous** *24* großzügig
**genuine** *19* echt
**get (deeply) into debt** *45* sich (tief) verschulden
**get a good press** *16* eine gute Presse haben
**get in touch** *17* (sich) in Verbindung setzen
**give directions** *11* den Weg beschreiben
**give it your best shot** *24* sein Bestes geben
**give notice** *54* kündigen
**given name** *21* Vorname
**globalization** *106* Globalisierung
**go bankrupt** *85* in Konkurs gehen
**go bust** *58* kaputtgehen
**go into liquidation** *99* Konkurs anmelden, abgewickelt werden
**go on** *70t* weitergehen
**gonna** *30* = going to
**goods** *42* Ware(n)
**goodwill** *98* immaterielle Vermögenswerte, Goodwill
**government** *13t* Regierung
**government bond** *65* Staatsanleihe
**gradual** *63* allmählich
**grain** *73* Getreide
**grant** *19* gewähren, erteilen, bewilligen
**gross** *61* Brutto-
**ground floor** *11* Erdgeschoss
**growth** *67* Wachstum
**guaranty** *83* Bürgschaft
**guidance** *25* Beratung
**guideline** *32* Hinweis

H

**halt** *113* anhalten
**handle** *47* umgehen mit
**handling charge** *79* Bearbeitungsgebühr
**hang on** *9* warte!
**hard drive** *40t* Festplatte
**hard-earned** *52* schwer verdient
**harm** *34* Schaden
**head** *44* fahren
**heading** *89* Überschrift
**headline** *58* Schlagzeile, Überschrift
**healthcare** *100* Gesundheitswesen
**heart attack** *70t* Herzinfarkt
**high street bank** *26* Großbank
**hire purchase** *42* Ratenkauf
**home improvements** *75* Renovierungsarbeiten
**home ownership** *86* Wohneigentum
**honestly** *24* ehrlich
**hospitality** *96* Gastfreundschaft
**housing market** *104* Immobilienmarkt
**huge** *67* riesig
**human being** *48* Mensch, menschliches Wesen

I

**I didn't catch that** *18* das habe ich nicht verstanden
**I don't know what got into me** *66* ich weiß nicht, was in mich gefahren ist
**identify** *36* festlegen, -stellen
**identity card** *21* Ausweis
**identity theft** *28* Identitätsdiebstahl
**illegal** *34* gesetzwidrig, illegal
**immediate** *68* sofort, umgehend
**impact** *73* (Aus-)Wirkung
**implication** *25* Auswirkung
**implicit** *111* stillschweigend, unausgesprochen
**impolite** *32* unhöflich
**in addition** *43* außerdem, darüber hinaus
**in arrears** *85* im Rückstand
**in contrast** *45* im Gegensatz
**in favour of** *110* zugunsten von
**in italics** *109* kursiv
**in progress** *98* in Arbeit
**in the black** *29* in den schwarzen Zahlen
**in the face of** *73* angesichts
**in the field of** *48* auf dem Gebiet von
**in the long run** *102* auf lange Sicht
**in the red** *29* in den roten Zahlen
**in theory** *44* theoretisch
**include** *27* einschließen, enthalten
**incompetent** *96* inkompetent, unfähig
**incorporate** *64* einbauen, einsetzen
**increase** *15* steigen, erhöhen, zunehmen
**increase** *64* Steigerung
**increasingly** *25* zunehmend
**individual** *61* (Einzel-) Person
**industrial glue** *108* Industrieklebstoff(e)
**inexperienced** *70* unerfahren
**influence** *80* beeinflussen
**inhabitant** *50* Einwohner/in
**initial charge** *67* Ausgabeaufschlag
**initial public offering (IPO)** *105* Börsengang
**insert** *34* einschieben, einführen
**insight** *36* Einblick
**install** *47* einrichten
**instalment** *42* Rate
**instant** *54* sofortig
**instant access** *28* Sofortzugang
**insurance** *28* Versicherung

**insurance policy** *12* Versicherung(spolice)
**insurance premium** *42* Versicherungsbeitrag
**insure** *95* versichern
**intend** *70* beabsichtigen, vorhaben
**interest (sing. only)** *27* Zinsen
**interest rate** *24* Zinssatz
**interest-only loan** *93* endfälliges Darlehen
**interior** *37* Innenausstattung
**international bank account number (IBAN)** *29* internationale Bankkontonummer
**interruption** *92* Unterbrechung
**introduce** *12* (sich) vorstellen
**inventory** *98* Inventar, Waren- und Lagerbestand
**invest** *9* anlegen, investieren
**investigate** *34* untersuchen, nachprüfen
**investor** *69* Investor/in, Anleger/in
**invoice** *107* Rechnung
**involve** *109* einschließen, beinhalten
**irrevocable** *110* unwiderruflich
**Islamic** *115* islamisch
**issue** *34* herausgeben; Ausgabe, Frage, Thema
**issuer** *45* Aussteller
**item** *38* Artikel, Gegenstand

### J

**jewellery** *83* Schmuck
**joint account** *19* gemeinsames Konto

### K

**keen** *17* (sehr) interessiert, eifrig
**keypad** *35* Tastenfeld, Tastatur

### L

**lackluster (AE)** *105* glanzlos
**ladder** *86* Leiter
**land-charge** *83* Grundschuld
**latter** *73* letzte(r,s)
**launch** *25* Einführung, Start
**lead manager** *104* Konsortialführer
**leading** *24* führend
**leaflet** *43* Broschüre, Prospekt
**leap** *63* springen
**learn on the job** *37t* bei der Arbeit / am Arbeitsplatz lernen
**legal** *99* juristisch, rechtlich
**legal department** *103t* Rechtsabteilung
**legislation** *73* Gesetzgebung
**leisure facility** *100* Freizeiteinrichtung
**lender** *80* Kreditgeber/in
**letter of credit** *108* Akkreditiv
**levy** *61* erheben
**liabilities** *98* Passiva, Verbindlichkeiten
**liability insurance** *91* Haftpflichtversicherung
**lien** *83* Pfandrecht
**life assurance** *83* Lebensversicherung
**limited** *10* begrenzt
**limited company (Ltd)** *99* Kapitalgesellschaft (KG), Gesellschaft mit beschränkter Haftung (GmbH)
**line of credit (AE)** *30* Dispositionskredit, Kreditlinie
**link** *69* Verbindung
**liquidity** *99* Liquidität
**list** *25* verzeichnen
**living expenses (pl. only)** *81t* Lebenskosten
**loading** *111* Verladung
**loan** *7* Kredit, Darlehen
**lobby** *8* Foyer, Eingangshalle
**location** *25* (Stand-)Ort
**log** *42* aufzeichnen
**long-term** *66* langfristig
**look forward to** *17* sich freuen auf
**loss** *42* Verlust
**lower** *78* herabsetzen
**lower case** *18* Kleinbuchstaben
**lump sum** *53* einmalige Summe

### M

**machinery** *83* Maschinen(park)
**maintenance** *81t* Unterhalt
**major** *47* Haupt-, wichtig
**make provision for** *62* Vorsorge treffen für
**maker** *64* Hersteller/in
**manage on one's own** *70t* alleine zurechtkommen
**manual trade** *7* Handwerk
**manufacturer** *73* Hersteller/in
**manufacturing company** *98* Herstellerfirma
**market** *97* vermarkten
**massive** *104* riesig
**match** *28* passen zu
**mattress** *54* Matratze
**mature** *70* fällig werden
**means of exchange** *115* Tauschmittel
**means of payment** *38* Zahlungsmittel, -modalität
**meanwhile** *58* inzwischen
**measure** *99* messen
**mediate** *71* vermitteln
**medium-term** *67* mittelfristig
**meeter-greeter** *8* Empfang(smitarbeiter/in)
**member of staff** *12* Mitarbeiter/in
**membership fee** *41* Mitgliedsbeitrag
**merger** *97* Fusion
**message** *17* Nachricht
**Middle-Eastern** *96* aus dem Nahen Osten
**mini statement** *27* Mini-Auszug
**miss** *31* versäumen
**misuse** *35* Missbrauch
**misuse** *44* missbrauchen
**Money Laundering Act** *22* Geldwäschegesetz
**money market account** *55* Geldmarktkonto
**morality** *73* Moral
**mortgage** *13t* Hypothek, Hypothekendarlehen
**mortgage bank** *58* Hypothekenbank
**move (home)** *86* umziehen
**move on to** *36* übergehen zu
**multi-modal transport** *112* Transport mit verschiedenen Verkehrsmitteln
**Muslim** *115* moslemisch
**my pleasure** *52* gern geschehen
**mystery** *34* Geheimnis, Rätsel

N

**nasty** *16* scheußlich, böse
**nationality** *21* Nationalität, Staatsangehörigkeit
**native speaker** *32* Muttersprachler/in
**need** *27* Bedürfnis
**negotiable** *112* übertragbar
**net** *51* Netto-
**net salary** *81t* Nettogehalt
**new shares** *104* junge Aktien
**newsagent** *47* Zeitungshändler/in
**nominal value** *115* Nennwert
**non-current assets** *98* Anlagevermögen
**non-refundable** *115* nicht rückerstattbar
**not necessarily** *66* nicht unbedingt
**notice account** *54* Festgeldkonto, Termingeldkonto
**notify** *44* benachrichtigen

O

**objective** *61* Ziel
**observe a period of notice** *54* eine Kündigungsfrist einhalten
**obtain** *67* erhalten
**occasional** *33* gelegentlich
**occupant** *89* Bewohner/in
**offend** *111* beleidigen
**offshore** *25* Übersee-
**old-fashioned** *7* veraltet
**omit** *98* weglassen
**on average** *81* im Durchschnitt
**on demand** *55* auf Abruf
**on maturity** *95* bei Fälligkeit
**on offer** *52* im Angebot
**on sale** *14* zum Verkauf
**on the job** *7* im Beruf, bei der Arbeit
**on your behalf** *67* in Ihrem Namen
**one thousand million (BE)** *50* Milliarde
**opening hours** *16* Geschäfts-, Öffnungszeiten
**open-plan** *9* Großraum(büro)
**opportunity** *25* Möglichkeit
**opportunity** *62* Chance, Gelegenheit
**oriented** *73* ausgerichtet, orientiert
**outlook** *113* Aussicht(en)
**outside the scope of** *61* außerhalb des Bereichs
**overcome** *15* überwinden
**overdraft** *12* Überziehung(skredit)
**overdraft** *13t* Dispositionskredit
**overdraft facility** *29* Dispositionskredit
**overdraw** *13t* überziehen
**overheads** *99* Betriebskosten
**overleaf** *25* umseitig
**overreact** *58* überreagieren
**overview** *36* Überblick, -sicht
**owe** *85* schulden

P

**pack sth in (coll.)** *81t* hinschmeißen
**package holiday** *14* Pauschalreise
**packing list** *108* Packliste
**paid off** *81t* abbezahlt
**panel** *34* Platte
**panic** *94* in Panik geraten
**partial** *42* Teil-
**pass away** *75* versterben
**patient** *58* geduldig
**pattern** *48* Muster
**payee** *39* Zahlungsempfänger/in
**paying-in book** *27* Einzahlungsbelegblock
**payment** *11* Zahlung
**payment in advance** *107* Zahlung im Voraus
**payment on open account** *107* Zahlung gegen Rechnung (mit offenem Zahlungsziel)
**peace of mind** *75* Sorgenfreiheit
**penalty fee** *53* Strafgebühr
**pension** *33* Rente, Pension
**pensioner** *62* Rentner/in, Pensionär/in
**percentage** *51* Prozentsatz
**perform** *63* abschneiden, sich entwickeln
**permanent contract** *13t* unbefristeter Vertrag
**personal banking manager** *7* Kundenberater/in
**personal quality** *37t* persönliche Eigenschaft
**personalized** *27* personalisiert
**persuade** *45* überreden
**pharmaceutical** *73* pharmazeutisch
**phenomenon** *106* Phänomen
**phishing** *15* Bankbetrug durch Datenklau
**piggy bank** *50* Sparschwein
**pilot scheme** *37t* Pilotprojekt
**pin-striped suit** *37t* Nadelstreifenanzug
**place of birth** *21* Geburtsort
**place of issue** *21* Ausstellungsort
**pledge** *83* Pfand
**pledge** *83* pfänden
**plunge** *113* abtauchen
**plunge** *63* (ab)stürzen
**polite** *6* höflich
**pollute** *73* verschmutzen
**pool** *66* sammeln, zusammenlegen
**pop into** *9* hineingehen
**popular** *6* beliebt
**popularity** *24* Beliebtheit
**portfolio** *14* Portefeuille, Depot
**potential** *28* potenziell
**precaution** *15* Vorsichtsmaßnahme
**predict** *73* vorhersagen
**preferential** *28* Vorzugs-
**premier customer** *25* Private-Banking Kunde/in
**premises** *14* Geschäft(sräume)
**present** *14* vorlegen, -stellen
**pressure** *6* Druck
**previous** *29* vorherig
**Prime Minister** *24* Premierminister/in
**priority** *73* Priorität
**privately-owned** *98* im Privatbesitz
**procedure** *19* Verfahren, Maßnahme
**proceeds (pl. only)** *61* Erlös, Erlöse
**profile** *82* Profil, Beschreibung
**profitable** *54* gewinnbringend
**prohibition** *115* Verbot
**prompt** *35* Stichwort, Vorgabe
**pronounce** *17t* aussprechen
**proof of identity** *19* Identitätsnachweis
**properly** *37t* korrekt, richtig

**property** *83* Immobilie, Grundeigentum
**property loan** *93* Baudarlehen
**pros and cons** *14* Für und Wider, Vor- und Nachteile
**prospect** *70* Aussicht
**prospective** *81* voraussichtlich
**protect** *20* schützen
**protection** *19* Schutz
**prove** *20* nachweisen
**provide** *25* liefern, (an)bieten
**provide for the future** *62* vorsorgen
**provisions** *98* Rückstellungen
**public limited company (plc)** *99* Aktiengesellschaft (AG)
**pump attendant** *48* Tankstellenwärter/in
**purchase** *47* Kauf
**purchase** *48* kaufen
**purpose** *22* Zweck
**purpose** *39* Verwendungszweck
**put sb in charge of sth** *102* jdm die Verantwortung für etw übertragen

## Q

**qualify** *37t* sich qualifizieren
**quarter** *40t* Quartal
**quay** *112* Kai
**query** *48* beanstanden, bezweifeln
**queue (BE)** *8* anstehen

## R

**rail travel** *100* Schienenverkehr
**railroad** *105* Eisenbahn
**raise** *54* erhöhen
**raise capital** *104* Kapital aufbringen
**rally** *63* Erholung
**rally** *63* sich erholen
**range** *25* Reihe
**rarely** *32* selten
**rate** *104* benoten, bewerten
**rating** *28* Bewertung
**rating** *65* Bewertung, Rating
**raw material** *98* Rohstoff
**reacquaint** *25* sich (wieder) vertraut machen mit
**react** *51* reagieren
**read between the lines** *111* zwischen den Zeilen lesen
**real estate (sing. only)** *66* Immobilien
**realty (AE)** *86* Immobilie
**reassurance** *58* Zusicherung
**rebound** *63* wieder steigen
**rebound** *63* Wiederanstieg
**receipt** *112* Quittung, Beleg
**receiver** *115* Empfänger/in
**recession** *52* Rezession, Wirtschaftsflaute
**recognise** *25* anerkennen
**recommend** *64* empfehlen
**recover** *63* sich erholen
**recruit** *99* (Personal) einstellen, rekrutieren
**redemption** *61* Auszahlung, Rückzahlung
**redundant** *85* arbeitslos
**reference** *19* Auskunft, Referenz
**reflect** *78* spiegeln
**refuse** *34* ablehnen
**regarding** *17* hinsichtlich
**regardless of** *102* unabhängig von
**register** *83* eintragen lassen
**regret** *32* Bedauern
**regulation** *19* Bestimmung, Vorschrift
**reimburse** *34* entschädigen
**reinvest** *67* wieder investieren
**relate to** *61* sich beziehen auf
**release** *107* freigeben
**release** *87* Freigabe
**relief** *24* Hilfe
**remaining** *45* restlich, verbleibend
**remove** *34* entfernen
**renovation** *83* Renovierung
**rent** *87* mieten
**repay** *45* tilgen, zurückzahlen
**repayment** *42* Rückzahlung, Tilgung
**repayment loan** *93* Annuitätsdarlehen
**repeatedly** *73* wiederholt
**replacement** *44* Ersatz
**represent** *24* vertreten, repräsentieren
**representative** *14* Vertreter/in
**reputation** *98* Ruf
**request** *61* bitten, beantragen
**required** *22* erforderlich
**research** *64* Forschung
**residence** *61* Wohnsitz
**residents' registration office** *19* Einwohnermeldeamt
**resist** *99* widerstehen
**resolve** *111* lösen
**responsible** *73* verantwortlich
**restore** *28* wieder holen, wieder herstellen
**retail banking** *14* Privatkundengeschäft
**retail outlet** *100* Einzelhandelsgeschäft
**retailer** *47* Einzelhändler/in
**retain** *61* einbehalten
**retained earnings** *98* Rücklagen
**retire** *70* in Rente/Pension gehen
**retirement** *62* Ruhestand
**return** *67* zurückgeben
**reveal** *104* enthüllen
**review** *17* überprüfen
**revoke** *41* widerrufen
**rights issue** *104* Bezugsrechtsemission
**ring the changes** *37t* variieren, für Abwechslung sorgen
**rise** *53* steigen
**risk tolerance** *70* Risikobereitschaft
**risk-tolerant** *70* risikobereit
**rob** *34* ausrauben
**roughly** *81* ungefähr
**round-table discussion** *97* Diskussionsrunde
**route** *94* Weg
**run a business** *103t* ein Unternehmen führen
**running costs** *70t* laufende Kosten

## S

**sacrifice** *73* opfern
**safe** *9* Tresor
**safety** *35* Sicherheit
**sailing** *78* Segeln
**salary** *7* Gehalt, Lohn
**sales geared** *37t* auf den Verkauf ausgerichtet
**salesperson** *43* Verkäufer/in
**sample** *108* Muster, Probe
**satisfaction** *16* Zufriedenheit
**satisfied** *17* zufrieden
**saver** *52* Sparer/in
**savers' tax-free allowance** *71* Sparerfreibetrag
**savings** *13t* Ersparnisse
**savings account** *12* Sparkonto

**savings and loan association (AE)** *87* Bausparkasse
**savings bank** *6* Sparkasse
**scale** *70* Skala, Maß(stab)
**scary** *58* beängstigend
**Schatz (German treasury bond)** *113* deutscher Schatzbrief
**scheme** *47* Programm, Projekt
**scholar** *115* Gelehrte/r
**score** *48* Punktzahl, Punktestand
**screen out** *73* ausschließen
**season ticket** *42* Jahres-, Zeitkarte, Abonnement
**section** *36* Teil, Abschnitt
**secure** *42* sicher
**secure** *83* sichern
**securities (pl. only)** *12* Wertpapiere
**security (no pl.)** *75* Kreditsicherheiten
**security** *8* Sicherheit
**seize** *102* ergreifen
**select** *70* auswählen
**selection** *67* Auswahl
**self-service terminal** *8* Selbstbedienungsterminal
**sell-off** *113* Ausverkauf
**senior** *12* vorgesetzt, leitend
**sense** *90* Sinn
**sentiment** *104* Stimmung
**separate** *15* getrennt, separat
**serious** *6* ernsthaft
**session** *113* (Börsen)sitzung
**set up** *27* einrichten
**set up** *85* gründen
**set up a business** *103* einen Existenz gründen
**set** *112* Satz
**set** *75* fest
**setback** *103* Rückschlag
**sex** *21* Geschlecht
**share** *52* Aktie
**share price** *104* Aktienkurs
**shareholder** *104* Aktionär/in, Anteilseigner/in
**ship** *108* verschiffen, versenden
**shipment** *111* Verschiffung, (Schiffs-)Ladung
**shipment** *64* Lieferung
**shipper** *110* Absender, Verschiffer
**shipping** *108* Versand, Fracht
**shortfall** *94* Deckungslücke
**shortly** *19* in Kürze, bald
**short-term** *98* kurzfristig
**show round** *8* herumführen
**sign** *18* unterschreiben
**signal** *105* signalisieren
**signature** *19* Unterschrift
**significant** *78* bedeutend
**similar** *27* ähnlich
**similarity** *8* Ähnlichkeit
**single parent** *85* Alleinerziehende/r
**sink** *113* sinken
**slash** *18* Schrägstrich
**slide** *113* abrutschen
**slide** *113* Abrutschen
**slight** *63* leicht
**slot** *34* Schlitz
**slowdown** *64* Rückgang
**slump** *113* abstürzen
**slump** *64* Sturz
**smooth** *78* glatt
**soap opera** *24* Fernsehserie, Seifenoper
**soar** *63* steil ansteigen, hochschnellen
**sole** *19* einzig, alleinig
**sole heir** *70t* Alleinerbe/-erbin
**solely** *22* (einzig und) allein
**solicitor's fee** *90* Anwaltskosten, Notargebühr
**solve** *34* lösen
**solvent** *58* solvent
**source** *6* Quelle
**specific** *107* genau, präzise
**specify** *112* angeben, festlegen
**specimen signature** *19* Unterschriftsprobe
**speculation** *115* Spekulation
**speculative** *70* spekulativ
**spin into** *58* hier: einzahlen
**split** *14* (auf)teilen
**spokesperson** *34* Sprecher/in
**spread** *67* verteilen
**stable** *63* stabil
**staff (pl. only)** *7* Personal, Mitarbeiter(stab)
**stage** *36* Phase, Abschnitt
**stand in line (AE)** *8* anstehen
**standardize** *97* standardisieren
**standing order** *27* Dauerauftrag
**star in** *24* eine Hauptrolle spielen in
**start out on one's own** *81t* sich selbstständig machen
**starving** *73* (ver)hungernd
**state** *24* bekannt geben, feststellen
**state** *56* staatlich
**state pension (fund)** *62* staatliche Rente(nkasse)
**statement** *8* (Konto-)Auszug
**statement printer** *8* Kontoauszugsdrucker
**steady** *63* stetig
**steep** *68* steil
**steer clear of** *94* einen Bogen machen um
**stock exchange** *52* (Wertpapier-)Börse
**stock listing** *105* Börsennotierung
**stop payment on** *44* sperren
**straight ahead** *8* geradeaus
**straightforward** *27* einfach, schlicht
**strict** *73* streng
**strike** *34* zuschlagen
**strip** *34* Streifen
**strongroom** *9* Stahlkammer, Tresorraum
**structure** *36* Aufbau, Struktur
**structured** *97* strukturiert
**stuck** *34* geklebt
**subject to** *78* vorausgesetzt
**subscription** *42* Abonnement
**subsidy** *56* Subvention
**successive** *113* aufeinander folgend
**suggestion** *14* Vorschlag
**suit** *27* entsprechen, passen zu
**suitable** *24* geeignet, passend
**summarize** *36* zusammenfassen
**supplier** *85* Lieferant
**supply** *61* liefern
**support** *25* Unterstützung, Hilfe
**suppose** *9* annehmen, vermuten
**surname** *12* Nach-, Familienname
**surrender value** *95* Rückkaufswert
**survey** *16* (Meinungs-) Umfrage
**sustainable** *73* nachhaltig
**swap** *18* tauschen
**SWIFT** *29* Code für internationale Überweisungen (Society for Worldwide Financial Telecommunication)

**syllable** *53* Silbe
**syndicated loan** *97* Konsortialkredit

T

**tailored** *28* maßgeschneidert
**take a break from** *80* unterbrechen
**take care** *7* pass auf dich auf!
**take possession of** *93* in Besitz nehmen
**takeover** *97* Übernahme
**target** *34* ins Visier nehmen
**target group** *36* Zielgruppe
**task** *6* Aufgabe
**tax** *56* Steuer
**tax authority** *61* Finanzamt
**tax evasion** *61* Steuerhinterziehung, Steuerflucht
**tax on investment earnings** *71* Zinsabschlagsteuer
**tax return** *61* Steuererklärung
**tax-efficient** *61* steuermindernd
**tax-free allowance** *71* Steuerfreibetrag
**teachings** *115* Lehren
**teller (AE)** *8* Kassierer/in
**temporary** *101* vorübergehend
**temptation** *99* Versuchung
**tend to** *73* tendieren zu, dazu neigen
**tent** *97* Zelt
**tepid** *105* lauwarm
**term** *54* Laufzeit
**term** *56* Ausdruck
**term deposit account** *90* Festgeldkonto
**terminology** *24* Terminologie
**terms of payment** *108* Zahlungsbedingungen
**text alert** *28* SMS-Benachrichtigung
**that won't cut any ice** *37t* das macht nichts her
**theft** *44* Diebstahl
**thief** *13t* Dieb
**think twice about** *52* es sich gut überlegen
**third party mandate** *19* Vollmacht
**threaten** *73* bedrohen
**through no fault of your own** *75* unverschuldet
**till** *8* Kasse
**title document** *83* Traditionspapier
**tolerate** *70* tolerieren
**tool** *98* Werkzeug
**top up** *27* (Karten-)Aufladung
**top up** *27* (mit Guthaben) aufladen
**topic** *37* Thema
**total** *81* sich belaufen auf
**trading** *105* (Börsen-)Handel
**trainee** *6* Auszubildende/r, Praktikant/in
**traineeship** *6* Ausbildung(sverhältnis), Praktikum
**transaction** *27* Zahlungseingang, -ausgang
**transfer** *112* übertragen
**transfer** *14* überweisen
**traveller's cheque** *44* Reisescheck
**treasury services** *97* Finanzdienstleistungen
**treat** *25* behandeln
**treatment** *69* Behandlung, Umgang
**tremendous** *73* gewaltig
**trigger** *58* auslösen
**trillion (AE)** *50* Billion
**trust** *103* Stiftung
**trust** *26* vertrauen
**trustee** *17* Treuhänder
**trustworthy** *6* vertrauenswürdig
**tumble** *113* purzeln
**turbulence** *63* Turbulenz, Aufruhr
**turn thirty** *66* die Dreißig überschreiten
**turnover** *97* Umsatz

U

**ultimate** *61* End-
**uncertain** *18* unsicher
**uncountable** *91* unzählbar
**underperform** *94* sein Ziel verfehlen
**underscore** *18* unterstreichen
**undertake** *45* unternehmen
**underwrite** *104* garantieren
**unemployed** *75* arbeitslos
**unemployment** *52* Arbeitslosigkeit
**unequal** *51* ungleich
**unit** *66* Investmentanteil, -zertifikat
**unsolicited mail** *45* nicht erbetene Post, Wurfsendung
**unwise** *84* unklug
**upside-down** *96* verkehrt herum
**upturn** *63* Anstieg
**upwards** *55* aufwärts
**urgent** *17t* dringend
**US$ denominated** *65* in US-Dollar
**usability** *47* Brauchbarkeit
**utility bill** *30* Rechnung für Strom-, Wasserversorger etc.

V

**vacation (AE)** *78* Urlaub
**valuable** *83* wertvoll, Wert-
**valuation point** *87* Bewertungspunkt
**value** *55* Wert
**valued at** *83* bewertet mit
**variable** *45* variable
**variety** *47* Vielfalt, Auswahl
**vary** *42* verändern, sich verändern
**vehicle** *83* Fahrzeug
**vending machine** *47* Verkaufsautomat
**venture** *115* Unternehmen, Unterfangen
**venturesome** *70* wagemutig
**vessel** *111* Schiff
**via** *39* über
**victim** *34* Opfer
**view** *27* durchsehen
**visible** *112* sichtbar
**visual aid** *36* Anschauungsmaterial
**volatile** *63* schwankend, unbeständig
**volume** *107* Volumen, Umfang

W

**wage(s)** *99* Lohn
**waistcoat** *37t* Weste
**ward** *24* (Kranken-)Station
**warehouse** *83* Lager(haus)
**warranty** *28* Garantie
**wealth** *51* Vermögen
**wealth management** *25* Vermögensverwaltung
**wealthy** *7* wohlhabend, reich
**wedding** *13t* Hochzeit
**welfare** *73* Wohlergehen
**well-advised** *64* gut beraten
**whereby** *61* wodurch
**whip sth up for sb (coll.)** *14* jdm (etw) zusammenstellen

**why on earth** *44* warum um Himmels willen
**widely** *32* weit (verbreitet)
**widespread** *73* weit verbreitet
**widow** *70t* Witwe
**willing** *52* gewillt (sein)
**wipe** *113* wischen
**withdraw** *8* abheben
**withdrawal** *19* Abhebung
**withdrawal form** *13t* Auszahlungsformular
**withhold** *61* abziehen
**withholding tax** *61* Quellensteuer
**wonder** *66* sich fragen
**work contract** *13t* Arbeitsvertrag
**work placement** *103* Praktikum
**worldwide** *25* weltweit
**worth** *83* im Wert von
**write off** *98* abschreiben

Y

**yield** *65* Rendite
**yield** *66* erwirtschaften, erzielen
**you can say that again** *66* das kann man wohl sagen
**Yours sincerely** *25* Mit freundlichen Grüßen

# Basic word list

Diese Liste enthält ca. 1000 Grundwörter, die in *Money Matters* New Edition als bekannt vorausgesetzt werden.

**bottom, at the ~** unten
**top, at the ~** oben
**left, on the ~** links
**right, on the ~** rechts
**a lot** viel, sehr
**a.m.** vormittags
**able** fähig, in der Lage
**about** über, etwa
**above** über, oben
**absolutely** absolut, völlig
**accept** annehmen, akzeptieren
**accident** Zufall, Unfall
**account** Bericht, Konto
**across** (quer) über
**action** Handlung
**active** aktiv, wirksam
**actor** Schauspieler
**actual** tatsächlich
**actually** tatsächlich
**add** zusammenzählen, hinzufügen
**address** Adresse
**advantage** Vorteil
**after** nach
**afterwards** danach, hinterher
**again** wieder
**against** gegen
**age** Zeitalter, Alter
**aged** alt
**ago** vor
**agree** vereinbaren
**agree to** zustimmen
**air** Luft
**all** alle(s)
**allow** erlauben, (zu)lassen
**allowed** erlaubt, dürfen
**almost** fast, beinahe
**alone** allein(e)
**already** schon, bereits
**also** auch, außerdem
**alternative** Alternative
**although** obwohl
**always** immer
**American** amerikanisch
**among** zwischen, unter
**amount** Summe, Betrag
**analyze** analysieren
**analysis** Analyse
**analyst** Analyst/in
**animal** Tier
**announce** ankündigen
**annual** jährlich
**another** noch eine
**answer** Antwort, Lösung; (be)antworten
**any** irgendetwas, -welche, jede
**anybody** jemand, jede/r
**anyone** jemand, jede/r
**anything** etwas, alles
**apartment** Wohnung
**appear** erscheinen, auftauchen
**apply** anwenden
**approximately** ungefähr, etwa
**Arab** Araber/in
**Arabian** arabisch
**argument** Argument
**around** herum
**arrange** arrangieren, vereinbaren
**arrangement** Anordnung
**arrive** ankommen
**article** Artikel
**artist** Künstler/in, Grafiker/in
**as well** auch, ebenfalls
**Asian** Asiate/Asiatin
**ask** fragen, bitten
**aspect** Aspekt, Seite
**at least** mindestens
**attractive** attraktiv, reizvoll
**automatic** automatisch
**automatically** automatisch
**automobile** Auto(mobil)
**average** Durchschnitt
**avoid** vermeiden
**away** weg, entfernt
**awful** schrecklich
**back** zurück
**backwards** rückwärts
**bad** schlecht, schlimm
**bag** Tasche
**banker** Bankier
**based on** basieren auf
**basic** grundsätzlich, einfach
**basically** im Grunde
**be** sein
**be on a diet** Diät halten
**be worried** fürchten
**because** weil
**become** werden
**bedroom** Schlafzimmer
**before** vor(her)
**begin** anfangen, beginnen
**behind** hinter, hinten
**believe** glauben
**below** unter, unten
**below** unterhalb, darunter
**beside** neben
**best** beste/r/s, , am besten
**better** besser
**between** zwischen
**big** groß
**bill** Rechnung
**bit** ein bisschen, etwas
**black** schwarz
**block** blockieren
**blueberry** Blaubeere
**bonus** Bonus
**book** Buch; buchen, bestellen
**born** geboren
**borrow** borgen, leihen
**both** beide
**bottom** Boden, Unterseite
**box** Kasten, Kästchen, Schachtel
**brackets** Klammern
**brainstorming** Ideen sammeln
**break** Pause; brechen
**break a record** einen Rekord brechen
**break the ice** das Eis brechen
**breakdown** Panne
**bright** hell
**bring** bringen, holen
**British** britisch
**build** (auf)bauen
**builder** Bauarbeiter/in
**building** Gebäude
**building society** Baugesellschaft
**business** Geschäft, Firma
**businessman** Geschäftsmann
**busy** beschäftigt, besetzt
**but** aber, sondern
**buy** kaufen
**buyer** Käufer/in
**bye** tschüs
**call** Anruf; (an)rufen
**called** genannt
**caller** Anrufer/in
**camera** Fotoapparat, Kamera
**can** dürfen, können
**cannot** nicht können
**capital** Kapital
**car** Auto
**car park** Parkhaus, -platz
**car showroom** Autosalon
**card** Karte
**career** Kariere, Laufbahn
**careful** vorsichtig, sorgfältig
**carry** tragen

**case** Fall
**case study** Fallstudie
**cash** Bargeld
**cash machine** Geldautomat
**cashier** Kassierer/in
**catch** fangen, erreichen
**cause** Ursache, Grund; verursachen
**central** zentral
**centre** Zentrum
**century** Jahrhundert
**certainly** sicherlich, bestimmt
**chance** Gelegenheit, Möglichkeit
**change** (Ver-)Änderung; (aus)wechseln, (sich) ändern
**charge** berechnen
**chat** Unterhaltung; sich unterhalten
**cheap** billig, günstig
**check** (über)prüfen
**chief** hauptsächlich
**child** Kind
**choice** Wahl, Auswahl
**choose** (aus)wählen
**city** (Groß-)Stadt
**class** Klasse
**classic** klassisch
**clean** reinigen, säubern; sauber
**clear** klar, deutlich
**client** Kunde/Kundin
**climate** Klima
**climb** klettern, steigen
**close** schließen
**clothing** Kleidung, Kleider
**colleague** Kollege, Kollegin
**collect** sammeln
**colour** Farbe
**coloured** farbig
**combination** Kombination
**combine** verbinden, kombinieren
**come** kommen
**common** üblich, gemeinsam
**communication** Kommunikation
**communicative** kommunikativ
**company** Firma, Unternehmen
**compare** vergleichen
**complete** vollständig; vervollständigen
**complex** komplex, vielfältig
**computer** Computer
**condition** Bedingung
**confrontation** Konfrontation
**congratulations** Glückwunsch
**connect** (miteinander) verbinden, anschließen
**connection** Verbindung
**consumer** Verbraucher/in
**contact** sich in Verbindung setzen mit, sich wenden an
**continue** fortsetzen
**conversation** Unterhaltung, Gespräch
**cool** ruhig
**copy** Kopie
**copy** kopieren
**correct(ly)** richtig
**cost** Kosten; kosten
**could** konnte/n, könnte/n
**count** zählen
**country** Land, Staat
**couple** Paar
**course** Kurs, Lehrgang
**cover** decken
**create** (er)schaffen, erstellen
**creative** kreativ, schöpferisch
**creativity** Kreativität, Ideenreichtum
**credit** Kredit
**crisis** Krise
**criticize** kritisieren
**crowded** belebt
**culture** Kultur
**cup** Tasse
**currency** Währung
**customer** Kunde, Kundin
**cut** schneiden
**daily** täglich
**danger** Gefahr
**dangerous** gefährlich
**dark** Dunkelheit; dunkel
**data** Daten
**date** Datum, Termin
**daughter** Tochter
**day** Tag
**deal** Geschäft
**dear** liebe/r
**death** Tod
**debit** Soll; belasten
**decide** (sich) entscheiden, beschließen
**decision** Entscheidung
**definition** Definition
**dentist** Zahnarzt/-ärztin
**department** Abteilung
**depend on** abhängen von
**describe** beschreiben
**desk** Schalter
**detail** Detail
**detective** Detektiv/in, Kriminalpolizist/in
**develop** entwickeln
**developed** entwickelt
**diagram** Grafik, Abbildung
**dialogue** Dialog
**difference** Unterschied
**different** anders, verschieden
**difficult** schwer, schwierig
**digital** digital
**direct** direkt, gerade
**direction** Richtung
**directly** direkt
**disadvantage** Nachteil, Schaden
**discover** entdecken, herausfinden, feststellen
**discuss** besprechen, diskutieren (über)
**discussion** Besprechung, Diskussion
**disorganized** schlecht organisiert
**document** Dokument, Papier
**dollar** Dollar
**door** Tür
**double** doppelt
**doubt** Zweifel; (be)zweifeln
**down** unten
**downstairs** (nach) unten
**draw** ziehen, zeichnen
**dream** Traum; träumen
**drink** Getränk; trinken
**drive** (Auto) fahren
**drop** Fall; fallen (lassen)
**during** während
**e.g. (for example)** zum Beispiel
**each** jede/r/s
**early** früh
**earn** verdienen
**easily** leicht
**east** Osten
**eastern** östlich
**easy** leicht, einfach
**eat** essen
**economy** Wirtschaft
**effective** effektiv, wirksam
**either** entweder
**electrician** Elektriker/in, Elektrotechniker/in
**electricity** Elektrizität, Strom
**electronic** elektronisch
**elevator** Lift, Aufzug
**else** andere/r/s
**elsewhere** woanders
**employed** beschäftigt
**end** Ende, Schluss; (be)enden
**end in** enden auf
**energetic** energisch
**energy** Energie

**enjoy** genießen, gefallen
**enough** ausreichend, genug
**enter** eintreten, eingeben
**entertainment** Unterhaltung
**environment** Umwelt, Umfeld
**equal** gleich
**equal** gleichen
**especially** besonders
**essential** wesentlich
**etc.** usw.
**European** europäisch
**even** sogar (noch)
**evening** Abend
**ever** je(mals)
**every** jede/r/s
**everybody** jede/r
**everyone** jede/r/s, alle
**everything** alles
**everywhere** überall
**exact** genau
**exactly** exakt, genau
**example** Beispiel
**excellent** ausgezeichnet, hervorragend
**except** außer
**excuse me** Verzeihung, Entschuldigung
**exercise** Übung
**exist** existieren
**expect** erwarten, annehmen
**expensive** teuer
**expert** Fachmann/frau
**explain** erklären
**explanation** Erklärung
**export** Export; exportieren
**exporter** Exporteur/in
**express** ausdrücken
**extra** zusätzlich
**extremely** äußerst
**eye** Auge
**face** Gesicht
**fact** Tatsache
**factor** Faktor
**fairly** ziemlich
**fall** Fall; fallen
**false** falsch
**family** Familie
**famous** berühmt
**far** weit (entfernt)
**fast** schnell
**father** Vater
**fax** Fax(gerät); faxen
**February** Februar
**fee** Gebühr
**feed** ernähren
**feel** (sich) fühlen
**feeling** Gefühl
**few** ein paar, wenig/e
**figure** Zahl, Ziffer
**fill** füllen, einsetzen
**filling station** Tankstelle
**finally** schließlich
**finance(s)** Finanz(en)
**financial** finanziell
**find** finden, suchen
**find out** herausfinden
**fine** gut, schön, fein
**finish** Ende; (be)enden
**firm** Firma; fest
**first** erste/r/s, zuerst
**fish** Fisch
**fit** fit
**fixed** festgelegt
**flat** flach; Wohnung
**flexible** flexibel
**flight** Flug
**floor** Etage, (Fuß-)Boden
**fluent** fließend
**fly** fliegen
**focus on** Blickpunkt auf
**folks** Leute, Menschen
**follow** (be)folgen
**following** folgend
**foot** Fuß
**football match** Fußballspiel
**forget** vergessen
**form** Form, Formular
**forward** vorwärts; befördern
**free** kostenlos, frei
**freelance** freiberuflich
**friend** Freund/in
**friendly** freundlich
**front** Vorderseite
**frustrated** frustriert
**full** voll
**fully** völlig
**fun** Spaß
**function** Funktion
**fund** Fonds
**fundamental** fundamental
**furniture** Möbel
**further** weitere
**future** Zukunft; (zu)künftig
**gallery** Galerie
**garden** Garten
**gas** Gas
**general** allgemein, generell, normal
**generally** im Allgemeinen, normalerweise
**geographic** geographisch
**get** holen, bekommen, werden
**gift** Geschenk
**give** geben
**glass** Glas
**global** global, Welt-
**go** gehen, fahren
**golden** golden
**good** gut
**good morning** guten Morgen
**goodbye** auf Wiedersehen
**good-looking** gut aussehend
**government** Regierung
**great** groß(artig)
**green** grün
**greet** (be)grüßen
**greetings** Grüße
**group** Gruppe
**grow** wachsen, anbauen
**guarantee** Garantie; garantieren
**guy** Bursche, Typ
**hairdresser** Friseur/Friseuse
**half** Hälfte; halb
**handout** Flug-, Merkblatt
**happen** passieren, geschehen
**happy** glücklich, froh, zufrieden
**hard** schwer
**hardly** kaum
**hate** hassen, nicht mögen
**have** haben
**head** Kopf
**health** Gesundheit
**hear** hören
**help** Hilfe; helfen
**helpful** hilfsbereit
**hide** verstecken, verbergen
**high** hoch; äußerst
**highly developed** hoch entwickelt
**hire** mieten, leihen, anstellen
**hit** Schlager; schlagen, treffen
**hold** abhalten, veranstalten
**holiday(s)** Ferien, Urlaub
**home** Zuhause, Heim; nach Hause
**hope to** hoffen zu
**horror** Entsetzen
**hospital** Krankenhaus
**hot-air balloon** Heißluftballon
**hour** Stunde
**house** Haus
**how** wie
**however** doch, jedoch
**huge** riesig
**hurt** schaden
**husband** (Ehe-)Mann
**idea** Idee, Gedanke
**ideal** ideal
**identical** identisch
**if** wenn, falls, ob
**ill** krank
**illness** Krankheit

**I'm afraid** leider
**imagine** sich vorstellen
**immediately** sofort, umgehend
**immigrant** Immigrations-
**import** Import; importieren
**important** wichtig
**importer** Importeur/in
**impossible** unmöglich
**improve** verbessern, sich bessern
**in fact** tatsächlich
**income** Einkommen
**incorrect** falsch
**indeed** tatsächlich
**Indian** indisch
**individual** individuell
**industry** Industrie
**inform** informieren
**information** Auskunft, Information(en)
**innovation** Innovation
**inside** innerhalb, drinnen
**instead** stattdessen, anstatt
**insurance** Versicherung
**integration** Integration
**interest** Interesse; Zins(en); interessieren
**interested** interessiert
**interesting** interessant
**into** in ... hinein
**invest** investieren
**investment** Investition
**invite** einladen
**Italian** italienisch
**January** Januar
**Japanese** japanisch
**join** beitreten, verbinden
**jump** springen
**just** einfach, nur, genau
**keep** (be)halten
**key** Schlüssel, Taste
**king** König
**know** kennen, wissen
**knowledge** Wissen, Kenntnis(se)
**Koran** Koran
**lack** Fehlen; fehlen
**land** Land
**language** Sprache
**large** groß, umfangreich
**last** letzte/r/s, zuletzt
**late** spät
**lately** in letzter Zeit
**law** Recht, Gesetz
**leader** Führer/in
**learn** lernen, erfahren
**least** wenigstens
**leave** (ver)lassen
**left** linke/r/s, links; übrig
**lend** leihen
**less** weniger, abzüglich
**let** erlauben, (zu)lassen, vermieten
**let's** lasst uns
**letter** Brief, Buchstabe
**level** Ebene
**lie** Lüge; (be)lügen
**life** Leben
**lifestyle** Lebensstil, Lifestyle
**lifetime** Leben
**lift** Fahrstuhl, Aufzug
**like** (ähnlich) wie; mögen, gern tun
**likely** wahrscheinlich
**limit** Grenze, Limit
**line** Linie, Zeile
**list** Liste; auflisten, notieren
**listen** zuhören
**listener** Zuhörer/in
**little** klein, wenig
**live** wohnen, leben
**local** örtlich, lokal
**long** lang
**look at** ansehen
**lose** verlieren
**loss** Verlust
**lots of/a lot of** viel, viele
**love** Liebe; lieben, sehr gern mögen
**low** niedrig
**luck** Glück
**lunch** Mittagessen
**machine** Maschine
**magazine** Zeitschrift
**magnetic** Magnet-
**mail** mit der Post versenden
**main** hauptsächlich, wichtigste
**mainly** hauptsächlich
**make** machen
**man** Mann, Mensch
**manage** (es) schaffen, verwalten
**management** Management, Verwaltung
**many** viele
**market** Markt
**married** verheiratet
**material** Material, Stoff
**matter** Sache
**may** dürfen, können, mögen
**maybe** vielleicht
**mean** bedeuten, meinen, heißen
**meaning** Bedeutung
**meaningful** bedeutend
**media** Medien
**medical** medizinisch, Arzt-
**medium** mittlere; Medium, Mittel
**meet** (zusammen)treffen, begegnen
**meeting** Konferenz, Besprechung
**member** Mitglied
**mention** erwähnen
**message** Mitteilung, Nachricht
**method** Methode, Verfahren
**midday** Mittag
**middle** Mitte
**might** könnte(n) (vielleicht)
**mind** Geist
**minimum** Minimum; minimal
**minute** Minute
**miss** verpassen, vermissen
**missing** fehlend
**mix** Mischung; mischen
**mobile phone** Mobiltelefon, Handy
**modernize** modernisieren
**moment** Moment
**money** Geld
**month** Monat
**monthly** monatlich
**more** mehr
**morning** Morgen
**most** meist
**mostly** hauptsächlich, meistens
**motor bike** Motorrad
**motorist** Autofahrer/in
**move** (sich) bewegen, umziehen
**Mr** Herr
**Mrs/Ms** Frau
**much** viel
**multi-millionaire** Multimillionär/in
**must** müssen
**name** Name; (be)nennen
**national** national, staatlich
**near** nahe
**nearby** nahe (gelegen)
**nearly** beinahe, fast
**necessary** nötig, erforderlich
**need** Bedarf; brauchen, benötigen
**negative** Verneinung; negativ
**neighbour** Nachbar/in
**nervous** nervös
**network** Sender, Netz(werk)
**never** nie(mals)
**news** Neuigkeit(en), Nachricht(en)
**newspaper** Zeitung

**next** nächst; danach
**night** Nacht
**no longer** nicht mehr
**none at all** überhaupt keine/r/s
**non-financial** nicht finanziell
**normally** normalerweise
**northern** nördlich
**note** Notiz; beachten, notieren
**notice** Notiz; bemerken
**now** nun, jetzt
**nowadays** heutzutage
**number** Nummer, Zahl
**o'clock** ... Uhr
**offer** Angebot; (an)bieten
**office** Büro, Amt
**officer** Beamter/Beamtin
**often** oft, häufig
**oil** Öl
**on board** an Bord
**once** einmal, einst, sobald
**online** online
**only** nur, einzig
**open** offen
**open** öffnen, beginnen
**operate** operieren
**opinion** Meinung, Einschätzung
**opposite** Gegenteil; gegensätzlich
**optimistic** optimistisch
**option** Option
**order** Bestellung, Reihenfolge; befehlen, bestellen, ordnen
**organization** Organisation
**organize** organisieren
**original** original, ursprünglich; Original
**other** andere/r/s
**out** aus
**outside** außer(halb)
**over** (vor)über
**overhead projector** Overheadprojektor
**overnight** über Nacht
**owe** schulden
**own** eigen; besitzen
**owner** Besitzer/in
**pack** packen
**page** Seite
**painting** Bild
**pair** Paar
**paper** Papier, Zeitung
**parameter** Parameter
**parent** Eltern(teil)
**parking space** (einzelner) Parkplatz
**part** Teil, Rolle
**particular** besondere, speziell
**particularly** besonders, bestimmt
**partner** Partner/in
**partnership** Partnerschaft
**pass** vorbeigehen, vergehen
**pass on** übergehen, weitergeben
**passenger** Passagier/in
**passport** Pass
**past** vorbei, nach; Vergangenheit
**patient** Patient/in
**pay** (be)zahlen; Gehalt
**people** Leute, Volk
**per cent** Prozent
**performance** Vorstellung
**perhaps** vielleicht, eventuell
**period** Zeit(raum)
**permanent** ständig
**permission** Erlaubnis
**person** Mensch, Person
**personal** persönlich
**petrol** Benzin
**phone** Telefon; anrufen
**phone call** (Telefon-)Anruf
**picture** Bild
**piece** Stück, Teil
**pin board** Pinnwand
**pity** schade
**place** Stelle, Platz; setzen, stellen
**plan** Plan; planen
**plane** Flugzeug
**planet** Planet
**plant** pflanzen
**plastic** Plastik
**play** spielen
**please** bitte
**p.m.** nachmittags
**pocket** Tasche
**pocket money** Taschengeld
**point of view** Standpunkt, Ansicht
**point** Punkt; Komma
**police** Polizei
**police officer** Polizist
**policy** Politik
**politics (pl. only)** (die) Politik
**poor** arm, schlecht, mangelhaft
**popular** beliebt, populär
**population** Bevölkerung
**port** Hafen
**position** Stellung
**positive** positiv, bejahend
**possibility** Möglichkeit
**possible** möglich, denkbar
**post** Post, Posten
**practically** praktisch
**practice** Praxis, Übung
**practise** (ein)üben
**precise** genau, präzise
**prefer** vorziehen, bevorzugen
**preparation** Vorbereitung
**present** Geschenk; gegenwärtig
**presentation** Vorstellung, Präsentation
**press** drücken
**press conference** Pressekonferenz
**pretty** hübsch
**price** (Kauf-)Preis
**print** drucken
**printer** Drucker/in
**private** privat, persönlich
**probably** wahrscheinlich
**problem** Problem
**produce** produzieren, herstellen
**producer** Produzent/in
**product** Produkt, Erzeugnis
**production** Produktion
**professional** professionell
**profit** Profit, Gewinn
**profit from** profitieren von
**project** Projekt
**provider** Anbieter/in
**public** öffentlich; Öffentlichkeit
**pull** ziehen
**purchase** Kauf; kaufen
**put** setzen, stellen, legen
**qualification** Qualifikation
**qualified** qualifiziert
**quality** Qualität
**quarter** Viertel
**question** Frage
**queue** Schlange
**quick** schnell, rasch
**quickly** schnell, rasch
**quick-thinking** schnell kombinierend
**quite** ziemlich, ganz
**rain** Regen; regnen
**raise** heben
**rapid** schnell, rasch
**reach** greifen, erreichen
**read** lesen
**reader** Leser/in, Lektüre
**ready** fertig, bereit
**real** echt, wirklich
**really** wirklich, eigentlich, tatsächlich
**reason** Grund, Begründung
**receive** erhalten, empfangen, bekommen
**recent** letzt, jüngst
**recently** neulich, kürzlich

**record** Aufzeichnung, Beleg; aufzeichnen; Platte; Rekord-
**recording studio** Aufnahmestudio
**reduce** reduzieren
**regatta** Regatta
**regional** regional
**regular** regelmäßig, regulär
**regularly** regelmäßig
**relationship** Beziehung, Verhältnis
**relevant** relevant
**remain** (ver)bleiben
**remember** sich erinnern, daran denken
**remind** (jdn) erinnern
**rent** Miete; mieten
**repeat** wiederholen
**report** Bericht; berichten
**resell** wieder verkaufen
**rest** Rast, Rest
**result** Resultat, Ergebnis; folgen
**return** zurückkehren, -gehen; Rückkehr
**return ticket** Rückfahrkarte
**reveal** enthüllen
**reverse** umkehren
**rewrite** umschreiben
**rich** reich, wohlhabend
**right** rechts, rechte/r/s, richtig; Recht
**ring through** durchrufen zu
**rise** Anstieg; ansteigen
**risk** Risiko; riskieren
**risky** riskant
**rock** Stein, Fels; schaukeln
**role** Rolle
**role-play** Rollenspiel
**room** Zimmer, Raum
**roughly** grob
**royal** königlich
**rule** Regel; herrschen
**run** laufen (lassen)
**rush** eilen, stürzen
**Russian** Russisch
**safe** Safe; sicher
**sale** (Schluss-)Verkauf
**salon** (Friseur-)Salon
**same** gleiche/r/s, der-, die-, dasselbe
**save** retten, sparen
**save up for** aufsparen fur
**say** sagen
**scene** Szene
**school** Schule
**screen** Bildschirm
**sea** See
**search** Suche; (durch)suchen
**seat** Sitz(platz)
**second** zweite/r/s; Sekunde
**secondly** zweitens
**secretary** Sekretär/in
**sector** Sektor, Bereich
**security system** Sicherheitssystem
**see** sehen
**seek** suchen
**seem** (er)scheinen
**sell** (sich) verkaufen
**seller** Verkäufer/in
**send** senden, schicken
**sentence** Satz
**serve** bedienen
**service** Kunden(dienst)
**set** Satz; setzen
**several** etliche, einige, mehrere
**share** (sich) teilen, gemeinsam (be)nutzen
**sharp** scharf
**shock** Schock, Schreck; erschüttern
**shop** Laden, Geschäft; einkaufen
**short** kurz, klein, knapp
**should** solle/n, sollte/n
**show** zeigen
**shut** schließen
**sign** (An-)Zeichen; unterschreiben
**signal** Signal
**silence** Stille, Schweigen
**similar** ähnlich
**simple** einfach
**simply** einfach
**since** da, weil, seit
**single** einzig, einzeln
**sit** sitzen, sich hinsetzen
**situation** Situation, Lage
**size** Größe
**sleep** schlafen
**slow** langsam; verlangsamen
**small** klein
**small talk** höfliche Unterhaltung
**smile** Lächeln; lächeln
**smoke** Rauch; rauchen
**smoker** Raucher/in
**social** sozial
**some** einige, etwas
**someone** jemand
**something** etwas
**sometime** irgendwann
**sometimes** manchmal
**son** Sohn
**soon** bald
**sorry** traurig; Verzeihung
**sort** Art, Sorte; sortieren
**sound** Geräusch, Klang, Laut; klingen
**space** (Zwischen-)Raum, Abstand, Platz, Weltall
**Spanish** Spanisch
**speak** sprechen, reden
**speaker** Sprecher/in
**special** besondere
**specialise** spezialisieren
**specialist** Spezialist/in
**specially** speziell
**spectacular** sensationell, spektakulär
**spell** buchstabieren, schreiben
**spelling** Schreibweise, Buchstabieren
**spend** ausgeben
**sporty** sportlich
**staff** Angestellte, Mitarbeiter/innen
**stairs** Treppe(n)
**stand for** stehen für
**standard** Norm, Standard, Maßstab; normal, üblich
**start** Beginn; anfangen, starten, beginnen
**statistic** Statistik
**status** Status
**stay** Aufenthalt; bleiben
**steal** stehlen
**step** Schritt
**still** still, trotzdem, (immer) noch
**stop** Halt; (an) halten, aufhören (mit)
**store** Laden, Geschäft
**strategy** Strategie, Taktik
**street** Straße
**strong** stark, kräftig
**student** Student/in, Lernende/r
**success** Erfolg
**successful** erfolgreich
**such** so, solch
**sum** Summe, Betrag
**sure** freilich, sicher
**surely** sicherlich
**table** Tisch, Tabelle
**taboo** tabu
**take** nehmen, bringen, dauern
**take a look at** ansehen, betrachten
**take out** herausnehmen
**take part in** teilnehmen an
**take-away** Außer-Haus-
**talk** Gespräch, Unterhaltung, Vortrag ; sprechen, reden

**tank** Tank
**target** Ziel
**tax** Steuer
**teach** unterrichten, lehren
**technology** Technik, Technologie
**telecommunications (pl. only)** Telekommunikation
**telephone** Telefon
**tell** sagen, erzählen
**than** als
**the States** die (Vereinigten) Staaten
**then** dann
**there** da, dort(hin(
**therefore** deshalb
**thing** Sache, Ding, Gegenstand
**think** denken, meinen, finden, glauben
**though** obwohl, doch
**thought** Gedanke
**through** durch
**throw** werfen
**ticket** Karte, Fahrschein
**till** bis
**time** Zeit, Mal
**tip** Hinweis, Tipp
**title** Bezeichnung
**today** heute
**together** zusammen
**toilet** Toilette, WC
**tomorrow** morgen
**too** zu, auch
**top** Spitze, Gipfel; Spitzen-
**total** (End-)Summe; völlig, (ins)gesamt
**totally** ganz
**towards** auf … zu
**town** Stadt
**trade** Handel
**train** Zug
**training** Training
**translation** Übersetzung
**transport** Transport, Verkehr
**travel** Reisen; reisen, fahren
**tree** Baum
**trend** Trend
**trip** Ausflug, Reise, Besuch
**trouble** Mühe, Umstände, Problem(e)
**truck** Lastwagen
**true** richtig, wahr
**try** versuchen, probieren
**turn** Wendung; wenden; (sich) drehen
**twice** zweimal
**type** erfassen, tippen
**unable** unfähig, nicht können
**unacceptable** unannehmbar, inakzeptabel
**unchanged** unverändert
**unclean** unsauber
**under** unter
**underground** unterirdisch
**underlined** unterstrichen
**underneath** darunter; unterhalb
**understand** verstehen, begreifen
**understanding** Verständnis
**unfortunately** leider
**uniform** Uniform
**university** Universität
**unless** wenn nicht, es sei denn
**unlike** anders als, im Gegensatz zu
**unlucky** unglücklich
**until** bis
**unusual** unüblich
**upstairs** oben
**use** Gebrauch; benutzen, verwenden
**useful** nützlich
**usually** normalerweise, gewöhnlich, meistens
**value** Wert
**version** Version, Fassung
**view** Ansicht
**VIP (=very important person)** Promi(nente/r)
**visit** Besuch; besuchen, besichtigen
**wait** warten
**walk** Spaziergang; (zu Fuß) gehen
**wall** Wand, Mauer
**want** wollen
**warn** warnen
**warning** Warnung
**watch** (Armband-)Uhr; beobachten, sehen
**way** Weg, Methode, Art (und Weise)
**weak** schwach
**week** Woche
**weekday** Wochentag
**weekend** Wochenende
**welcome** Willkommen; willkommen
**well** gesund, gut, also
**west** Westen
**western** westlich
**what** was, welche/r/s
**whatever** was auch immer
**when** wenn, als, wann
**whenever** immer wenn
**where** wo(hin)
**whether** ob
**which** welche/r/s
**while** während
**who** wer, der/die/das, welche(r/s)
**whole** ganz
**whose** dessen, wessen
**why** warum
**wide** breit, weit
**widescreen** Großbildschirm
**wife** (Ehe-)Frau
**will** Wille; werde(n), wollen
**wish** Wunsch; wünschen
**with** mit, bei
**within** innerhalb (von), in
**without** ohne
**woman** Frau
**won't** wird nicht
**word** Wort
**work** Arbeit, Werk; funktionieren, arbeiten
**worker** Arbeiter/in
**world** Welt
**worry** sich Sorgen machen
**worse** schlechter, schlimmer
**worth** wert
**would** würde/n
**write** schreiben
**wrong** falsch
**yacht** Jacht
**year** Jahr
**yesterday** gestern
**yet** noch
**young** jung
**zero** Null

# Banking word list: German – English

**Die folgende Liste enthält ca. 650 Fachbegriffe aus dem Bankwesen.**

**(haftendes) Eigenkapital** equity capital
**abbuchen** debit
**Abbuchung** debit (entry)
**abheben** withdraw
**Abhebung** withdrawal
**Ablaufdatum** date of expiry, expiry date
**Abrechnung(stag)** settlement (day)
**Abteilung** department
**abtreten** assign
**Abtretung** assignment
**abzahlen** pay off
**abziehen** deduct
**Abzug** deduction
**Akkreditiv** letter of credit, documentary credit
**Aktie** share, stock (AE)
**Aktiengesellschaft (AG)** public limited company (plc)
**Aktienkurs** share price
**Aktionär/in** shareholder
**Aktiva** assets
**Akzeptanzstelle** point of sale
**Allgemeine Geschäftsbedingungen** General Business Conditions
**an der Börse notiert** listed on the stock exchange
**an die Börse gehen** go public
**Anfrage** inquiry
**Angebot** offer
**Angebot und Nachfrage** supply and demand
**Angestellte/r** clerk, employee
**Anlage** investment
**Anlageberater/in** investment consultant
**Anlagevermögen** non-current assets
**anlegen** invest
**Anleger/in** investor
**Anleihe(papier)** bond
**Annuitätsdarlehen** repayment loan
**Anteil** share
**Antragsformular** application form
**Antragsteller/in** applicant
**Arbeitgeber/in** employer
**Arbeitnehmer/in** employee
**auf eigene Rechnung handeln** act on one's own account
**Aufenthaltserlaubnis** residence permit
**Aufenthaltsnachweis** proof of legal residence
**Aufschwung** upturn, rise
**Ausbildung(sverhältnis)** traineeship
**Ausführung** transaction
**Ausgabe** issue
**Ausgabe(n)** expenditure (pl. only)
**Ausgabeaufschlag** initial charge
**ausgeben** issue
**ausgeübter Beruf** occupation
**Auslagen** costs
**Außenhandel** foreign trade
**ausspähen** spy out
**Aussteller** issuer
**Ausstellungsdatum** date of issue
**Ausstellungsort** place of issue
**Auszubildende/r** trainee
**Baisse** bear market
**Bankleitzahl** bank sort code
**bankrott** bankrupt
**Banktresor** strongroom
**Bargeld** cash
**Bargeldautomat** cash dispenser
**bargeldlos** cash-free, cashless
**Barscheck** open cheque
**Baudarlehen** property loan
**Bausparkasse** building society
**Bausparvertrag** building society policy
**beantragen** apply (for)
**Bearbeitungsgebühr** handling, arrangement fee
**Begleichung** settlement
**Beitrag** contribution
**belasten** debit
**Beleg** receipt
**Berater/in** adviser
**Beratungsgepräch** consultation
**berechnen** charge
**Beruf** profession
**Berufsschule** vocational school
**bestätigen** confirm, endorse
**besteuert werden** be taxed
**Bestimmungsort** destination
**Betrag** amount
**betragen** amount to
**betriebliche Altersversorgung** company pension
**Betriebskosten** running costs, overheads
**Betrug** fraud
**Betrüger/in** swindler
**betrügerisch** fraudulent
**beurteilen** assess
**bevollmächtigen** authorize
**Bewertungspunkt** valuation point
**bewilligen** grant
**bezahlen** pay, honour
**Bezahlung** payment, settlement
**Bezugsrechtsemission** rights issue
**Bilanz** balance (sheet)
**Billion** (BE) billion, (AE) trillion
**Börse** stock exchange, stock market
**Börseneinführung** listing
**Börsengang** flotation, IPO (initial public offering)
**Broschüre** brochure
**brutto** gross
**Bruttoinlandsprodukt (BIP)** GDP (gross domestic product)
**Buchung** entry
**Bürge** guarantor
**Bürgschaft** guarantee
**Dachfonds** fund of funds
**Darlehen** loan
**Dauerauftrag** standing order
**Deckung** cover
**Deckungslücke** shortfall
**Depot** portfolio
**Depot (im ~ der Bank)** in the custody of the bank
**Depotkonto** safe custody account
**Devisen** foreign exchange
**Diebstahl** theft
**Dienst(leistung)** service
**Disagio** discount

**Dispositionskredit** overdraft facility
**Dividende** dividend
**Dokumente gegen bar/ Zahlung** documents against payment
**Dokumenteninkasso** collection of documents
**echt** genuine
**ec-Karte** debit card
**effektiver Jahreszins** APR (annual percentage rate), true APR
**Eigenkapital** equity (capital)
**eine Hypothek aufnehmen** take out a mortgage
**eingeben** key in
**Einkommen** income
**Einkünfte** income
**Einlagensicherungsfonds** financial services compensation scheme
**Einmalanlage** lump sum investment
**Einrichtung** setting-up
**einschätzen** assess
**Eintrag** entry
**Einwohnermeldeamt** residents' registration office
**einzahlen** pay in, pay into
**Einzahler/in** payer
**Einzahlung** deposit
**einziehen** claim
**Einzugsermächtigung** direct debit
**Einzugsverfahren** direct debit
**Emission** flotation, issue
**Emissionsbank** issuing house
**Emittent** issuer
**emittieren** issue
**Empfänger/in** recipient
**endfälliges Darlehen** interest-only loan
**Entgelt** fee
**Entsprechung** equivalent
**erben** inherit
**ermächtigen** authorize
**Ersatz** replacement
**ersetzen** replace
**Ersparnisse** savings
**erstatten** reimburse, refund
**Erstattung** refund
**Erstnotierung** first listing
**Ertrag** yield
**Erwerb** acquisition
**erwirtschaften** yield, make
**erzielen** yield
**Europäische Zentralbank** European
**fällig werden** fall due, mature
**Fälligkeit** maturity
**Fälligkeit(sdatum)** redemption date, maturity date, due date
**fälschen** forge
**Familienname** surname
**Familienstand** marital status
**Festgeldkonto** term deposit account, notice account
**Filiale** branch
**Filialleiter/in** branch manager
**Finanzamt** tax authority
**Finanzierung** financing
**Firmendarlehen** corporate loan
**Firmenkunde** corporate client
**Firmenkunden** corporate business
**Fonds** fund
**Forderungen** provisions for, receivables, trade debts
**Frachtgut** consignment, freight (no plural)
**Freiberufler** self-employed person
**Freigabe** release
**Freistellungsantrag** application for tax exemption
**Fremdkapital** creditors
**Fremdwährung(en)** forex = foreign exchange
**führen (Konten)** keep (accounts)
**Fusion** merger
**Gebühr** charge, fee
**gebührenfrei** free of charge
**Geburtsdatum** date of birth
**Geburtsname** name at birth
**Geburtsort** place of birth
**Gegenwert** equivalent
**gegenzeichnen** countersign
**Gehalt** salary
**Gehaltskonto** current account,
**Geheimnummer** code number, PIN
**Geldautomat** ATM, cash dispenser
**Geldwäschegesetz** Money Laundering Act
**Gemeinschaftskonto** joint account
**genehmigen** approve
**Geschäftskunde/in** corporate client
**Geschäftszeiten** opening hours
**Gesellschaft mit beschränkter Haftung (GmbH)** private limited company (Ltd)
**gewähren** grant
**Gewinn** profit
**Gewinn- und Verlustrechnung** profit and loss account
**Girokonto** checking account (AE), current account
**Großbank** high street bank
**Grundschuld eintragen** register a land-charge
**gültig** valid
**günstig** favourable
**Güterstand** system of marital property
**Guthaben** credit balance
**Guthabenzinsen** credit interest
**gutheißen** approve
**gutschreiben** credit
**Gutschrift** credit (entry)
**Habensaldo** credit balance
**haftbar** liable
**halbjährlich** half-yearly
**Handelsrechnung** commercial invoice
**Handelsvolumen** volume of trade
**Handlungsvollmacht** power of attorney
**Hauptgeschäftsführer/in** chief executive (officer)
**Hauptstelle** head office
**Hausse** bull market
**Höhe** amount
**Hypothek aufnehmen** take out a mortgage
**Hypothekenbank** mortgage bank
**im Rückstand** in arrears
**immaterielle(s) Vermögen(swerte)** intangible assets
**Immobilien** real estate
**in Umlauf** in circulation
**Indossament** endorsement
**indossieren** endorse
**Inkassoauftrag erteilen** place a collection order
**Insolvenz** insolvency

**institutionelle/r Fonds-manager/in** institutional fund manager
**Inventar** inventory
**investieren** invest
**Investition** investment
**Investmentanteile** units
**Investmentfonds** unit trust, investment fund
**Investor/in** investor
**Jahreshauptversammlung** annual general meeting (AGM)
**jährlich** annual(ly)
**Kai** quay
**Kapital aufbringen** raise capital
**Kapitalanleger/in** investor
**Kapitalversicherung (als Rente auszahlbar)** annuity assurance
**Kapitalversicherung** life assurance, endowment insurance
**Karteneinzug** slot (for inserting cards)
**Kassa gegen Dokumente** documents against payment
**Kasse** till
**Kassierer/in** cashier
**Kaufpreis** purchase price
**Kaufvertrag** contract of sale
**Kleinanleger/in** retail investor
**Kleinkredit** personal loan
**Kollege/Kollegin** colleague
**Konkurs** bankruptcy
**Konkurs (in ~ gehen)** go bankrupt
**Konnossement** bill of lading
**Konsortialführer** lead manager
**Konsortialkredit** syndicated loan
**Konsortium** syndicate
**Konto** account
**Konto mit Kündigung(sfrist)** notice account
**Kontoauszug** bank statement
**Kontoauszugsdrucker** statement printer
**Kontoinhaber/in** account holder
**Kontokorrentkonto** current account
**Kontokorrentschuldner** trade debtors
**Kontosperrung** blocking an account
**Kontostand** balance
**Kontoüberziehung** overdraft
**kostenlos** free of charge
**Kredit** loan, credit (no plural)
**Kreditgeber/in** lender
**Kreditinstitut** bank
**Kreditkarte** credit card
**Kreditnehmer/in** borrower
**kreditwürdig** creditworthy
**Kreditwürdigkeit** creditworthiness
**Kunde/Kundin** customer
**Kundenberater/in** customer service officer
**Kundenberatung** customer service
**kündigen** give notice
**Kündigungsfrist** period of notice
**Kurs-Gewinn-Verhältnis** price-earnings ratio
**kurzfristig** short-term
**Ladung** shipment
**Lager(bestand)** stocks
**Lager(haus)** warehouse
**Lagerbestände** inventory
**Lagerschein** warrant
**langfristig** long-term
**Lastschrift** debit, direct debit
**Lebenshaltungskosten** living expenses
**Lebensversicherung** life assurance, life insurance
**Legitimation** proof of identity
**Leitzins** base rate
**Lieferung** consignment, shipment, delivery
**Lohn** salary, wage
**löschen** cancel
**Mahnung** reminder
**Miete; mieten** rent
**Milliarde** (BE) thousand million, (AE) billion
**Mindeszahlung** minimum payment
**Missbrauch** misuse
**Misstrauen** mistrust
**Mitantragsteller/in** co-applicant
**mittelfristig** medium-term
**mitunterzeichnen** co-sign
**Münze** coin
**Nachfrage** demand
**Nennwert** denomination, nominal value
**netto** net
**nichtselbständige Arbeit** employment
**Nichtveranlagungs-bescheinigung** certificate of exemption
**Obligation** bond, debenture
**Orderscheck** order cheque
**Packliste** packing list
**Passiva** liabilities
**Pension** pension
**Pensionierung** retirement
**Personal** staff
**Personalausweis** proof of identity, identity card
**Pfand** pledge
**pfänden** pledge
**Pfandrecht** lien
**plündern** plunder, raid
**Portefeuille** portfolio
**Praktikant/in** trainee, work experience student
**Praktikum** period of work experience
**Präsentation** presentation
**Preisfindung** bookbuilding
**Privatkundengeschäft** retail banking
**Provision** commission
**prüfen** examine
**Quellensteuer** withholding tax
**Quittung** receipt
**Rate** instalment
**Ratenkauf** hire purchase
**realisieren** realize
**Rechnung** invoice, bill
**reingezeichnet** clean on board
**Reisescheck** traveller's cheque
**Rekordhoch** record high
**Rendite** return, yield
**Rente** pension
**Rentenpapier** bond
**Rentner/in** pensioner
**Reserven** reserves
**Rezession** recession
**risikobereit** risk-tolerant
**Risikobereitschaft** risk tolerance
**Risikokapital** venture capital
**rückgängig machen** revoke
**Rückkaufswert** surrender value

**Rücklagen** reserves, retained earnings
**Rückstellungen für Verbindlichkeiten und Forderungen** provisions for liabilities and charges
**Rückzahlung** repayment, redemption
**Ruhestand** retirement
**Sach(anlage) vermögen** tangible assets
**Saldo** balance
**Schalter** counter
**Scheck** cheque
**Schiff** vessel
**Schiffsladung** shipment
**schriftlich** in writing
**SCHUFA** German banks' credit reference agency
**SCHUFA-Klausel** SCHUFA declaration
**Schuld(en)** debt
**schulden** owe
**Schuldner** debtor
**Schuldverschreibung** debenture
**schwanken** fluctuate
**Schwankung** fluctuation
**Schwellenländer** emerging markets
**selbstständig** self-employed
**selbstständige Tätigkeit** self-employment
**Selbstauskunft** voluntary disclosure
**Sendung** consignment, shipment
**Seriennummer** serial number
**Sicherheit(en)** collateral, security
**Sicherheitsvorkehrung** safety precaution
**Sicherungsübereignung** assignment by bill of sale
**Solidaritätszuschlag** solidarity tax
**Soll** debit
**Soll(saldo)** debit balance
**Sorten** foreign currency
**sparen** save
**Sparkasse** savings bank
**Sparkonto** deposit account, savings account
**Sparplan** savings scheme, plan
**Sparschwein** piggy bank
**Spediteur/in** freight forwarder, forwarding agent
**spekulativ** speculative
**sperren** stop (payment on)
**staatliche Förderungen** government support/incentives
**Staatsanleihen** government bonds
**Stahlkammer** strongroom
**Stammaktie** equity, ordinary share
**Stammaktien** equities, ordinary shares
**Standardwert** blue chip
**Steuer** tax
**steuerfrei** tax-free
**Steuerfreibetrag** tax-free allowance
**Steuerhinterziehung** tax evasion
**Steuerklärung** tax return
**Strafgebühr** penalty fee
**Strafzinsen** penalty interest
**Stückelung** denominations
**subventionieren** subsidize
**Summe** amount, total
**Tätigkeit** occupation
**Teilrückzahlung** partial repayment, instalment
**Termin** appointment
**Termingeldkonto** notice account
**tilgen** pay back, pay off, repay
**Tilgung** repayment
**Traditionspapier** title document
**Tresor(raum)** strongroom
**Überbringerscheck** bearer cheque
**Übernahme** takeover
**überschreiten** exceed
**übersteigen** exceed
**übertragbar** negotiable
**übertragen** assign
**überweisen** transfer
**Überweisung** credit transfer, remittance
**überziehen** overdraw
**Überziehungskredit** overdraft
**Umlaufvermögen, -kapital** current assets
**Umsatz** turnover
**umtauschen** change
**Umtauschkurs** exchange rate
**unbefugt** unauthorized
**unbeständig** volatile
**ungesicherte Schuldverschreibungen** junk bonds
**Unterhaltskosten** running costs
**Unterhaltungszahlungen** maintenance (payments)
**Unternehmer/in** entrepreneur
**unterschätzen** underestimate
**unterschreiben** sign
**Unterschrift** signature
**Unterschriftsprobe** specimen signature
**Untersuchung** inquiry
**unwiderruflich** irrevocable
**Ursprungszeugnis** certificate of origin
**Verbindlichkeiten** liabilities
**Verbindlichkeiten** accounts payable
**verdächtig** suspicious
**Verfallsdatum** expiry date
**verfügbar** available
**verfügbares Einkommen** disposable income
**Verfügbarkeit** availability
**verfügen über** dispose of
**Verladehafen** port of loading
**Verladung** loading
**Verlust** loss
**Vermögen(swerte)** assets
**Vermögensberater/in** investment consultant
**Vermögensverteilung** wealth distribution
**Vermögensverwaltung** asset management
**vermögenswirksam** asset-building
**verpfänden** pledge
**Verrechnungsscheck** crossed cheque
**Versand** dispatch
**Verschiffer** shipper
**Verschiffung** shipment
**verschlüsselt** encrypted
**verschuldet** in debt
**versichern** insure
**Versicherung(spolice)** insurance (policy)
**Versicherungsbeitrag** insurance premium
**Vertrag** contract
**vertraulich** confidential
**Verwendungszweck** purpose
**verzinsen** pay interest on
**vierteljährlich** quarterly

**Vollmacht** authority for per pro signatory, third party mandate
**vorausgesetzt** subject to
**Vorlage** presentation
**vorlegen** present
**Vorname** first name, given name
**vorrätig** in stock
**Vorsorge treffen für** make provision for
**vorsorgen** provide for the future
**Vorstand** board of directors
**Vorzugsaktien** preference shares
**Währung** currency
**Warenausfuhr** exports, exported goods
**Wechsel** bill of exchange
**Wechselkurs** exchange rate, rate of exchange
**wechseln** change
**Werktag** working day
**Wertbezeichnung** denomination
**Wertpapierbestand** Portfolio
**Wertpapierbörse** stock market, stock exchange
**Wertpapiere** securities (pl. only), stocks and shares
**Wertstellung** value
**wertvoll** valuable
**widerrufen** revoke
**wohlhabend** affluent, wealthy
**Wohnverhältnisse** residential status
**Zahlung** settlement, payment
**Zahlung gegen Rechnung (mit offenem Zahlungsziel)** payment on open account
**Zahlungsbedingungen** terms of payment
**Zahlungsempfänger/in** beneficiary, payee
**Zahlungsmittel** means of payment
**zahlungsunfähig werden** default
**Zahlungsunfähigkeit** insolvency, default
**Zahlungsweise** method of payment
**zeichnen** subscribe to
**Zeichnungsfrist** subscription period
**Zentrale** head office
**Zins(en)** interest (no plural)
**Zinsabschlagsteuer** tax on investment earnings
**Zinssatz** rate of interest, interest rate
**zu pari** at par
**zugunsten von** in favour of
**Zulassung** listing
**zurückverfolgen** trace
**zurückzahlen** pay back, pay off, repay
**Zusammenschluss** merger
**Zweck** purpose
**Zweig(stelle)** branch

# List of irregular verbs

**be** – was/were – been *sein*
**bear** – bore – borne *tragen*
**become** – became – become *werden*
**begin** – began – begun *anfangen, beginnen*
**break** – broke – broken *(zer)brechen*
**bring** – brought – brought *bringen, holen*
**build** – built – built *(auf)bauen*
**burn** – burnt – burnt *brennen*
**buy** – bought – bought *kaufen*
**catch** – caught – caught *fangen, erreichen*
**choose** – chose – chosen *(aus)wählen*
**come** – came – come *kommen*
**cost** – cost – cost *kosten*
**cut** – cut – cut *reduzieren; schneiden*
**deal** – dealt – dealt *handeln*
**do** – did – done *tun, machen*
**draw** – drew – drawn *zeichnen*
**drink** – drank – drunk *trinken*
**drive** – drove – driven *fahren*
**fall** – fell – fallen *(hin)fallen, sinken*
**feel** – felt – felt *(sich) fühlen*
**find** – found – found *finden*
**fly** – flew – flown *fliegen*
**forget** – forgot – forgotten *vergessen*
**get** – got – got *holen, bekommen, werden*
**give** – gave – given *geben*
**go** – went – gone *gehen, fahren*
**grow** – grew – grown *wachsen, anbauen*
**have** – had – had *haben*
**hear** – heard – heard *hören*
**hold** – held – held *halten, fassen*
**keep** – kept – kept *aufbewahren*
**know** – knew – known *kennen, wissen*
**lead** – led – led *führen, bringen*
**learn** – learnt – learnt *lernen, erfahren*
**leave** – left – left *(ver)lassen*
**let** – let – let *erlauben, lassen*
**lose** – lost – lost *verlieren*
**make** – made – made *machen, herstellen*
**mean** – meant – meant *bedeuten, meinen*
**meet** – met – met *(sich) treffen*
**pay** – paid – paid *(be)zahlen*
**put** – put – put *setzen, stellen, legen*
**read** – read – read *lesen*
**ride** – rode – ridden *fahren*
**ring** – rang – rung *klingeln*
**rise** – rose – risen *steigen*
**say** – said – said *sagen*
**sell** – sold – sold *(sich) verkaufen*
**send** – sent – sent *senden, schicken*
**set** – set – set *(ein)stellen*
**speak** – spoke – spoken *sprechen, reden*
**spell** – spelt – spelt *buchstabieren, schreiben*
**spend** – spent – spent *ausgeben; verbringen*
**stand** – stood – stood *stehen, aushalten*
**take** – took – taken *nehmen, bringen, dauern*
**tell** – told – told *sagen*
**think** – thought – thought *denken, meinen*
**understand** – understood – understood *verstehen*
**wear** – wore – worn *tragen*
**write** – wrote – written *schreiben*

## List of geographical names

**Austria** ['ɒstriə] Österreich
**Asia** ['eɪʃə] Asien
**Athens** ['æθɪnz] Athen
**Baltic Sea** [ˌbɔːltɪk 'siː] Ostsee
**Bavaria** [bə'veəriə] Bayern
**Czech Republic, Czechia** [tʃek rɪ'pʌblɪk] Tschechische Republik, Tschechien
**Denmark** ['denmɑːk] Dänemark
**Estonia** [ɛs'toʊniə] Estland
**Europe** ['jʊərəp] Europa
**Far East** [ˌfɑːr 'iːst] Ferner Osten
**Federal Republic of Germany** [ˌfedərəl rɪˌpʌblɪk əv 'dʒɜːməni] Bundesrepublik Deutschland
**Great Britain** [ˌgreɪt 'brɪtn] Großbritannien
**Greece** ['griːs] Griechenland
**Ireland** ['aɪələnd] Irland
**Italy** ['ɪtəli] Italien
**Latvia** ['lætviə] Lettland
**Lithuania** [ˌlɪθju'eɪniə] Litauen
**Malaysia** [mə'leɪziə] Malaysien
**Middle East** ['mɪdl iːst] Naher Osten
**Moscow** ['mɒskəʊ] Moskau
**Munich** ['mjuːnɪk] München
**Norway** ['nɔːweɪ] Norwegen
**Nuremberg** ['njʊərəmbɜːg] Nürnberg
**Poland** ['pəʊlənd] Polen
**Republic of Belarus** [rɪ'pʌblɪk əv ˌbelə'ruːs] Republik Weißrussland
**Rome** [rəʊm] Rom
**Russia** ['rʌʃə] Russland
**Scotland** ['skɒtlənd] Schottland
**South Africa** [saʊθ 'æfrɪkə] Südafrika
**South America** [ˌsaʊθ ə'merɪkə] Südamerika
**South-East Asia** [ˌsaʊθiːst 'eɪʃə] Südostasien
**Spain** ['speɪn] Spanien
**Sweden** ['swiːdn] Schweden
**Switzerland** ['swɪtsələnd] (die) Schweiz
**Ukraine** [juː'kreɪn] Ukraine
**United Arab Emirates** [ju'naɪtɪd 'ærəb 'emɪrəts] Vereinigte Arabische Emirate
**United Kingdom** [juˌnaɪtɪd 'kɪŋdəm] Vereinigtes Königreich
**United States of America** [juˌnaɪtɪd 'steɪts əv ə'merɪkə] Vereinigte Staaten von Amerika
**Vienna** [vi'enə] Wien
**Vietnam** [ˌviːet'næm] Vietnam
**Wales** ['weɪlz] Wales
**Warsaw** ['wɔːsɔː] Warschau

# Acknowledgements

**Fotos**
Titelfoto: Corbis/Zefa/Joson
RF: Alamy: S. 12/1 / Tetra Images, S. 12/2 / L. Hims, S. 12/4/IS 336, S. 12 / image 100, S. 62/3 / RadiusImages, S. 74/2 / Aurora Open;
Corbis: S. 12/3 / Fancy / Veer, S. 12/5 / J. Lauritz;
Comstock: S. 21;
Istockphoto: S. 86/2;
Shutterstock: S. 33, S. 35, S. 38/2/3/4, S. 49, S. 74/1, S. 74/3, S. 74/5, S. 86/3, S. 86/4, S. 86/5, S. 88, S. 115, 128, 130, 133;
V. Maly: S. 38/1;
RM: Alamy: S. 37 / D. Pearson, S. 38/5 / D. Hurst, S. 62/1 / TPH, S. 74/4 / E. Buttarelli, S. 86/1 / D. Robertson, S. 106/1 / J. Wiedel;
Fotofinder: S. 62/2 / ecopix / A. Froese, S. 106/2 / Visum,
Picture Alliance: S. 58 / A. Rain, S. 100 / epa Star, S. 105 / epa YM, S. 106/3 / M. Gambarini;
Ullstein bild: S. 114/1, S. 114/2, S. 114/3;
Cinetext: S. 24

**Texte**
S. 15: Hamburger Abendblatt, 30. 08. 07;
S. 24: 7 Days, 17. 03. 06;
S. 48: The Economist, 23. 09. 06;
S. 58: The International Herald Tribune, 15.–16. 09. 07;
S. 59: Die Welt, 15. 09. 07;
S. 64: The International Herald Tribune, 23. 01. 08;
S. 65: Frankfurter Allgemeine Zeitung, 27. 02. 08;
S. 65: The Financial Times, 07. 02. 08;
S. 99: The Daily Telegraph, 11. 03. 08;
S. 105: Frankfurter Allgemeine Zeitung, 07. 11. 07;
S. 105: The International Herald Tribune, 11. 03. 08

S. 137: abridged from BBC News – Business, http://www.bbc.co.uk/news/business-16596949, 18.01.12
S. 139: abridged from The UK Card Association, http://www.theukcardsassociation.org.uk/wm_documents/decade_of_cards_final.pdf, 10.12.12

Wir danken allen Instituten, Firmen und Personen, die bei der Erstellung dieses Lehrwerks mit Materialien und Informationen behilflich waren.